21726 -2

GN
473
C87

Curley, Richard T.

Elders, shades, and
women

Elders, Shades,
and Women

Elders, Shades, and Women
Ceremonial Change in Lango, Uganda

RICHARD T. CURLEY

UNIVERSITY OF CALIFORNIA PRESS
BERKELEY, LOS ANGELES, LONDON

University of California Press
Berkeley and Los Angeles, California
University of California Press, Ltd.
London, England
Copyright © 1973, by
The Regents of the University of California
ISBN: 0-520-02149-5
Library of Congress Catalog Card Number: 70-634788
Printed in the United States of America

TO BIRDIE

81006

Contents

TABLES

FIGURES

Acknowledgments

This book, like all anthropological studies, required the assistance and cooperation of many people.

In 1964, Professor Elizabeth Colson conducted a graduate seminar on spirit possession in Africa, and my participation in the seminar stimulated interest in a topic that is central to this study. Professor Colson also read the manuscript at various stages and offered valuable advice.

The field work in Uganda was supported by the Foreign Area Fellowship Program of the American Council of Learned Societies and by the Social Science Research Council. Professor Melvin Perlman initially suggested that I do research in Lango District, and he offered assistance, criticism, and advice throughout the research and writing. I am also grateful to Professors Aidan Southall and John Middleton for their suggestions concerning the feasibility of doing field work in Lango District.

The field work was carried out with the cooperation of the Makerere Institute of Social Research. I am grateful to Dr. Josef Gugler and other members of the Institute staff for their assistance. Miss Mildred Brown, Mr. Matthew Okai, Mr. Isaac Ojok, and Mr. Otim, the *rwot* of Moroto County, introduced us to Lango District and offered advice on several occasions. Mr. John Odwe was my research assistant, interpreter, informant, and friend in Obanya Kura.

Alberta Curley assisted in the field work, and her interest in the material and participation in the project led to many fruitful discussions and new ways of looking at the data. She also spent many hours typing and tabulating data, and the study owes much to her. Ed Ottonello offered valuable criticisms. Linda Krone and Lynn Rives assisted with the preparation of the manuscript.

Tod Ruhstaller drew the illustrations. Rephah Berg read and criticized the manuscript with great care. Max Knight saw the manuscript through its final stages.

My greatest debt, however, is to the subjects of this study, the people of Obanya Kura. Their hospitality and willingness to teach made this study possible.

R.T.C.

I

Introduction

POINTS OF DEPARTURE

This study concerns social change among the people of Lango District, northern Uganda. Its focal point is the ceremonial life of a single community in Lango and how this life has changed in the past fifty years. It covers the period since the imposition of British colonial rule on Lango District and the beginning of extensive contact between Langi[1] and Europeans. The field work on which this study is based was carried out in Lango District from October 1965 until March 1967. The research covered a number of aspects of Lango culture which are only incidentally related to ceremonial change and which are therefore not included in this book. However, I have included some descriptive material so that the reader can understand the social and cultural context of ceremonial change.

In selecting a problem for field work, my attention was first drawn to the Nilotic peoples of Uganda and the Republic of the Sudan. It became apparent to me in reading the literature on these societies that a great deal of ethnographic work is yet to be done (Beattie 1956; Evans-Pritchard 1960). Several inquiries indicated that field work in the southern Sudan was impossible because of the political situation there. The Langi of Uganda

1. The word "Lango" can be used as an adjective: "the Lango people"; "a Lango spear." It can also be used as a singular noun to refer to a Lango person: "I am a Lango by tribe." However, the plural noun that means "the Lango people" is correctly "Langi." Hence, the title of Driberg's study *The Lango* (1923) is actually incorrect. In this study I adhere to Lango usage; I therefore use "Langi" to refer to more than one Lango person.

1

appeared a good choice: little ethnographic work had been done
in Lango since 1938, and the government and people of Uganda
had long been noted for their cooperation with researchers. Moreover, Lango seemed suitable for the study of several theoretical
problems that I wished to investigate.

My investigation had two primary goals. The first was to collect ethnographic data among a people whose culture had not
been greatly disrupted by external influences. For this purpose
it was essential to study a community in which present-day practices could be seen as a continuation of precontact practices, and
in which informants were likely to remember something of the
precontact situation. I wished to avoid communities lying within the sphere of rapidly growing townships, and communities
affected by radical innovations such as a group farm or a nearby
industrial plant. My principal requirements, then, were that the
community's subsistence patterns be similar to what they had
been in the precolonial period and that social change in the community could be treated as a process of adaptation and accretion
rather than one of discontinuity.

The second goal was to study the changes in the roles of men
and women and to see how these changes affected relations between the sexes and social organization in general. An initial as-
sumption was that the roles of both men and women would be
adapting to new economic conditions, such as the introduction of
cash crops and participation in a market economy, which forced
some Langi to deal with the outside world and some to leave their
villages to become wage laborers in townships and industrial
sites. I had a special interest in studying how the absence of a
fairly large percentage of the adult-male population would affect
village social organization. From journal and newspaper accounts
of current developments in Uganda, I received the impression
that labor migration was common in Lango, so that its effect on
village social organization could be studied there—although, as
it turned out later, such accounts overstated the importance of
labor migration as a feature of Lango life.

Another good reason for studying Lango lay in the realm of
published source material. The Langi were the subject of one
of the most complete studies to have been written on a sub-
Saharan African society in the first decades of this century. Jack

H. Driberg was sent to Lango District in 1914 and served there for five years, first as assistant district commissioner and later as district commissioner. While serving in Lango he undertook ethnographic and linguistic investigations which resulted in his publication of *The Lango* in 1923. This work was thoughtfully written and it contains much valuable information, although there are lacunae which can be frustrating when one tries to understand 1917 Lango society in a systematic fashion. For example, Driberg included much useful information about Lango religion and social organization, but not enough to allow one to understand them in the light of theoretical developments that have taken place in anthropology since Driberg's day. Nevertheless, I expected that *The Lango* would provide me with a good general picture of precontact Lango culture and would be especially helpful in the study of social change. For these general purposes it has been a valuable source.

A second important written source is T. T. S. Hayley, *The Anatomy of Lango Religion and Groups* (1947). Hayley's field work was limited to a period of six months in 1936–37, but his book offers an excellent description of Lango ceremonial activities and beliefs as well as many data on social organization. The existence of both these written sources presented the possibility of comparing data from three well-separated periods in Lango history: 1914–1917, 1936–1937, and 1966.

LANGO DISTRICT

Lango District (see Map 1) lies between latitudes 1°30′ North and 2°44′ North, and between longitudes 32°15′ and 33°15′ East. It covers 5700 square miles, including 500 square miles of open water and swamps. The gently rolling terrain lies at an elevation of 3000–4000 feet. The most outstanding geological formations are occasional outcrops of granite, many of them visible from a considerable distance. In the southern part of Lango District there are fewer hills, and streams and swamps become more frequent as one moves southward toward Lake Kioga, which forms most of the southern border of the district. Lango District is adjacent to Teso to the east, Karamoja to the northeast, Acholi to the north and northwest, and Nyoro to the southwest.

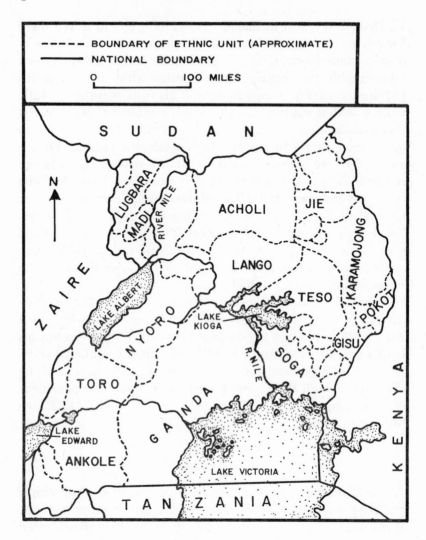

MAP I

MAJOR ETHNIC UNITS OF UGANDA

The vegetation of Lango has been well described by Driberg (1923:45). The predominant growth is elephant grass (*Pennisetum purpureum*), which grows to a height of six feet and is found in all parts of the district. Small trees and various kinds of scrub are common, and large trees occasionally break the monotony of the savanna. The shea butternut tree (*Butyrospermum parkii*) is common in the northern part of the district, the Borassus palm (*Borassus aethiopum*) in the south and west (Langdale-Brown 1960). Fuel requirements and slash-and-burn agriculture have resulted in considerable deforestation, and now the only true forests are in the forest reserves which have been set aside by the Uganda government throughout Lango.

All but a few of the 400,000 Lango people live in this setting. The official borders of Lango District virtually coincide with the territorial limits of the Langi. Population pressure has not been intense enough to impel Lango expansion into other areas, and there are only a few Lango settlements outside the district. Most of these are in Acholi District, where interaction with the Acholi is facilitated by linguistic similarities between the Acholi and Lango languages.[2]

Lira is the administrative and commercial center of Lango, chosen by colonial officers because it is in the geographical center of the district. Lira has a population of 6000, many of whom are non Lango. During my field work, virtually all the forty small shops, or *duka*, that line the main street were operated by Asian traders. These shops offered a variety of merchandise for sale to the Langi, who came from the countryside to make purchases and to enjoy the excitement of town life. In addition, Lira contains several buildings that house the administrative offices of the Uganda government and the Lango District government (Dahlberg 1971). There are also several churches, a large hospital, social clubs, secondary schools, a landing strip, a golf course, four bars, and a marketplace which is open daily. Lira has been served by a railroad line since 1964, when East African Railways opened a line to Pakwach, in the West Nile District of Uganda. Lira is a principal station on this line, which transports most of the cotton grown in Lango, Acholi, and West Nile districts and provides passenger service to Kampala and elsewhere in East Africa. There

2. The linguistic and cultural similarities between the Lango and Acholi peoples sometimes lead to a sense of common ethnicity in the commercial and industrial centers of Uganda, whose residents have diverse ethnic origins. Writing of Kampala, Parkin notes that "these Nilotes come to understand each others' [*sic*] dialects. A loose superfraternity exists between them, especially since Interlacustrine Bantu until recently referred to them all as 'barbarians' or 'foreigners'" (Parkin 1969:201). Similar ethnic groupings elsewhere in Africa have been labeled "super-tribalism" by Jean Rouch (1956).

are two highway routes to Kampala, one passing east of Lake
Kioga and the other west of it. Kampala is 260 miles away by the
latter route, and 290 miles away by the former. Within Lango
District itself, there are few paved roads, but a good system of
all-weather murram roads is maintained.

There are six counties in Lango: Moroto, Erute, Oyam,
Kwania, Maruzi, and Dokolo. In all of these the principal source
of cash income is the cultivation of cotton. Millet and sorghum,
long the most important food crops, are grown in all the counties
along with sweet potatoes, cassava, and several legumes, chiefly
cowpeas and groundnuts. All Langi place a high value on cattle,
and these too are found throughout the district, as are goats,
sheep, and chickens. Visits to all six counties showed that in
spite of this common economic pattern, there are significant
regional differences which are due to variation in geography and
in the pattern of social change.

The annual rainfall becomes heavier as one travels south from
Lira toward Lake Kioga, and a greater percentage of the land is
swampland, which is utilized only for fishing and, during the
dry season, when the grass cover on the regular grazing land is
diminished, for grazing cattle. In addition, the southern portion
of Lango—i.e., the greater part of Kwania, Maruzi, and Dokolo
counties—is affected by the tsetse fly, which inhibits cattle raising.
Consequently, cattle are fewer, and the average Lango owns
fewer cattle, in those counties than in the three northern counties. The southern area also has a greater population density,
with a resultant pressure on the land available for agriculture.
Possibly because of the relative scarcity of land, the inhabitants
of Kwania, Dokolo, and Maruzi counties have been more recep-
tive to agricultural and technical innovations. The introduction
of new crops, the adoption of the motor-driven tractor for cultivation, and the establishment of an agricultural cooperative
union have all taken place more rapidly in the southern area.
A recent innovation is the development of large group farms in
several localities in the southern part of the district. As might be
expected, such developments have had their effects on many
aspects of traditional Lango life, most notably in the decreasing
importance of the communal labor groups, and the difficulty of
maintaining the informal system of land tenure.

SELECTING A FIELD SITE

From what could be learned during several casual visits to southern Lango District, not many young men were leaving the district as labor migrants, but the trading centers of Dokolo, Aduku, Ngai, and Aboke had many non-Lango people, most of whom came from other districts in the north of Uganda to seek work in the cotton ginneries and trading centers of Lango. The three southern counties did not appear to meet the requirements of the study: few Langi were leaving to become labor migrants, and it would have been difficult to find a community of Langi in this area that was not undergoing rapid change.

Throughout my preliminary survey of Lango District, the matter of choosing a field site was affected by considerations of where I would be allowed to live. Government officials granted me permission to reside in a government rest camp, but only four rest camps were available. Three of these were in the southern counties, and one was in the northeastern section of the district, in Moroto County. A visit to Moroto County indicated that the communal work group was the basis of the agricultural system there, and that with the exception of the ox-drawn plow, there had been no radical agricultural innovations in recent years. My first impression was that Moroto County had less traffic on its roads, fewer trading centers, and fewer people wearing long trousers and other European-style clothing—all rough indications that the area was not so densely populated, so ethnically heterogeneous, or so caught up in the processes of change as were the three southern counties. Moroto seemed like a good choice for the ethnographic study of a Lango community, and perhaps of labor migration.

In November 1965, my wife and I took up residence in the government rest camp near Aloi, in Moroto County. We remained there until March 1967. This rest camp is located in an area known locally as Obanya Kura ("God is waiting for me"). The rest camp (see Map 2) is twenty-four miles east of Lira and is not far from the county offices of Moroto County. Among the most significant features of the area are a government clinic slightly more than a mile east of the camp, and the trading center at Aloi, two and one-half miles west. Aloi is at the junction of five roads and is served by buses, taxis, and railroad. The railroad station facilitates the shipment of cotton processed at the Aloi ginnery of the Lango Co-operative Society. Aloi also has a bar, and five small shops (operated by Asian traders until November 1972), which stock a narrow range of merchandise: kerosene, soap, cigarettes, beer, cloth, ready-made clothing, sandals, hoes, spare parts for bicycles. During my field work, about 100 non-

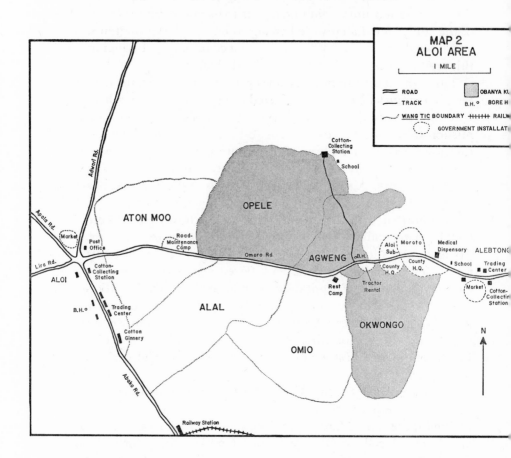

MAP 2
ALOI AREA

1 MILE

Lango people lived in Aloi: the Asian traders, some of their employees, and some of the ginnery workers.

After hiring a young Lango man to work as an interpreter and research assistant, my next problem was to select a residential area for study. This problem existed because of Lango residential patterns: the Langi do not live in villages; rather, each family has its isolated household. Distances between households vary greatly. Some households are immediately adjacent to their nearest neighbors, and others are 400 yards away. Where does one begin in the ethnographic study of such an area? And—still more problematic—where does one end? During the initial two-week period set aside for language study and talking with my assistant and others about general features of Lango culture, I could get no information about a discrete community as such.[3] There appeared to be two possible solutions: first, to delineate a circular area with a radius of, say, one mile and with the rest camp at the center. In this arbitrary fashion I could have defined an area of research. The second possibility was to decide on some convenient number of homesteads—say, 100—and limit the study to the residents of those homesteads.

With these alternatives in mind, I made a map of the area that surrounds the rest camp and attempted to familiarize myself with the location of the 172 homesteads within this area. I undertook a census of the area to obtain demographic and genealogical information. The census was useful in several ways: first, the genealogies derived from it proved valuable; second, it was a good way to introduce myself to the residents of the area and assure them that my intentions were honorable; and third, it demonstrated that there was a satisfactory way of delineating an area of research.

In responding to the questions I asked during the census, informants were able to name the area in which they lived and could describe a network of relations based on the exchange of labor within each area. Driberg (1923:171) and Hayley (1947:38) both noted the existence of the communal labor group called the *wang tic* ("work eye"), which is a group of male household heads who regularly work together in one another's fields. The areal

3. For a discussion of a similar ethnographic problem, see Alan Harwood's description of communities among the Safwa of Tanzania (1970:4).

aspects of the *wang tic* were not discussed by Driberg or Hayley,
but in 1965 it was possible for me to delineate the boundaries of
six work-group areas. The boundaries change when a member of
the work group decides to expand his agricultural land or when
a member decides to stop working with one work group and affiliate himself with a neighboring work group. By and large, however, the boundaries of the work group area are recognized and
respected. Each work group has a headman, called the *aduong
wang tic* ("work-eye elder"), whose authority is limited to matters
concerning agricultural labor and land disputes. There is also
a system of neighborhood courts. In four of the six work-group
areas I mapped, each area had its own neighborhood court. The
two remaining work-group areas were served by a single neighborhood court. To sum up, there were four reasons for considering the work-group area to be the residential basis of a significant
social group: the ability of informants to delineate the boundaries; the network of labor within the area; the office of headman; and the relations of the neighborhood-court system to the
work-group area. These reasons justify the use of the term "neighborhood," which I shall regularly use to refer to the *wang tic*.

During the preliminary survey I collected census data for four
neighborhoods. These four neighborhoods contained 740 people,
and I decided that field work based on the techniques of partic-
ipant observation would not be feasible with such a large number
of people. I therefore selected three neighborhoods for thorough
study: Agweng, Opele, and Okwongo. These three neighborhoods included 172 households with a total of 603 people. The
neighborhoods were contiguous, and all the households were
within a forty-minute walk from the rest camp. These three
neighborhoods constitute the area of Obanya Kura.

LABOR MIGRATION

One of the goals of the census was to collect information on
the incidence of labor migration in the area. In doing so, I
learned that labor migration is not widespread and that it plays a
minor role in the economic and social life of Obanya Kura. Table
I shows the number of men in Obanya Kura who have held jobs
outside the Aloi area for a period of more than two months.

The figures do not include men attending school outside Aloi, nor do they include several men who served in the King's African Rifles during World War II. Table I also shows the number of women who have spent more than two monthes outside the Aloi area. Most of the women were not employed while they were living away; they were accompanying their husbands.

TABLE I

Incidence of Labor Migration in Obanya Kura

Neighborhood	People who had been absent for a period of two months at some time in the past		People who were absent in January 1966		Population
	Men	*Women*	*Men*	*Women*	
Opele	4	3	2	1	224
Agweng	4	3	2	0	234
Okwongo	4	1	3	1	145

These figures suggested to me that labor migration was not a suitable topic of investigation for a long period of field work. After completing the survey, I decided to collect general ethnographic information on the economic and social organization of the community, and I set out to measure fields, observe agricultural practices, and interview residents about the activities of the neighborhood. By interviewing older informants about the precontact and early-contact periods, I attempted to trace some of the developments that had occurred after the introduction of a cash-crop economy and the establishment of colonial administration.

PROBLEMS IN THE STUDY OF LANGO RELIGION

During the first few months of living in Obanya Kura, I attended a number of religious ceremonies and made some inquiries about religious beliefs and practices. The first ceremonies that I observed were curing ceremonies, in which patients were treated for spirit possession. My attention was drawn to these ceremonies partly because they were rich in symbol and drama and partly because they offered insights into the social life of the community: many of the patients in these ceremonies had become possessed as the result of conflicts among their kinsmen. Another salient feature of the possession ceremonies was that much of the ritual employed by the participants was heavily laden with symbols obviously derived from the experience of social change.

At first I was only incidentally interested in the ceremonies, seeking in them background information on social organization. After witnessing several of them, however, I came to believe that the ceremonies themselves could serve as an excellent focal point for a study of social change. They seemed to dramatize areas of Lango life in which the effects of change were being felt deeply, particularly within the sphere of husband-wife relationships. All the shamans and patients I interviewed described spiritual problems that one can relate to the changing nature of male-female role obligations. Thus, the ceremonies used religious symbols to enact and resolve social conflicts, many of which were the result of social change. This topic became more exciting when I was told repeatedly that the possession dance, although not a new phenomenon, had increased greatly in popularity during the past fifty years and that many more female shamans were conducting the dance than during earlier times. Here was a further suggestion that the possession ceremony was related to the whole phenomenon of change, and that its popularity was due to its ability to explain and resolve personal and social problems new to the Langi.

During the last twelve months of my stay, most of my research was in the realm of religion. I sought out ethnographic details of religious ceremonies, life histories of shamans and other practitioners, and information on what might be called the social meaning of religious ceremonies—who attended ceremonies, who paid for them, under what circumstances a person's kinsmen held ceremonies for him, and so forth. These, of course, are broad topics for investigation, and they drew me well outside religious matters in the course of research. It is a truism in anthropology that one does not study a single dimension of a culture without examining its relations to the rest of the culture. This principle holds especially true in the study of religion, which is interrelated with all aspects of cultural and social life. The realization of this principle inculcates a feeling of futility in the ethnographer, however, for it decrees that, like Samuel Johnson's educated man, he must know a little about everything and a lot about one thing. In an effort to keep the research within reasonable proportions, I attempted to limit myself to the following broad topics: (1) the ethnographic description of ceremonies and a study of their social meanings; (2) the study of social organization and the nature of role relations within the community; and (3) the reconstruction of the changes in Lango ceremonial activities and social organization since 1914.

CEREMONIAL COMPLEXES

There are three ceremonial complexes in Lango: (1) a set of ceremonies performed by clan elders; (2) a cycle of ceremonies performed for married women and their children; and (3) spirit-possession ceremonies. This study attempts to demonstrate that each of these three ceremonial complexes serves a different set of cultural needs and that during the course of social change each of them has changed in a different way. For these reasons, each ceremonial complex will be described in a separate chapter (Chapters III, IV, and V). In order to place religious change in a wider social setting, Chapter II offers a description of Lango social organization. The information presented in Chapter II is central to the explanation of why Lango ceremonies changed as they did.

Etogo Ceremonies

The first ceremonial complex to be considered is a set of ceremonies performed by a group of elders representing several clans. These groups are called *etogo,* and their activities are limited to ceremonial matters. The *etogo* perform curing ceremonies, they direct the funeral ceremonies of important men, and they perform rainmaking and other ritual activities that are meant to ensure the well-being of the community as a whole. An important feature of the *etogo* is that it binds clans together in an alliance which serves the political function of integrating the clans and reducing conflict between them. Thus, the *etogo* can be seen as a cross-cutting mechanism which facilitates the peaceful coexistence of patrilineal clans living in the same area.

Now, however, *etogo* ceremonies are the least important of the three ceremonial complexes. Several *etogo* ceremonies have been forgotten, and only the older men take much interest in the *etogo*. In Obanya Kura, I had occasion to witness only four *etogo* ceremonies performed during the course of my research. A number of other *etogo* ceremonies were described to me, but many of these are no longer practiced and are significant only as an aspect of Lango memory culture. In Chapter III I shall consider the status of the *etogo* both in the past and in the present, and offer an explanation of the decline of the institution. I shall present evidence to show that the *etogo* and its ceremonies are no longer performing a vital function in Lango because a radically different type of political system was introduced during the colonial period. Hayley pointed out (1947:90) that intervillage warfare, cattle raiding, and protracted feuds between clans were reduced considerably after the establishment of a bureaucratic government and a system of local chiefs and courts in Lango District. As the political organization of Lango changed with the introduction of the *Pax Britannica,* so too did the religious institutions that had given ritual sanction and meaning to the precolonial political organization. The decline of the *etogo* can be explained by reference to the changes that were taking place in the political life of Lango.

There are, of course, other reasons for the decline of the *etogo* ceremonies. They were affected by changes that took place in the Lango economy after the introduction of cotton. Since 1914 the Langi have become cultivators who not only grow their own foodstuff but also raise cotton which is sold in overseas markets and which ties the individual cultivator to the world economy. New food crops have been introduced, agricultural techniques have been improved, and a system of markets has been established throughout most of Uganda. These changes have had their effects on Lango social organization, for they have given the Langi a measure of protection from the vicissitudes of the environment. The food supply is more certain now than when food shortages and famine occurred from time to time. During periods of food shortage, redistribution of the available land could be effected through the expedient of intervillage warfare and cattle raiding. Under that system, alliances between clans and lineages were necessary for protection or for mobilizing several clans to raid an outside group. The *etogo* provided a way for the Langi to attain such alliances. Within their own areas the *etogo* also functioned to redistribute food among their members. There is no longer any need for a group that serves these functions. A Lango man can grow all the food he needs; if for some reason he cannot, he can buy food in the markets with money earned from the sale of his cotton.

This is not to suggest that the functions of the *etogo* ceremonies were entirely economic and political and that consequently the decline of the *etogo* is to be explained solely as a result of economic and political changes. There were other reasons, and they will be discussed.

Kwer *Ceremonies*

The Langi believe strongly in the efficacy and desirability of *kwer* ceremonies, and the ceremonies are held frequently. Some of the eight ceremonies in the *kwer* series have died out, but the institution is still viable. I attended about twenty-five performances of *kwer* ceremonies, and many others were described to me. The chapter on *kwer* ceremonies is devoted to a description of the ceremonies and an attempt to account for their persistence. Simply stated, the *kwer* persist because they represent an attempt to solve through symbolic means a problem that is basic to all patrilineal systems: the problem of incorporating a woman into her husband's localized descent group. The strong ideology of patrilineality, coinciding with a virilocal rule of residence, means that a wife is an outsider in the home of her husband. The *kwer* ceremonies attempt to resolve the problem of incorporation through symbolic means, and at the same time to assure a woman that she and her children will enjoy good health as long as they remain with her husband.

Spirit-Possession Ceremonies

The chapter on spirit possession describes the beliefs and activities associated with possession. It also discusses the increasing popularity of the ceremonies and offers some explanations. One explanation is to be found in changing aspects of the husband-wife relationship. Lango women have achieved a modicum of economic independence from their husbands: theoretically a wife controls all the money that comes into a household through the sale of cotton. She can also earn money by selling food at the market. However, this newly achieved economic position of women exists within a social system that offers women very little real mobility. Money earned by women is often appropriated by their husbands, and women's personal freedom is greatly restricted. Their economic gains turn out to be a Pyrrhic victory, for in the end they are still expected to submit to the rule of men. The life histories of shamans repeatedly state this theme, and this inability of women to make real gains has led them to participate in possession ceremonies that call attention to their plight and sometimes, give them a greater degree of control over their own lives and over their husbands.

The relations between the status of women and spirit possession has received some attention in anthropological literature. I. M. Lewis (1966, 1971) has reviewed the subject and cites ethnographic examples from the Chinese of Singapore (Elliot 1955: 71), the Luvale of Zambia (White 1961:48), the Hausa of Nigeria (Mary Smith 1954:271), the Taita of Kenya (Harris 1957), the Tonga of Zambia (Colson 1958:137; 1969:69–103), and other groups. The problem, as described by Mary Smith (1954:272), is roughly the same in all these societies: the "inability of the Hausa women to participate adequately in the ceremonial and public life of Islam leaves a gap which is filled by the spirit possession cult." Lewis uses these examples to show that spirit possession is associated with the "war between the sexes" (1966:319). He argues that spirit possession is likely to be found "in traditionally male dominated societies." Lewis sees possession ceremonies as a vigorous response to deprivation, and as found most commonly in societies in which women are "peripheral" (1966:321).

In a rejoinder to Lewis' article, Peter J. Wilson presents an alternative hypothesis: "Spirit possession and similar states seem more closely correlated with social situations which regularly, though not necessarily, give rise to conflict, competition, tension, rivalry, or jealousy between members of the same sex rather than

between members of the opposite sex" (1967:366). The data from
Lango tend to support Lewis' hypothesis rather than Wilson's.
That is, they suggest that spirit possession is more closely related to male-female conflict than to conflict among females.
However, these data also show that the phrase "war between the
sexes" is a somewhat extreme description of what is actually taking place and that women use spirit possession as a means of
gaining advantages rather than engaging in "war" with males.

CONCLUSION

I am not attempting to demonstrate that religious practices are
determined solely by economic conditions nor that they serve
economic functions exclusively. Ceremonies can serve many
functions, not the least of which is providing a set of concepts
through which people can order their lives and understand many
of the imponderables around them. Recent literature in anthropology has stimulated interest in the question of how religious symbols perform these functions (Douglas 1967; Beidelman
1964, 1966a, 1966b; Turner 1967). The study of ceremonial
change in Lango suggests some explanations of how religious
symbols are sometimes replaced by others and sometimes abandoned entirely. The economic and sociological reasons for religious change can be explained by reference to some of the
broader events of culture change in Lango and to some of the
enduring features of Lango social life.

II

The Changing Social Structure: Neighbors and Kinsmen

INTRODUCTION

Ever since the pioneering works of Malinowski (1925, 1927) and Evans-Pritchard (1937), anthropological studies of religion have been concerned not merely with recording data on religious belief and ritual but with studying the relations between religious phenomena and other aspects of society. Many social anthropologists working in Africa have sought an understanding of social forms and processes through the analysis of belief and ritual. These anthropologists would share with Monica Wilson the view that "Men express in ritual what moves them most, and since the form of expression is conventionalized and obligatory, it is the values of the group that are revealed. I see in the study of ritual the key to an understanding of the essential constitution of human societies" (1954:24).

If religious phenomena are the key to our understanding of social organization, the converse is also true: belief and ceremony cannot be understood without reference to their social context. Ceremonies are enacted by groups of people, and the formation of these groups is based largely on the kinship and residential groupings prevailing among the people. Similarly, changes in ceremonial life arise out of changes in the mode of subsistence, new forms of social relations, and new ideologies.

This chapter deals with the social background against which

ceremonial change has taken place in Lango. It discusses (1) the residential and kinship groupings prevailing in Obanya Kura[1]; (2) the status of women within the extended family; and (3) the ways this status has been affected by social change.

SUBSISTENCE

The people of Obanya Kura are subsistence cultivators whose staples are millet, sorghum, cowpeas, groundnuts, cassava, and potatoes. Each household grows all the food required by its members except a few supplementary foods and condiments, which can be purchased at a market or at a shop in a nearby town. In addition to food crops, the cultivators of Obanya Kura produce cotton, which is sold yearly as a cash crop. During the harvest season of 1966, the men in one neighborhood earned, on the average, 425 East African shillings ($45.50) from the sale of their cotton. They used this money to pay taxes, to buy clothing and other household items, and to pay the school fees of any children who were attending school.

In Lango, as in much of East Africa, the cultivation of crops is carried out in conjunction with cattle raising, and every man strives for a large herd of cattle. It is likely that in the past cattle were a vital part of the food supply, constituting a reserve for periods when food crops failed. At present, cattle are slaughtered for meat on ceremonial occasions, and they provide very little milk. Apart from their rather limited value as a source of food, the economic significance of cattle now centers on three activities: their use as draft animals, their sale in the marketplace, and their value as an indication of social status. The ox-drawn metal plow was introduced into Moroto County in 1955, and it has become increasingly popular as a means of clearing land. At present, one out of three households owns a metal plow, and plows are often loaned to other households. In recent years, the Uganda government has encouraged the sale of cattle at monthly cattle auctions held in various parts of Lango District. The men of Obanya Kura

1. It is worth noting that there are no age grades or age sets in Lango at present. In the past, there were age sets, and Driberg (1923:234–247) has a brief description of initiation into the age sets, although they were already beginning to disappear by 1920. Hayley (1947) also has a description of initiations, which he compiled from the statements of very old informants.

sell their cattle to agents who then transport them to Kampala for slaughter. Cattle sales are high from August through December, when cash reserves are low.

Cattle are also used as a means of converting surplus wealth into a visible form which enhances the status of the owner. Not only is the possession of a large herd itself an indication of one's high status, but cattle can be used as bridewealth or distributed as gifts to kinsmen and neighbors in such a way that the donor builds up a following of people who are obligated to him. Because of their significance as status symbols and their place in the marriage system, cattle loom large in Lango culture. Individual cows are named, cattle form the subject of numerous songs, and disputes over cattle are frequent and sometimes disruptive of social relations.

In Obanya Kura married men own an average of five cattle. Generally speaking, the size of a man's herd is determined partly by his position in the life cycle. A newly married man is not likely to own any cattle, having recently spent his cattle as bridewealth. Later he might accumulate more cattle, but he will probably spend some on subsequent marriages. Over time, however, he should be able to build up his herd to ten or twelve cows. As his children reach the age of marriage he might acquire eight to twelve cows at once, following the marriage of a daughter—or he might be obliged to give out an equal number to assist a son in marrying. Thus, herd size fluctuates markedly throughout a man's life. His herd will probably be largest when he is about fifty years old. In later years his agricultural productivity might decline, so that he will not have the surplus income to purchase additional cattle. Furthermore, he might become physically unable to look after his herd and personally incapable of recruiting a younger man to care for it. As a rule, cattle do not figure importantly in inheritance proceedings; during my work in Obanya Kura no man over sixty controlled cattle.

THE NEIGHBORHOOD (WANG TIC)

Land in Obanya Kura is held communally—or, to be more precise, it is *controlled* communally, since no person or group actually owns land. The approximate boundaries of each neighborhood are known, and the right to use the land within those boundaries is under the control of the adult males of the community and is supervised by an elected official—the neighborhood headman (*aduong wang tic*). The population pressure in Obanya Kura is not so great as in other parts of Lango District, and there are few disputes over land. People are not overly concerned with the boundaries of their neighborhood or of the plots that they work. Only three land disputes occurred in Obanya Kura during my research; one of them occurred when a government facility was built on a field cultivated by a local resident, and the other two arose out of confusion over who had usufruct rights to the land. All the disputes were settled amicably without consulting the neighborhood headman. Very often a man residing in one neighborhood cultivates crops on land in another neighborhood, and this is an acceptable arrangement, as long as he has been granted permission by the neighborhood headman.

The right to use a plot of land can be acquired in three ways. First, one man can transfer his rights to a piece of land to another man. The most frequent instance of this occurs when a father gives his son the right to use the land that the father has been cultivating. Or, in the same way, a man simply grants a plot to another man regardless of their relationship. Second, a man inherits land that had been cultivated by his father. The rule of inheritance remains unchanged from that described by Driberg: "Normally a man's eldest son is declared his heir . . . [and] is bound to distribute a reasonable amount to his uterine brothers" (1923:174). Like the transfer of land from a living man to his son, the transfer can take place within the context of the family only, so that it is not necessary to consult the neighborhood headman or other neighbors. Third, a man can approach the neighborhood headman and ask his permission to cultivate a particular plot. This is necessary when a newcomer moves into a neighborhood to take up residence, and only once in the recent history of Obanya Kura has such a request been denied.

There are no means by which a person can buy land or the right to use it. Until recent years, the idea of land ownership was barely conceivable to Langi, but in 1964 the question of land tenure became charged with political significance. A large group of Langi, responding to rumors that Lango District was to be surveyed and land titles were to be granted, massed before the offices of the District government in Lira and demanded that the existing system be maintained. The meeting was precipitated by an allegation that land tenure would open the way to European settlement in Lango District similar to that in the highlands of western Kenya. Since then, the issue has remained dormant in spite of population pressure and numerous land disputes in the southern part of Lango District.

This incident illustrates the strong attachment that Langi have to the idea of not owning the land, an attachment that was strengthened by the fear of European encroachment. This does not mean, however, that Langi view land as a scarce commodity. In most of Lango District land is certainly not in short supply, and population pressure is not yet sufficient to cause a land short-age—even though the system of shifting cultivation requires that much of the land lie fallow at any given time. People in Obanya Kura tend to take land for granted, although it is unlikely that they will continue to do so.

The present system of usufruct rights underlies many features of Lango social organization: when we consider the way land is allocated and used, we realize how dependent the individual cul-tivator is on his kinsmen and neighbors. For example, a man can be banished from his neighborhood if he antagonizes neighbors by refusal to participate in the communal work activities or by antisocial behavior, such as stealing, adultery, and misuse of lands. The neighborhood headman can hold a meeting of the residents of the neighborhood, and if they vote accordingly, the transgressor is banished from the community. This occurred in Agweng neighborhood in 1959, after a young man antagonized his neighbors by repeated acts of hostility, including verbal and physical assaults, and by refusal to take part in communal labor. Eventually, one man, a nonkinsman, accused him of trying to commit adultery. The charge was never substantiated, but it led to a vote to expropriate the lands of the wrongdoer. He had no choice but to migrate with his wife and children to another neighborhood, where he activated other kinship bonds.[2]

2. It is likely that the whole system of the *wang tic*, including its control over the land, became more important during the colonial period. Colson (1971:197) has discussed the effect of colonial rule in creating systems of communal control

Each *wang tic* is named. The name refers to the geographical territory rather than to a social group; residence in a *wang tic* does not confer any particular social identity upon a person. A person will say, "I live in Agweng," rather than "I am a member of Agweng" or "I am an Agweng." But living in a neighborhood and using its land entails more than cultivating one's own crops. It carries with it the realization that one is ultimately dependent on one's neighbors and that to maintain good relations with them one must fulfill certain obligations. The most explicit such obligation is to assist neighbors in agricultural labor when called upon to do so.

The system of communal labor is more active during certain periods of the yearly agricultural cycle. When the dry season ends, in late February or early March, the rains begin to soften the ground, and men must clear their fields and prepare the soil for planting millet. Then additional fields must be cleared for cotton planting, which continues until May. In order to clear land, a man first asks his wife to prepare about ten gallons of millet beer. Much planning is called for in this effort, because beer takes three weeks to prepare; a man must determine in advance when he wants his fields cleared. He informs the neighborhood headman of the date; it is the responsibility of the neighborhood headman to notify other men in the neighborhood of their assignments for work. All married men in the neighborhood are expected to appear in the fields of the host on the appointed day. It is customary for them to work from sunrise until shortly after noon, when they take a brief rest, wash themselves with water brought to them by the host's wife, and then begin to drink beer.

The sociability of neighborhood life is expressed in beer drinking, during which groups of men sit around beer pots. After a work party, large pots of beer are served, and generally ten or twelve men are seated around each beer pot. The beer has the consistency of gruel and has a very low alcohol content. Warm water is added to it from time to time, and it is sucked from the pot through drinking reeds, two or three men taking turns drink-

---

of the land throughout Africa. Reliable historical information is not available on this point, although it may be significant that neither Driberg or Hayley described the *wang tic* as a group that has control over land.

ing through the same reed. Beer drinking is the most important form of commensality in Lango, and beer, like cattle, is a popular topic of conversation. One man sometimes greets another with the question, "Have you found any beer?" or "Where's the beer?" Women sell beer on market days, and men pay one shilling for a place at the pot where they can continue drinking until the beer has been consumed. In the late afternoon, women sometimes sell beer in their yards, and groups of four or five women gather to gossip and enjoy one another's company.

Serving beer to one's neighbors after a work party is not considered payment for the labor, but it is a necessary gesture of good will if a man is to maintain his standing in the neighborhood. A man "pays" for his neighbor's services later, when the neighbor invites him to work in his fields, and a man who fails to appear is considered derelict in his responsibility. If a man persistently fails to work in his neighbors' fields as requested, the members of the *wang tic* can exclude him from the communal work activities, although they do not take his fields from him.

Not all agricultural work is done by the *wang tic*, nor do the communal work parties continue throughout the year. *Wang tic* labor is employed only for the heavy work, which is the responsibility of men. According to the sexual division of labor, men clear the land before planting and plow the fields. Men and women share the work of weeding and harvesting, although women spend more time at this work than men. These time-consuming but less strenuous tasks are often carried out by work groups of four or five people, in an institution called *alea* (from *leyo*, "to share, to alternate"). In *alea*, a group of neighbors agree to work in one another's fields, spending a day in each member's fields and then beginning again in the fields of the first member. Unlike the larger *wang tic* work parties, *alea* work parties do not necessarily culminate in beer drinking. Another difference is that *alea* work parties are especially popular among women, whereas women do not participate as laborers in *wang tic* work parties.

An example of the *wang tic* system in action is a work party that took place in early April of 1966. Okeng[3] is a thirty-eight-year-old man with two wives. He lives in Agweng neighborhood,

3. To protect informants, the Lango names used throughout this book are fictitious.

and three of his brothers and his aged father live nearby. Okeng cultivates three acres of cotton and two and one-half acres of millet. The rains had just begun to soften the ground, so that it was time for him to consider planting his fields. Okeng's wife had prepared twelve gallons of beer, and on Monday morning Okeng walked a quarter mile to the house of the neighborhood headman and asked whether the men of the *wang tic* could work in his fields on Thursday. The headman informed Okeng that there were to be work parties on Tuesday and Wednesday and that he would notify the men to appear in Okeng's field on Thursday. On Tuesday and Wednesday Okeng went to work in the fields of his neighbors with the men of the *wang tic*. On Tuesday eleven men, all from Agweng neighborhood, worked together, and on Wednesday fifteen men worked together.

Okeng has the reputation of being a man who "stays well" with his neighbors. On Thursday, eighteen men appeared in his fields and worked for about four hours in the morning, managing to clear almost three acres of land and hoe the soil to prepare it for planting. All the men were residents of Okeng's neighborhood except his father's brother and his father's brother's son, who lived together less than a half mile away in another neighborhood. The beer flowed freely in the afternoon, and those who had worked in the morning were joined by additional guests. Every guest who had not worked was a woman, an old man, or an able-bodied man from another *wang tic*. It is improper for an able-bodied man to appear at a beer party in his own *wang tic* if he was asked to work in the work party that day and did not. This rule is carefully observed.

About forty people gathered for the beer party at Okeng's house and remained until dark. Okeng considered the day to have been a success for him, and he later cultivated the remainder of his fields by recruiting his younger brother, another lineage member in the neighborhood, and his father's brother's son to work in his fields for two days.

The foregoing example illustrates several features of *wang tic* work activities. The activities are coordinated by the neighborhood headman, but his authority is minimal; he cannot apply sanctions if a member of the *wang tic* does not appear for work. Consequently, the size of the work parties is flexible, because each member of the *wang tic* decides for himself whether to work on a given day. His first consideration is whether the man whose fields are to be cleared is likely to reciprocate by returning the labor. Therefore, a man's past work record is taken into consideration, and Okeng happened to have the reputation of one who is willing to work for others. Okeng wisely enhanced his reputation on this occasion by appearing at the two work parties that preceded his. He admitted to me that he did not particularly want to work on those days, but he knew that failure to work would affect the turnout at his own work party.

Belonging to a neighborhood requires more of a person than participating in communal work activities. Each neighborhood has an informal court, which operates apart from the regular government court. The neighborhood members appoint five men to hear cases; these men meet (more or less regularly) once each week throughout the year. They also meet in a special session when an urgent case arises. The neighborhood courts were originally established by the district government in the 1930s, and they were seen as an adjunct to the government courts. The neighborhood courts handle cases thought too petty to be brought before the government courts. A typical agenda for a neighborhood-court meeting consisted of three cases: a theft of two chickens, an argument between a husband and wife over a minor household incident, and a debt of ten shillings. The neighborhood-court elders are free to offer their opinions and admonish the wrongdoers. But the court has no authority to sanction an offender through the use of fines or imprisonment.

The neighborhood, here defined as the land under the control of a single communal work group, is a more meaningful entity for men than for women. One reason is that the duties of motherhood restrict a woman's mobility. Furthermore, women are expected to perform numerous household tasks, like sorting cotton, shelling peas, and preparing food. Women simply do not have the leisure time to walk a half mile to spend an afternoon visiting in the community. Women do make such visits, but not as frequently as men; and when they do visit, one is likely to find a group of four or five women, compared with the typical men's group of ten to fifteen. Age is also a factor, for older women who are no longer charged with the care of infants are freer to visit within the *wang tic* than young married women. In general, though, women's social networks, as seen in their visiting patterns and in their *alea* work activities, are restricted to a smaller residential area and include only four or five neighboring households.

On the other hand, women attend the twice-weekly markets more often than men do, and to attend they must walk about a mile from Obanya Kura. If a women is to attend the market she completes her household tasks in early morning, leaves for the market in midmorning, and remains at the market until late afternoon selling beer or small amounts of produce. Apart from economic considerations, there is a good reason that women show a keener interest in the market than men. The reason has to do with the virilocal rule of residence. At the market a woman sees consanguineal kinsmen and former neighbors from her natal *wang tic*. Hence she can obtain news from her mother or request a favor of her brother, and generally maintain ties with her consanguineal kinsmen.

The significance of the neighborhood as a social network is derived largely from its relation to the land and from the pattern of subsistence in which groups of men work communally. It is not a closed community, for men who live in adjacent neighborhoods are free to work with the men of another *wang tic*, and a man would certainly not confine his visiting to his own *wang tic*. But the communality of the *wang tic* is not experienced as intensely by women. A young married woman does not even know all the members of her husband's *wang tic*, nor does she know the geographical boundaries of the *wang tic*. She may attend the neighborhood court, but for the first few years of marriage a woman has fewer acquaintances than her husband does, and she relies on visits to the market to maintain contact with her consanguineal relatives.

THE PRINCIPLE OF DESCENT AND DESCENT GROUPS

In the foregoing description of the neighborhood we have not discussed kinship ties between households. But Lango is a patrilineal, virilocal society, and Langi, therefore, tend to form local lineages, one of which can come to make up the majority of members in any *wang tic.* Or, failing to form a majority, the members of one patrilineage may become a plurality and so come to dominate the life of the *wang tic.*

Table II shows something of the relation between descent

TABLE II

Clan and Lineage Composition of the Three Neighborhoods in Obanya Kura

Agweng neighborhood		Opele neighborhood		Okwongo neighborhood	
Number of households	Number of individuals	Number of households	Number of individuals	Number of households	Number of individuals
Ocukuru me Oki		**Raki**		**Oki me Okwerocuga**	
a. 7	36	a. 14	104	a. 10	57
b. 1	7	b. 1	4	b. 1	14
8	43	c. 3	15	11	71
		d. 2	18		
Atek me Ober		20	141	**Ocukuru me Alilo**	
3	11			4	17
Raki		**Ocukuru me Oki**		**Raki**	
a. 5	35	1	7	a. 1	3
b. 1	5			b. 1	4
6	40	**Ocukuru me Ogorayit**		2	7
		4	25		
Okaruwok				**Atek me Okweruwe**	
a. 11	62	**Oki me Ngura**		4	21
b. 1	10	a. 2	11		
12	72	b. 1	6	**Ocukuru me Mea**	
		3	17	a. 2	10
Oki me Ngura				b. 1	9
1	8	**Omolotar**		c. 3	10
		8	34	6	29
Ocukuru me Okwerokwac					
2	12				
Ober me pala					
8	48	—	—	—	—
40	234	36	224	27	145

Obanya Kura: total households 103; total population 603

NOTE: Lower-case letters denote lineages of a clan.

groups and neighborhoods by listing the clan affiliation of adults in the three neighborhoods of Obanya Kura. This table also shows that a clan may be represented in a neighborhood by more than one local lineage; local lineages are denoted by the letters "a," "b," "c," and "d." Women are tabulated with the clans of their husbands.

The local lineage, however, is only one of several types of kin group. The others are the satellite household, the household, the *jo doggola*, and the clan. We shall examine each of these groups, beginning with the smallest, which can be referred to as a homestead, or "satellite" household.

THE SATELLITE HOUSEHOLD

Virtually all Lango men state a preference for polygyny, although it is an ideal that not all men can afford. Of 96 married men in Obanya Kura, 21 were living in polygynous unions at the time of the study, and only 1 had more than two wives. Polygyny in Lango serves as an example of the well-known distinction between "real" and "ideal" culture: an estimate of the incidence of polygyny based on what men say about the desirability of polygyny would be unduly high.

The establishment of satellite households relates directly to the incidence of polygyny, for a Lango man builds a separate household for each wife. The satellite household is composed of a wife, her unmarried offspring, and possibly a son who has been married for a year or two and the son's wife. A young Lango man resides at his mother's household until he takes it upon himself, usually at the behest of his wife, to build a separate residence.

Figure 1 shows the physical arrangement of a satellite household. The household occupies a clearing about 30 yards in diameter and includes a main house, a kitchen, and two small houses. In addition, it has a kraal, or cattle byre, although many Lango households do not have kraals attached to them. A group of three or four men combine their herds and build a single kraal at the house of one of the men.

The oldest son in the household built one of the two smaller houses shown in Figure 1 for himself when he was about fifteen years old, and several months later he built one for his older

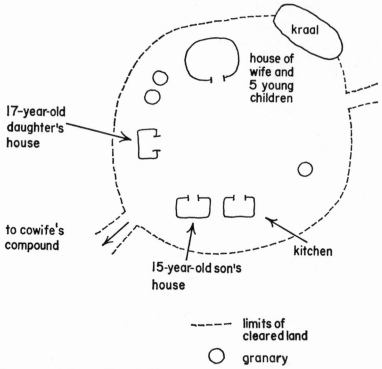

Figure 1: A Lango Household

sister. Parents do not consider it desirable to sleep in the same house with their children who have reached puberty, and adolescents are encouraged to build their own small houses. From the point of view of the youth, a separate house is preferable because it offers the possibility of taking in lovers at night, a practice that the parents accept.

The satellite household in Figure 1 is occupied by a man's senior wife, and a path connects it to the household of the second wife, about 120 yards away in a separate clearing. Because tall grass abounds in Lango, other households are not visible as one stands in a yard and looks out across the bush, a condition that enhances the quality of isolation of the household.

A Lango husband is expected to divide his time more or less equally in each of the satellite households, sleeping for three or four consecutive nights in one and then going to the other. He takes all his meals at the household where he is sleeping. The husband is also expected to stop in at the other satellite household a few times each day.

Husbands are expected to treat each wife equally, but in actuality, men tend to favor one wife over another—to spend more time at her house and offer her more assistance. The senior wife has an advantage over the junior wife in competing for the assistance and support of the husband. Furthermore, the senior wife, having resided in the neighborhood longer, has developed friendships with her husband's clansmen and is more likely to obtain assistance from them than is the junior co-wife. The ranking of the wives varies, of course, with such factors as age, the fertility of the woman, her industriousness, and her disposition, but a junior co-wife has to be especially aggressive and pleasing to the husband if she is to usurp the privileged position of the senior wife.

The satellite household is also the basic unit of agricultural production and consumption in Lango, for agricultural lands are assigned to each household, which has exclusive rights to the produce of those fields. This fact is an especially important aspect of the relationship between husband and wife, for although a man may inherit fields or may acquire them through the *wang tic*, the wife controls the fields and their produce. Moreover, a husband should allocate his fields equally between his wives, and the wife retains control of a field as long as she is living in the *wang tic* with her husband. A husband knows at all times which fields are held by which of his wives, and he is expected to assist each wife in the heavy agricultural labor required in her fields. When members of the *wang tic* are called to cultivate, they perform their day's work in the fields of one wife, and it is she who makes beer for them, from millet grown in her own fields. If *wang tic* labor is required in the fields of the other wife, the *wang tic* members return on another day, and the other wife makes beer.

Each satellite household is a separate economic unit. According to Lango ideals a man should see that each wife is provided for equally. He should provide each wife with equal field acreage, with an eye toward equalizing the food supply and cash income of each household. Traditionally, all agricultural produce was controlled by the wife, but the introduction of cash-crop cultivation has made this ideal less workable. The cotton is packed in bales and delivered to purchasing agents by the men, who receive the payment. If the ideal of equal distribution were to be adhered to, a man would keep in a separate lot the cotton grown by each wife, and would hand over to each wife the payment for her lot. The distribution of income is a source of contention between husband and wife and between co-wives. Husbands sometimes conceal cash from their wives or demand money from their wives for personal purchases.

With respect to household resources other than money, women have considerable authority, and men openly acknowledge that household property is held in the name of the wife of the household. Thus, a man does not own cattle in his own name; the cattle belong to each household and are held in the name of his wife. If he wishes to sell a cow he must obtain permission from his wife, and this is a frequent source of conflict in the family, for wives often object to the sale of cows on the grounds that the husband is squandering the future bridewealth of a son. The bridewealth received upon the marriage of a daughter should also remain under the authority of the mother of the girl, to be redistributed within the household, usually to the oldest unmarried son, who will use it for his own bridewealth.

A developmental cycle (Goody 1958) characterizes Lango domestic groups: the composition of each household changes over time with births, marriages, and deaths. A young married son, after staying with his wife for about a year in the household of his mother, builds a house of his own in a separate clearing nearby. (Daughters leave the households of their mothers altogether when they marry and take up residence at their husbands' households.) This practice means that a new satellite household is formed about one year after each marriage.

THE HOUSEHOLD

The most common familial living arrangement in Lango varies slightly from the satellite household. The nuclear family is found in monogamous marital unions, wherein the husband maintains his residence permanently in the house of his wife and does not have the problem of dividing his fields, cattle, and other property between wives. Every married man is involved in such an arrangement, at least during the first years of marriage, and he continues as the head of a single household unless he marries a second wife.

In physical arrangement, the household of a nuclear family is similar to a satellite household, although a man who maintains only one household builds larger buildings in the single household and puts more effort into upkeep. Similarly, the agricultural produce will not be divided between wives, so that the wife in such a household has more cash income than the wife in a polygynous arrangement. One reason is that a large part of the agricultural labor is done by men; if a man has more than one wife his labor must be divided between their fields, and a husband's work output will not necessarily increase if he takes a second wife. Furthermore, a wife in a polygynous marriage is given less land to work than a woman in a monogamous marriage. Of 25 sample households in Obanya Kura whose fields I measured, there were 6 polygynous unions, each of them including two wives. The amount of land cultivated by the wives of one man averaged 4.2 acres. The wives in monogamous unions cultivated 3.8 acres, whereas women who had co-wives cultivated 2.2 acres.

The benefits that accrue to a woman in a monogamous union may be temporary, however, because a man who cultivates successfully with the assistance of his wife may accumulate so much wealth over several years that he can afford a second wife. A leveling mechanism is in effect, reinforced by the ideal of polygyny. The leveling mechanism, similar to that described by Manning Nash (1966:72–79), ensures that no married woman will enjoy an especially privileged position in the community. When a man has earned an income sufficient to support his wife in a prosperous household, he will also have converted some of his wealth into cattle and will be motivated by the desire to marry again and attain prestige for himself as the father of many children. Lango men say that the most noble condition for a man is to be the "elder of many people": "To be an old man and to be able to walk among many children and grandchildren and watch them working in fields which you yourself once worked." This state can best be achieved by marrying polygynously and by providing bridewealth for one's sons so they will be able to marry and remain in the neighborhood.

As offspring marry, the household shrinks, and eventually a man and his wife are left in a household with no children but with their sons living in separate domiciles close by. This situation gives rise to a local lineage, which is a group of patrilineally related men, their wives, and their unmarried children occupying a portion of land within a *wang tic*. The local lineage is of shallow generational depth, representing three or four generations descended from a man who is still alive or one who died only recently. In Obanya Kura, local lineages varied in size from one to fourteen households and hence varied considerably in their influence and importance in the community.

The households of the members of a local lineage are, typically, adjacent to one another, so that each lineage occupies a niche, or section, of the *wang tic*. As one walks through a neighborhood, informants point out that this area is the "land of Okello," referring to the oldest member of the lineage that dominates the area. As a lineage increases in size, the members may find it necessary to take land and perhaps build their houses in a neighboring *wang tic*. This often leads to a rearrangement of the boundaries of the *wang tic*, for the newcomers may wish to continue cultivating land with the members of their lineage and not wish to affiliate themselves with the residents of their new neighborhood. The realignment of the boundaries is less problematic to the residents than to the ethnographer striving to impose permanent boundaries on the *wang tic*. The boundaries of the *wang tic* are known, but they are flexible and are constantly subject to change as required by the people who live on the land.

Local lineages expand as a result of natural increase, and a local lineage can also expand its size and influence in an area by inviting members of its patrilineal clan to take up residence with it. This process was at work in Opele, one of the three *wang tic* of Obanya Kura, where a single lineage virtually controlled the *wang tic*. Opele was originally settled in about 1920, when Langi were still living in villages of "from ten to one hundred and fifty huts" (Driberg 1923:71). At that time members of a single lineage belonging to the Raki clan occupied a village that had been the object of several cattle raids and attacks by members of a lineage engaged in a blood feud with the Raki. To protect themselves, the Raki moved *en masse* to the area of Opele, built homesteads for themselves, and cultivated lands together as the members of a single *wang tic*. They brought with them two men who were not of the Raki clan but who were affinally related, having married Raki women. Gradually, members of other Raki lineages moved into Opele, and they were accepted into the *wang tic* dominated by the Raki clan and its affines. After a while, three young men of the Raki clan who lived in other areas were invited to join the Raki of Opele. These newcomers were not closely related to the Raki of Opele; in fact, two of the men were not able to trace their genealogical relationship to the Raki of Opele. One of these newcomers was invited to move to Opele because land was scarce in the *wang tic* of his father, and the other two came because the Raki of Opele offered to assist them in the payment of their bridewealths. A young man whose father cannot afford to assist him in gathering bridewealth has no alternative but to seek assistance from a clansman or a mother's brother, and generally he moves from the father's home to the *wang tic* of the person who assists him.

The result of all these migrations was that in 1966, in Opele, a single lineage of the Raki clan comprised fourteen households and occupied about a third of the *wang tic* lands. But there were also members of three other Raki lineages, the offshoots of the three "outside" Raki who had moved into Opele. There were thus four local lineages of the Raki clan in Opele.

The Raki example illustrates several features of the role of a local lineage in the life of a *wang tic*. Members of the four Raki lineages controlled the neighborhood court, and a Raki man was neighborhood headman. There was certainly no hostility between the Raki people and the others in Opele, but it was clear that the Raki, particularly through the large lineage that had originally settled in Opele, controlled the distribution of land in the *wang tic*. This lineage had expanded to such a degree that its land formed the most densely settled portion of Opele. Although land was not actually scarce, several young men of Raki found it easier to obtain land in one or another neighboring *wang tic* and consequently moved out of Opele. As long as land is available in other areas, therefore, there is a limit to the number of people a local lineage can have before it begins to disperse as young men move elsewhere. Such men cannot strictly be considered members of the local lineage, although they may return frequently to visit and may seek assistance from the local lineage (A. Curley 1971:67–71).

THE JO DOGGOLA ("PEOPLE OF THE DOORWAY)"

When the members of a local lineage become so numerous that young men can obtain land more easily in other neighborhoods, the lineage begins to disperse. (In Opele a lineage of only fourteen households was already expanding into other neighborhoods.) Lineages disperse for other reasons, too. Men move away from their parental homes to seek assistance in obtaining bridewealth, or because of unpleasant relations with other members of the *wang tic*, or (rarely) because they have been deprived of lands in the *wang tic*. Consequently, descent ties are not coterminous with residential ties, for everyone has agnatic kinsmen outside his own *wang tic*.

The *jo doggola* is a dispersed lineage with a depth of about six generations, members of which trace their ancestry to a known ancestor. Unlike the local lineage, which exists only as an analytical concept that I devised to describe a feature of Lango social organization, the *jo doggola* can be defined and discussed by Langi. The term *jo doggola* means "people of the doorway" and can be formally defined as "the group that can be called upon to assist in the payment of blood money should a member of the group kill an outsider." The payment of blood money is required whenever one person is believed to have caused the death of a person in another lineage. There is little distinction between murder and accidental killing, so that if a man accidentally spears his hunting companion he is required to pay seven cows to a close senior male kinsman of the victim. The blood money, called *gelo kwor* ("to pay for the body"), is collected from seven senior male kinsmen of the transgressor. These men are prominent elders in the local lineages that make up the *jo doggola*. The men are dispersed throughout an area with a radius of about twelve miles, the distance regarded as one day's walk.

Of eight deaths of adult males during the period 1963–1966 in Obanya Kura, six were considered to have been natural deaths; that is, the persons died of illness. The remaining two were considered to have been the fault of other persons. As far as I could ascertain, one of the killings was clearly a murder and the other was an accident. In both instances, the survivors collected partial blood payment from the lineages of the men who were judged to have been at fault. One payment was five cows, and the other was four cows. Many people commented on how difficult it was to collect the full seven cows, and some bitterness remained between the various parties over the unpaid portion of the blood payments.

Figure 2 depicts the dispersal pattern of one *jo doggola*. It is based on an incident that occurred in 1961: a man in Obanya Kura had committed a murder and had to gather the blood payment of seven cows from consanguineal kinsmen in his *jo doggola*.

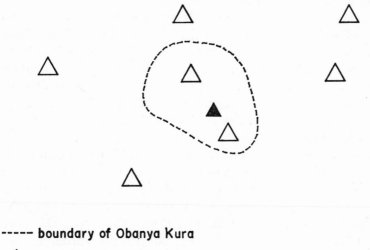

----- boundary of Obanya Kura

△ male kinsman who paid one cow to the lineage of the victim

▲ offender

|——————————|
5 miles

Figure 2: Dispersal of Senior Males in a *Jo Doggola*

The *jo doggola*, therefore, represents the group of agnatic kinsmen whom one can conveniently visit and whom one may ask for assistance, the group that we would term the maximal lineage. Donation of cattle for payment of blood money is only one form of assistance that members of a *jo doggola* may be asked to provide one another. For example, a young man has the right to ask a member of his *jo doggola* for bridewealth cattle, and he may take up residence with a member of his *jo doggola* after marriage.

The dispersal of kinsmen whose help one may ask offers a distinct advantage in a society where subsistence is threatened by local food shortages and epizootics of cattle disease. The bond between *jo doggola* members is such that they are obliged to support one another, and a man can migrate to the *wang tic* of a *jo doggola* member when faced with a scarcity of land in his own *wang tic*. In Chapter III, we shall see that this network of kinship is widened further by the interrelation of clans to one another in a ceremonial linkage called the *etogo*.

The *jo doggola* is not a corporate group, nor is its membership known with certainty by those who belong to it. Its composition constantly changes as the local lineages grow and as men migrate. The composition of the *jo doggola* is determined by the combination of residence and genealogical relationship. When a man migrates to a new area, his kinship ties to those whom he left behind will matter little, since he will be too far away to maintain regular contact. But over the course of time he may become accommodated into the *jo doggola*, even though his precise genealogical relationship to the other members is not known. Genealogy is not terribly important in Lango, and people seldom keep careful account of the names and relationships of ancestors beyond the third ascending generation. Since no lineage leaders or offices are associated with any kinship group in Lango, there is no single point of reference that one can employ to delineate the composition of a *jo doggola*. The closest thing to a reference point is the founder of the lineage, but it is not uncommon for two men who claim to be in the same *jo doggola* to disagree over who the founder is. It is not accurate, therefore, to describe Lango social organization as a segmentary lineage system, the segments of which are articulated at several levels; Lango organization does not fit the model that has been described by Evans-Pritchard (1940) for the Nuer. It is possible that during the precolonial period Lango groups were articulated into a more coherent system than that which presently exists, but there is little evidence that this was so.[4] This possibility is suggested by the existence of two political offices in traditional Lango whose titles, *rwot* and *jago*, can both be translated as "chief." But neither the *rwot* nor the *jago* appears to have been the head of a lineage, a clan, or any other group (Driberg 1923; Tarantino 1949*a* 1949*b*). Rather, the offices appear to have been associated with military leadership during brief periods when a *rwot*, assisted by several *jagi*, would organize a war party. The offices were temporary and entailed military control over a geographical area in Lango rather than leadership of a descent group. The offices of *jago* and *rwot* disappeared after 1914, when colonial rule was established. During the early colonial period Lango warfare was ended through the use of Ganda agents and small military detachments. The terms *rwot* and *jago* were retained, but their original meanings were lost, and they were applied to Lango administrative officers who were trained and appointed by the Uganda government.

The *jo doggola*, then, has never been a clearly defined group of consanguineal kinsmen with a recognized leader. Today its importance is that an individual can use *jo doggola* relationships to obtain assistance from kinsmen who live outside his home area. The *jo doggola* is important ceremonially: invitations to certain ceremonies are extended to all members of a *jo doggola* or to representatives of the local lineages that make up the *jo doggola*. For example, the largest of the *kwer* ceremonies, the Bringing Beer for the Ankle Bells, is an occasion when the entire *jo doggola* should be invited.

Informants describe the *jo doggola* as a group that can consume the meat of one cow without gorging themselves and without anyone's going away hungry. That would mean a group of about 120 adults. This estimate of the number of adults in a *jo doggola* is as good as any. It includes women who have married in, al-

4. Work is currently being done on precolonial Lango political affairs by John Tosh of the University of London. See Tosh (1971).

though, strictly speaking, these women are not members of their husbands' *jo doggola*; they remain in the *jo doggola* of their fathers.

The Lango Clan is a named, exogamous, patrilineal descent group, the members of which consider themselves to be descended from a common mythical ancestor. Members of a clan follow prohibitions associated with that clan, and these and other prohibitions are observed by women who marry male members of the clan. Members of a clan consider themselves to be related to one another for some purposes and frequently use kinship terms in addressing and referring to clansmen even though the actual relationship may be remote. Today only two aspects of clanship affect interpersonal relations in any significant way: the marriage-regulating functions of the clan and the affection arising out of the significance of patrilineality in Lango ideology.

A man cannot marry a woman in his patrilineal clan or in the patrilineal clan of his mother. Because clans are dispersed widely over Lango District, the names of clans are sometimes changed and the taboos associated with each clan become altered, and there is sometimes confusion over whether two people belong to the same clan and whether they are permitted to marry. The greater the distance between the homes of two prospective marriage partners, the greater is the possibility that confusion over clan affiliation will arise. The advice of older people may be sought to clarify the genealogical relationship between the descent groups of the two marriage partners. At present, young people tend to disregard the elders and to go ahead with the marriage arrangements, especially if the proposed marriage is between a man and a woman who is believed to be in his mother's clan. If there is any doubt at all about the clan membership of the woman, the couple is likely to go ahead with the marriage proceedings. Older people sometimes remark that such marriages indicate a breakdown of the whole idea of clanship and will have disastrous biological consequences. It is difficult to determine whether these statements actually reflect a decrease of the significance of clanship in Lango, or whether people have always interpreted clan membership loosely when it stood in the way of a particular marriage. It is certainly true that younger people—those under thirty—are unaware of and uninterested in the mythological basis of their own clans and that many are not even certain of the name of their clan or the taboos associated with it.

A young woman is instructed by her husband's mother in the observances of the clan which both women have married into. This custom has the somewhat paradoxical result that, although the clans are patrilineal, the principal repositories of clan traditions are women. It is considered important for women to be aware of the observances, because most of them are thought to affect fertility and the health of children. If a woman fails to observe the regulations of her husband's clan, her negligence might be used as an explanation for the sickness of her child or for her barrenness. Examples of these observances are the following: not sitting on the skin of a duiker; never drinking water from a gourd; always wearing a wrist bracelet made of the skin of a bushbuck.

Ties of affection between members of the same clan are significant when a man emigrates from a *wang tic* to take up residence in another part of Lango District. The newcomer associates himself with a distant clansman in the area and may be accommodated into a local lineage even though he cannot trace his genealogical relationship to its members.

Establishing relationships based on clan membership is attaining a new significance in Lango as more men engage in wage labor in and outside Lango District. As noted in Chapter I, labor migration has not yet affected the lives of many people in Obanya Kura, but several young men who had worked in Lira and other towns related that they formed friendships in the new setting on the basis of clanship, seeking out drinking companions among members of their own clan from other areas in Lango and sometimes calling upon them for assistance in finding a job, a meal, or a place to live. I was told that clanship operates in the same way in some sections of Kampala and other industrial townships of Uganda[5], although it was not possible to obtain precise information on the matter.

5. Parkin (1969:128–149) discusses agnatic ties among Nilotic migrants in Kampala.

To conclude, the principle of patrilineal descent is a feature of Lango ideology, but aside from its function of regulating marriage, it is most important within small local groups of shallow generational depth which I have called local lineages. Within these groups, there are agricultural cooperation in the context of the *wang tic,* common participation in ceremonies, and frequent claims on fellow lineage members for support and assistance. Patrilineality in Lango can be fully understood only when seen in relation to residence and subsistence activities.

WOMEN IN LANGO SOCIETY

Territorial Exogamy

The rule of clan exogamy is readily acknowledged by all, but endogamic marriages sometimes take place when the clan membership of two persons is ambiguous.[6] However, another type of exogamy is important in Lango social organization. It is not discussed so explicitly as clan exogamy, nor is it surrounded by the same sort of interdictions. This is territorial exogamy—the practice of marrying outside one's neighborhood. Territorial exogamy is evident in the census statistics from Obanya Kura, which show that 96 percent of married women had married *into* the neighborhoods in which they were residing; that is, their natal homes were not in the neighborhoods of their husbands. The average distance between a wife's natal homestead and her post marital residence is six miles, a distance that permits visiting between a wife and her natal homestead. During the first few years of marriage a wife returns to her parents' home about once a month (except during the first few months of marriage, when she is forbidden to).

Related to this pattern of territorial exogamy is a rule of mother-in-law avoidance which is imposed upon married men.[7]

6. I recorded three instances in which marriage partners were told by older kinsmen that they should not marry because they belonged to the same clan. In each instance, however, there was sufficient ambiguity about the clan affiliation of at least one partner that the marriage was allowed to take place. I did not hear of any instances in which two persons were actually prevented from marrying because of the rules of exogamy.

7. For a theoretical discussion of mother-in-law avoidance see Radcliffe-Brown (1952: 92,108).

A man must not look at the mother of his wife nor any classificatory mother-in-law—that is, any woman who has married into the local lineage of his wife's father and who is of the same generation as his wife's father. A man may talk with his mother-in-law, in a formal conversation in which the man remains within a house and the mother-in-law stands outside the house, with a wall between them. Formerly, if a man did see his mother-in-law, he was obliged to recompense his wife's father with a payment of one bull, but there has been no instance of such a payment in Obanya Kura since 1962. Although mother-in-law avoidance is not a barrier to neighborhood endogamy, the avoidance makes it inconvenient for a man to marry within his neighborhood, and Lango men readily acknowledge that if they marry outside their neighborhood it will be easier for them to cooperate with and visit the members of their own *wang tic*. For most men, mother-in-law avoidance is a problem only at the marketplace, where an accidental encounter with one's mother-in-law is likely. During visits and ceremonies, the probability of such an encounter is minimized by the precaution of separating men and women.

From the man's point of view, there are other reasons that it is undesirable to marry a woman in one's own neighborhood. Men complain that a wife's interest will be divided between her natal home and her married home if the two are near each other: a wife can be called upon to work in the fields of her parents or to assist her mother in household tasks, and she will not fulfill her wifely obligations satisfactorily. Equally important is the husband's concern that minor domestic squabbles will cause the wife to leave him and take refuge at the home of her parents. To a very great extent, a husband must answer to his wife's brothers for any alleged mistreatment of the wife, and men contend that living near the wife's brothers subjects a man to the control of the wife's brothers and can lead to animosity and the eventual dissolution of the marriage.

The example of Tomasi Okello shows some of the sorts of transactions that can take place between a man and his wife's brothers. Okello made arrangements to mary Mirici, whose family home was 5.5 miles from Okello's home—no more than the average distance. He agreed to pay 12 cows and 900 shillings in bridewealth, but he had considerable difficulty collecting the cows. As the marriage time drew near, he had collected only 11 cows, but Mirici's kinsmen agreed to the marriage on the condition that Okello pay the additional cow later. Mirici had two brothers; one was already married, but the other brother, Opio, was expecting to use the bridewealth from Mirici's marriage so that he could get married himself.[8] Several weeks after Mirici moved to Okello's house, Opio came to visit and began to inquire about the payment of the additional cow. Okello assured Opio that the cow was forthcoming, but later complained that Opio was pressing him needlessly and was trying to cause trouble. The additional cow was not paid as long as I was in Obanya Kura, and Okello eventually began to say that he did not really owe a cow and had never promised to pay it.

In July, when Okello and Mirici had been married for fourteen months, Mirici's mother sent word to Mirici that there was much work to be done around her natal home and asked her to come and help. Mirici asked her husband whether it would be all right for her to go, and he tried to dissuade her from going. Mirici disregarded Okello's injunctions and went to her mother's house, taking her infant with her. She stayed for three days, and Okello told people that he was very angry with her, since there was much weeding to be done in his own fields. When Mirici returned, Okello chastised her severely. In August, they had another argument, and Okello beat her. News of the beating prompted Opio to visit Okello to find out why he had beaten Mirici. Opio had a very strong interest in the marriage of Mirici, because if she were divorced and the bridewealth had to be returned, he would be unable to use the bridewealth for his own marriage. Opio was in a difficult situation: he was obliged to look after his sister as her protector and as a man who had a special relation to her children, but he also had to appease Okello lest Okello decide to divorce Mirici. Opio ended by siding with Okello and chastising his sister for "bringing trouble" to the home of her husband.

One week later, Opio reappeared at Okello's house and asked

8. Each male is "cattle-linked" to a sister whose bridewealth will be used to provide at least some of the cattle for his own marriage. This arrangement is similar to the cattle linkage of the Lovedu, described by Krige (1939).

Okello to loan him fifteen shillings to help pay a court fine. Okello loaned him the money but complained to others about having to make the loan. The fifteen shillings were never repaid, and Opio even requested additional loans from Okello. By this time, Okello had come to regard his brother-in-law as a permanent thorn in his side, but there was little that he could do about it. Okello was fond of his wife, and since she had already borne one child and was pregnant with another, he had no reason to divorce her.

Lango men also argue that, in the event of a divorce, it is not easy to get one's bridewealth returned if the wife's father and brother live close by. Divorce cases often involve protracted disputes between affines, and if the wife's brothers live in the same neighborhood, they can impose extralegal pressures on the husband to avoid having to return the bridewealth.

It is difficult to assess the validity of the men's reasons because there are so few marriages within the neighborhood that one cannot readily observe the social processes at work. In any event, the fact that 96 percent of marriages are between residents of different neighborhoods shows that men are sufficiently motivated by those reasons to seek wives outside their neighborhoods.

INCORPORATION INTO HOUSEHOLD, LOCAL LINEAGE, AND NEIGHBORHOOD

For a woman, territorial exogamy creates a number of impositions and requires personal adjustments following marriage which are far greater than those required of men. These personal adjustments can be seen on three levels: (1) acceptance of a woman into a household; (2) incorporation into her husband's local lineage; and (3) adjustment to a new neighborhood.

Marriage arrangements are protracted, and they include lengthy discussions over the payment of bridewealth. Upon the completion of bridewealth payment, the woman takes up residence at her husband's household, bringing with her only a few personal possessions. From the beginning, she must make a great effort to satisfy her mother-in-law and her husband, to comport herself as meekly and unobtrusively as possible, and to display a willingness to work hard and assume household responsibilities.

A young wife must not look her mother-in-law directly in the eye and must not speak to strangers or to any men except her husband and his brothers. The first few months of marriage are particularly important, for the wife is closely observed: her personality and willingness to work are discussed by the mother-in-law, and, most important, it is hoped that she will show signs of pregnancy. If a marriage continues for two years without a pregnancy, the husband has the right to divorce his wife, and is entitled to have his bridewealth repaid. A young wife is fully aware of this and fears the stigma attached to barrenness.

The first signs of pregnancy add immensely to the status of a wife, and entitle her to request a house of her own if her husband has not yet provided her one. Once a wife is set up in her own household, she is able to exert her personality more fully than was possible while she remained at her mother-in-law's household. Gradually, her husband assigns his fields to her, and she may begin to sell surplus crops in the marketplace, assume the responsibility of managing the fields, and make beer for members of the *wang tic.*

Meanwhile, the woman acquires a place in the local lineage of her husband. She comes to participate in a joking relationship with her husband's brothers and work in *alea* groups with other women of the local lineage. She is designated as the "co-wife" (*nyeko*) of the wives of her husband's real and classificatory brothers. After the first few months of marriage, she is entitled to visit her parents, and may bring her mother-in-law or some of her co-wives with her to exchange food and hospitality. If she becomes ill, she can rely on the assistance of the women who have married into her husband's lineage, and her relationship with them is symbolized by the observance of the same set of prohibitions— the prohibitions of her husband's clan, which are taught to her during the first few months of her marriage.

The acceptance of a young woman into the neighborhood at large differs somewhat from her acceptance into the local lineage of her husband, for she does not classify all the women of the neighborhood as co-wives or as affinal kinsmen. Gradually, she comes to participate in the economic and social life of the neighborhood as she visits other households in the *wang tic* and works in the field with other women of the *wang tic,* walks to the market with them, and visits with them. At first she may restrict her social relations within the neighborhood to a few women who came from her own neighborhood and have also married into the new area, and some of these women may even be related to her consanguineally. If a woman is to participate effectively in a neighborhood, however, she must widen her ties to associate with women whom she did not know before and women to whom she is not related.

At some point, she may require medical assistance and may be advised to consult a female adept in the neighborhood. Discussing her condition with women in the neighborhood, and perhaps having a spirit-possession dance performed for her, she becomes the object of much attention from women in the neighborhood. In Chapter V we shall see that spirit possession and the activities associated with it form one of the main preoccupations of women and are a frequent topic of conversation.

The adjustment to household, local lineage, and neighborhood is a great problem for women in a patrilineal, virilocal society. Lango men never face the same sorts of problems, for they are raised in a neighborhood and know all its members from an early age. Women sometimes jokingly refer to themselves as "stranger" or "visitor," but it is a joke born of anxiety as well as joviality.

The problems associated with the incorporation of women are dramatized in the *kwer* ceremonial complex. The *kwer* ceremonies illustrate the ambiguous position of a woman, who is born into her father's clan but must alter her clan affiliation at marriage. Of all the ethnographer's questions, perhaps the most difficult to answer was this: "Does a married woman belong to the clan of her husband or to the clan of her father?" Some informants said that a woman remains in her father's clan throughout her life. Others said that a woman does not belong to any clan until she marries and learns the totemic observances of her husband's clan. A few men argued that the concept of clan is altogether irrelevant for women, since the existence of a clan depends solely on its male members. The varied and complicated responses to this question were due not to ignorance of the issues but to a real problem inherent in a patrilineal, virilocal society.

Women and Social Change

Although Lango women must be incorporated into the residential and descent groups of their husbands, one must not
presume that women are entirely without rights. A woman can
initiate legal proceedings against any man, including her husband. Moreover, as a woman grows older she can attain high
status within the lineage and the neighborhood as a woman who
works hard and sees that her sons are provided with bridewealth
and that her daughters are married for a high bridewealth. Lango
ideas about the relation between the sexes do include notions
of male superiority and of the desirability of male domination
over women, but they also heed the obvious fact that lineages
depend on the procreative powers of women and that ties of affection between mothers and children are greater than those between fathers and children.

The foregoing features of Lango life remain much as they
were during Driberg's study. Since then, however, numerous
changes have taken place in Lango society.

First, a large number of changes have taken place in the realm
of political organization. After colonial rule was established, an
administrative system was introduced, and hostilities between
kinship and residential groups were virtually brought to a halt,
allowing us to speak of a *Pax Britannica*. Among the first reper-
cussions of colonial rule was a tendency toward the abandonment
of the village and a dispersal of residents into isolated homesteads. At the same time, a court system and an administrative
apparatus were provided, allowing people to obtain redress of
grievances and allowing the government to implement its
policies.

Schools were introduced in Lango after 1920 and, although
people had to pay a fee to send their children to school, the
schools became increasingly popular. An elementary school was
accessible to the people of Obanya Kura, and junior and senior
secondary schools were established in Lango District.[9] Because
parents must pay school fees, they may have to decide not to send
some of their children to school, and many of the decisions are

9. In 1966, there were 34 children from Obanya Kura attending elementary
schools, an average of 0.3 per household. There were 5 children in junior secondary
school, and 3 in secondary school.

made according to sex. Parents rightly regard education as a financial investment that will reap returns for them later in life if their children obtain salaried jobs. Girls are considered to be a higher risk because many girls leave school before the completion of their education in order to marry. Furthermore, there are many more tasks for young girls to perform around the house than for young boys. Consequently, few girls are sent to primary school. As a child advances in school, the tuition fee becomes greater each year, and more children are forced to drop out for financial reasons. Here again, girls are selected out of the educational system.

Government administration has brought numerous other innovations into the lives of the Langi. One innovation that affects people most immediately is the system of free medical care. The clinic in Obanya Kura is extremely popular; unfortunately, it lacks the equipment and personnel to meet the medical needs of the people adequately. The people see the government medical system as a supplement to traditional Lango curing practices, including the ceremonies that form the subject of this study. The persistence of the *kwer* ceremonies and the increasing popularity of spirit-possession activities is due partly to the fact that the people of Obanya Kura continue to suffer illnesses, the bulk of which cannot be treated at government medical facilities. Because obstetric complications are numerous and because child care is the province of women, Lango women are more affected than men by the availability of health facilities. Women visit the clinic more often than men and discuss in greater detail the merits and inadequacies of various medical assistants and medicines.

In the previous chapter, we referred to economic change in Lango, particularly the introduction of cotton as a cash crop, the use of money as a medium of exchange, and the establishment of a cotton-marketing system and shops which allow people to exchange surplus crops for consumer goods. The greater share of these consumer goods, however, is sold to men. Apart from clothing and a few household items, women are not really able to make major purchases. The most valuable material possession of most households is a bicycle, but women are usually not taught to ride one, and it is almost unknown for a man to give his wife permission to use the bicycle.

In spite of the fact that a woman has nominal control over the material resources of the household, those resources can rarely be used to the woman's advantage. Technically, a Lango woman does not own property, and in the event of a divorce, the property reverts to her husband. Similarly, a wife can supplement the household income by trading in the marketplace, but there are few, if any, ways in which she can spend the money to improve her own status. A woman who accumulates money in this way is expected to use it for the bridewealth of her sons or to give it to her husband.

Conclusion

Social change in Lango has not given women any substantial means of improving their status. Men have access to education, the possibility of wage labor, and the ability to purchase consumer goods which enhance their status within the community, but women do not. The most important qualities for a woman are still her ability to bear children and to adjust to life in her husband's family.

This process of differential social change has been noted for other African societies (LeVine 1966), and it is intrinsically related to two of the ceremonial complexes we shall describe: *kwer* ceremonies and spirit-possession ceremonies. Women are still faced with the problem of incorporation, which is dramatized in the *kwer* ceremonies, and one can safely predict that those ceremonies will continue to be practiced as long as the present pattern of patrilineality and virilocality persists and as long as women are denied access to the principal economic assets of the household.

The spirit-possession complex is directly related to differential social change, and in spirit-possession ceremonies the themes of sexual antagonism and the inability of women to possess consumer items are dramatized. This is not to say that sexual antagonism is a regular feature of Lango life or that women violently object to differential social change. Differential access to status is never discussed, but it is acknowledged through the symbolism of the possession dance.

III

Etogo: *Ceremonies of the Elders*

Named groups of elders perform a wide range of ceremonies for the purposes of curing people and controlling the forces of nature, such as lightning and rain. These ceremonies and the elders who perform them are called *etogo*, and they constitute an important domain in Lango religion. *Etogo* activities are organized partly along kinship lines, and they encourage relations among descent groups cohabiting in an area. The functional significance of the *etogo* is more apparent in ethnohistorical studies, since many *etogo* activities are no longer practiced in Lango. *Etogo* still exist, however, and some of the ceremonies are still performed, but they are being replaced by new forms of social groupings and alternative ceremonial activities. In this chapter, we shall examine the function of the *etogo* in Lango social organization, describe some of the *etogo* ceremonies performed in recent years in Obanya Kura, and explain the recent decline of the *etogo*. First it is necessary to look at the basic organization of the *etogo* as it relates to ties of kinship and residence.

ETOGO ORGANIZATION

An *etogo* is defined as "the male elders of several clans that are joined in a permanent or semipermanent relation for ceremonial purposes." In theory, every married male belongs to an *etogo* and is entitled to attend its ceremonies. However, a man does not gain full status in an *etogo* until his father has died. After that, he is recognized as an elder and can be called upon to assist in performing *etogo ceremonies*. If a man dies before his son has married, the boy does not become an *etogo* elder as soon as he is married, but must wait until his oldest child has reached the age of marriage. The distinction between young men and elders pervades *etogo* gatherings: the two age groups are seated in different clusters and are given different foods, and the elders expect deference from the young men, at least for the duration of the event.

Obanya Kura is a locality consisting of three distinct neighborhoods, and it can be called a vicinage. Within a vicinage all the men in one clan belong to the same *etogo*. Patrilineal descent, therefore, is one of the basic organizing principles of the *etogo*, for it decrees that a man belongs to the *etogo* of his father. Patrilineality does not, however, determine which other clans will be aligned with his own in the same *etogo*. That is determined by two principles which I shall call "ideology of alliance" and "locality." Briefly, by "ideology of alliance" I refer to the Lango belief that each clan is bound to certain other clans in a permanent ceremonial grouping, the *etogo*, and that no matter where one travels in Lango District one will always find the same clans joined to one another. Langi believe, then, that the same clans are always bound together in a ceremonial relation which remains the same through space and time. The principle of locality is derived from ethnographic observations rather than from Lango ideology. It pertains to the difficulty of maintaining effective *etogo* relations over a large area. In other words, although Lango ideology asserts that the same clans are always bound to one another in *etogo* linkages, in actuality the linkages vary from one locale to the next. These two principles can best be illustrated by referring to actual *etogo* organization in Obanya Kura.

I asked seventeen men forty-five years of age or older which clans were in their *etogo*. Their responses are reported in Table III. In the table, the *etogo* are shown as clusters of clans, so that it is possible to identify three *etogo*.

Each clan stands in an *etogo* relation with about five other clans. This alliance may be based on kinship, but it need not be. All the clans belonging to the Etogo me Mea are Ocukuru, and it is believed that these clans are related to one another through common descent. The links are vague, however, for it is said that the Ocukuru groups segmented into different clans very early in Lango history. Thus they are distinct clans, each having its own food taboos and each forming an exogamic group. Elders of the Etogo me Mea say, "We are related to one another, but we are not so close as brothers in a clan." Elders of the Etogo me

TABLE III

Etogo Affiliation of Clans in Obanya Kura

		Informant																
ogo	Clan	Augustino Otianga	Matan Oyuru	Ipila	Resnia Ongura	Aloncius Ongare	Baranabo Adea	Dicon Adicu	Angelus Oguol	John Ocen	Lakan Odyang	Ekora	Erikano Oiine	Benjamin Abenyo	Omara Nua	Ongom Ongeo	Otwi	Yokadina Oguvang
	Ober me Wi Cogo	X		X														
la	Atek me Jo Aber	X	X	X														
	Ober me Pala	X	X	X														
	Okwero We	X	X	X	X													
	Omolo	X	X	X														
	Otikokin							X		X								
	Oki me Ngura					X	X	X		X	X	X	X					
ki	Okaruwok					X	X	X		X	X	X						
	Owumolao					X	X	X	X	X								
	Raki					X	X	X	X	X	X		X					
	Oki me Bura					X	X	X										
	Ngurapuc	X				X	X	X	X		X							
	Ocukuru me Alilo													X	X	X	X	
	Ocukuru me Mea													X	X	X	X	X
Iea	Ocukuru me Okwerokwac													X	X	X		X
	Ocukuru me Ogorayit										X			X	X	X	X	X
	Ocukuru me Atek													X	X	X		X
	Ocukuru me Oki													X	X	X	X	X
	Pedi			X														
	Oki me Wan Odyang	X										X						
	Okwero Kic	X																
	Oki me Okwero Cuga							X										

NOTE: An "X" indicates that the man considered that clan to be in his *etogo*.

Mea are not concerned with the genealogical relationship of the clans in their *etogo*, and they do not describe their *etogo* affiliations in the idiom of kinship. Rather, they state that all the clans in their *etogo* are bound to one another for ceremonial assistance because those clans have long been associated with one another and because they have always been able to perform effective ceremonies for one another. The same is true of the other two *etogo* of Obanya Kura, which claim no genealogical relationships among the clans.

Thus far, the description of *etogo* accords with Lango ideology. But Langi say that the groupings of clans in *etogo* are constant throughout Lango District. This claim introduces the problem of locality—how the *etogo* are distributed. Here the description of *etogo* organization becomes complicated, for there is a discrepancy between informants' statements and ethnographic observations. The statements represent a sort of charter which gives *etogo* their authority and permits them to operate in an orderly way. For example, a man who belongs to the Etogo me Oki believes that his *etogo* is an ancient ceremonial alliance and that if he should move to another area in Lango District he can easily locate the members of his *etogo* and call on them for assistance if he needs to have a ceremony performed. He believes that the elders of this clan have always and everywhere been associated with the same five clans, and that these clans have always performed ceremonies for one another.

When we consider the number of clans in Lango District, however, it becomes apparent that there is a fallacy in the charter. I did not attempt to compile an exhaustive list of clans, but Driberg listed more than 115 (1923:192–204), and my own notes contain many clan names not on his list. The number of clans is certainly well over 100, and the clans are widely but unevenly dispersed. Within the three neighborhoods in Obanya Kura, 13 clans are represented. If a man migrates from one vicinage to another he is not likely to find members of all the clans that made up his home *etogo*. He may find men belonging to some of the clans and they may all be in the same *etogo*, but this *etogo* will also include other clans, which did not belong to his original *etogo*. In short, he will find himself affiliated with an *etogo* that has a very different clan composition from the one he previously belonged to.

Another point to consider is the number of *etogo* that are active in a given area. I did not visit any area other than Obanya Kura to obtain information on *etogo*, but I asked Obanya Kura residents who had lived in other vicinages about *etogo* organization in their previous homes. Their responses indicate that a vicinage has from three to five active *etogo*. The population is simply not dense enough in Lango to support more *etogo* than that. *Etogo* composition depends largely on which clans happen to reside in the area. *Etogo* composition cannot be as fixed as Langi believe, for the *etogo* must be flexible enough to accommodate new members.

Not only does the clan composition change from one area to the next, but the names of the *etogo* are different. The three *etogo* in Obanya Kura are named Mea, Oki, and Pala. The *etogo* name "Mea" is taken from "Ocukuru me Mea," the name of a clan whose members were numerous in the area during the 1930s. "Oki" is the name of a man who lived two generations ago and who was very active in his *etogo*. The name "Pala" indicates that several men in Obanya Kura who belong to this *etogo* came from the area known as Apala. All the names have obvious local referents, a further indication that *etogo* are not fixed throughout Lango.

In considering the relation between locality and *etogo* organization, there is another point at which the Lango model of the *etogo* is misleading. The Langi describe their *etogo* as groups of men, and Hayley (1947:48–52) also spoke of *etogo* "groups." The concept of "group" is misleading, for *etogo* are not bounded, nor do they have a fixed membership. The personnel of an *etogo* fluctuates markedly depending upon the location of the ceremony. This inherent flexibility can best be described using the concept of "field" (Jay 1964:138).

The concept of the *etogo* as a social field can be illustrated by an actual incident: A man named Ogwal belonged to the clan Ocukuru me Oki, and his *etogo* included five other clans. An *etogo* ceremony was to be held at his house, but it was not feasible to invite all elders of the six clans from all over Lango District. Such an invitation would presume that several hundred men were willing to travel distances of up to sixty miles to attend a ceremony at the house of a stranger. Moreover, a ritual group of such a large number of people would mean that the elders of Ogwal's *etogo* would be spending most of their time attending ceremonies if they were to meet their reciprocal *etogo* obligations. Instead, news was circulated to the effect that an *etogo* ceremony was to be held at Ogwal's house and that the elders in his *etogo* should attend. Those who attended came from a limited area whose size depended on such factors as the status of Ogwal and the importance of the ceremony. All the men who attended came from less than five miles away.

Ogwal's clansman, Ituku, lived ten miles from Ogwal. Ituku held an *etogo* ceremony which also attracted elders from a distance of five miles.

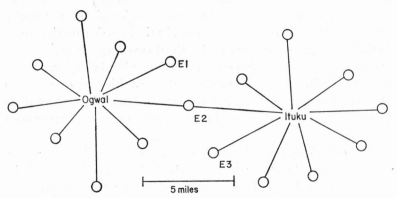

Figure 3:   Diagrammatic Representation of Elders Attending Ceremonies

In Figure 3 each outlying circle represents an elder who attended one of the ceremonies, and the length of the line represents the distance between his home and the place where the ceremony was held. This example demonstrates that there is no single entity which we can refer to as an *etogo* group. To describe the membership of an *etogo* we must consider it over time. The *etogo* field is organized along egocentric lines, for its membership depends on the location of the ceremony.

Table III offers further testimony to the flexibility of the *etogo*. It shows that three *etogo* were active in Obanya Kura, but

that some informants disagreed over which clans belonged to
each *etogo*. They disagreed because some of them named clans in
the Aloi area only. For example, five informants in the Etogo
me Oki did not acknowledge that the Oki me Bura clan was in
their *etogo*, and three stated that it was. No men of Oki me Bura
live in the area. Since the members of Oki me Bura do not
regularly participate in the *etogo* activities of the area, the place
of this clan in the *etogo* is acknowledged by only a few. In general, the responses indicate that the *etogo* is a local phenomenon
including whatever clans happen to be in the area, and that the
etogo is not an indissoluble phratry extending throughout Lango
District.[1]

THE FUNCTION OF THE ETOGO

The Langi recognize the importance of descent and the ideology of alliance among clans as two important factors in *etogo*
organization, but they overlook the factor of locality—the problem of maintaining *etogo* of uniform clan composition throughout Lango when the clans are unevenly dispersed. There is a
logical explanation, though, both for the Lango model and for
the actual deviation. The explanation derives from the functional significance of the *etogo* as an institution that cuts across
clan lines.

The manifest function of the *etogo* is seen in its ceremonial
activities, which fall into two categories. First, the *etogo* are responsible for relations between the living and the dead. Second,
the *etogo* perform a series of ceremonies called *gato* ("blessing")
ceremonies, which serve either to protect people from or to cure

1. We have noted the discrepancy between the Lango view of the *etogo* and the
realities of *etogo* organization. Such discrepancies between ideology and social action have been commented on by several students of African religion in their descriptions of culturally similar situations (Lienhardt 1961:25; Middleton 1960:21;
Evans-Pritchard 1956:311–322). The explanation for these discrepancies may be
that many African belief systems are directed primarily at solving fundamental
problems of existence rather than developing intellectually coherent models of
social reality. Thus, the Lango belief that the *etogo* is unchanging in its composition does not conform to social reality, but this matters little because the real
purpose of the etogo is to conduct ceremonies that are necessary to the well-being
of the community. In fact, the fiction incorporated into the belief system actually
permits the *etogo* to operate more effectively. Lango religion is marked above all
by its pragmatism, a quality that has been noted in other African religious systems
(Evans-Pritchard 1937; Horton 1964).

them of a variety of misfortunes. These ceremonies (to be discussed later) include the *gato bwoc*, a cure for impotence; the *gator twor*, a general curing ceremony; and the *gato kot*, a cure for persons who have been struck by lightning and a way of preventing lightning from striking them in the future. Some *etogo* ceremonies are performed for the well-being of a single person, some for that of a particular group of people, and some for that of the community as a whole. All *etogo* ceremonies stress the theme of cooperation by members of different clans and emphasize values that are important to the solidarity of the community.

Older men and women believe that, if the *etogo* did not exist, illness would not be cured, men would not be able to overcome the natural elements, and people would not get along well with their neighbors. "Without the *etogo* men would not stay well together" is a sentiment often voiced by informants. No doubt it expresses the ability of the *etogo* to cut across lines of clanship and promote efforts toward solidarity.

The origin of the *etogo* is unclear to Langi, but all express the view that it was established at an early period in Lango history to allow people to assist one another in performing curing ceremonies and in burying the dead. This account also states that during this early period, clans were much smaller than they are now. Migration was frequent, and a man might migrate into an area to support himself. He could rely on *etogo* members for support because *etogo* members have a sacred obligation to assist one another even if they belong to different clans. Given the flexibility of the *etogo*, he could easily attach himself to a group of *etogo* elders and participate in the ceremonial life of the community. In this way, a man would be able to develop interpersonal ties with neighbors which would affect his membership in the communal work group and the sharing of essential goods within the vicinage.

If this account contains an element of truth, the *etogo* system facilitated internal migration of nuclear families and other small kin groups. My own observations tend to support this view, for when a man moves into an area it is a simple matter for him to attach himself to an *etogo*. It is true that few people migrate into areas where they have no kinsmen, but the *etogo* group allows a newcomer to expand his social network. After all, the *etogo* members are said to be "near brothers"—which makes the *etogo* members something close to fictive kinsmen. The institution of the *etogo* was entirely compatible with an ecological system of shifting agriculture, movable wealth in the form of livestock, and periodic hardships induced by drought, locusts, small-scale warfare, and cattle diseases. Migration was, and to some extent still is, the most reasonable solution to many of these problems. Roughly 31 percent of the men living in Obanya Kura moved into the area from elsewhere.

The example of Ogwal illustrates the flexibility of the *etogo*. In 1944, Ogwal moved into Opele, one of the three neighborhoods of Obanya Kura. He was then about twenty-five years old and had a wife and one child. Ogwal had been living with his father and two brothers in Omoro, an area about twelve miles from Obanya Kura. Ogwal was not faring well in his home in Omoro; his relations with his father and his brothers were bad, and he believed that he had been cheated out of several cows. The arguments with his agnatic kinsmen centered on the issue of the cows but extended into other aspects of Ogwal's life in Omoro. His wife complained that Ogwal's brothers and their wives stole food from her and that her mother-in-law placed excessive demands upon her. Ogwal's brothers refused to work in his fields, and even persuaded the residents of the *wang tic* not to assist Ogwal.

Frustrated with his situation in Omoro, Ogwal paid several visits to Opele and made contact with Okulu, a member of his mother's clan who had lived in Opele for about three years. Okulu was a member of the Ober me Pala clan, and Ogwal was a member of the Okwero We clan. In Omoro, these two clans belonged to different *etogo*. When Ogwal moved to Opele he took up residence near Okulu, who served as his benefactor. Okulu helped Ogwal obtain permission to cultivate fields in the new neighborhood, and Okulu's brothers assisted Ogwal in building a house. Ogwal also began to attend *etogo* ceremonies with Okulu, even though there were no members of Ogwal's clan in Okulu's *etogo*. However, by attending *etogo* ceremonies and by aligning himself with Okulu and other members of the *etogo*, Ogwal gradually came to be considered a member of the *etogo*.

When I talked with Ogwal about these matters he stated quite firmly that his clan, Okwero We, was in the same *etogo* that Okulu belonged to. Upon analyzing his account, however, it became apparent that Ogwal had merely attached himself to the *etogo* when he moved into the new neighborhood. In doing so, he was able to build up his ties to the kin group that was sponsoring him in his new home. Over time, most people had come to believe that Ogwal's clan was bound in a close relation with the other clans of the *etogo*, but the history of the etogo demonstrates that Ogwal's clan is now in that *etogo* in Opele because Ogwal affiliated himself with the *etogo*, so that later his sons came to be accepted into it. The composition of the *etogo* groups in Ogwal's former neighborhood was very different from the *etogo* composition in his new neighborhood, yet the charter of the *etogo* was flexible enough to accommodate Ogwal. This flexibility permitted Ogwal to adapt more successfully to his new environment than if he had not been able to affiliate with any group.

Seen in the context of migration, the flexibility of the *etogo* system has an adaptational value.[2] As long as there is uncertainty about which clans belong to the *etogo*, the possibility is open for newcomers to affiliate with the group. If the clan composition of an *etogo* were entirely fixed, many men would be left out of the *etogo* system in their areas. In describing the organization of the *etogo*, we noted that, in spite of the flexibility, *etogo* elders subscribe to the view that the clan composition of their group is unchanging and that the elders bear a great obligation to one another. Although this belief does not accord with the facts of *etogo* affiliation, the belief is itself fundamental to the *etogo* system. It is a convenient fiction which imparts to each *etogo* the quality of permanence and instills in individuals a sense of allegiance which would probably not exist if the fiction were not maintained so steadfastly. If it were openly acknowledged that *etogo* affiliation is flexible and that membership in the groups is not fixed, the authority of the *etogo* to perform interclan ceremonies would be weakened. And the *etogo* would be ineffective as a mechanism for cutting across clan ties throughout Lango society. A man would not be able to migrate into a new area with the

2. The ability of religious systems to serve as adaptive mechanisms has been studied by Rappaport (1968) and Moore (1957).

assurance that he would be able to affiliate himself with the same *etogo* in which he had participated at his earlier residence (or with any *etogo*). He would find himself not only among non-kinsmen but also among people who belonged to alien *etogo* and who were unable to assist him in the performance of necessary rituals. The newcomer is not likely to worry about the problem until he needs to have a ritual performed. When the occasion arises, he will request the assistance of neighbors and any kins-men who live nearby, and informally a decision will be made to hold an *etogo* ceremony for him. Thereafter he will consider that the clans represented at this ceremony compose his *etogo* "group." An example of this process can be seen in the case of Augustino Otianga, one of the informants in Table III.

This man has lived in Okwongo for many years, but his clan is not indigenous to the neighborhood, and few of his clansmen live there. In 1965, lightning struck the kraal near his house, injuring a cow. When lightning strikes, it is customary to invite the *etogo* elders to perform a lightning blessing. However, Otianga was un-certain which people in his vicinage were in his *etogo*. He sought advice from two senior men in his vicinage, and they agreed to supervise the ceremony and invited other men to assist them. These men belonged to four clans, and Otianga has come to think of these four clans as the clans (besides his own) in his *etogo*. The example illustrates two organizational features of the *etogo*: its egocentric nature; and its flexibility, which allows a migrant to be accommodated into the ceremonial life of his new vicinage. Moreover, Otianga's example illustrates the prevalence of the belief that *etogo* membership is fixed; Otianga, like other Lango men, expresses the conviction that the clans in his *etogo* "group" are immutably bound together.

CEREMONIES

We have seen that the *etogo* is not a permanent group, in that Langi usually cannot describe the boundaries of the group nor can the outside observer discern any boundaries. Moreover, *etogo* membership is not significant in daily activities: one does not seek out the company of an *etogo* elder as such, nor are there any fac-tions or cleavages in the community based on *etogo* lines. The

TABLE IV

Summary of Data on *Etogo* Ceremonies

		Number of times performed in Obanya Kura during field work	Year last performed in Obanya Kura
	Exhuming the Bones	2	
Ceremonies that	Blessing the Sick	4	
restore relations	Praying for the Sick	3	
with ancestral	Blessing the Impotent	2	
spirits	Rain Blessing	2	
	Standing on the Grave	6	
	Grave Opening	0	1964
Funerary	Mixing the Funeral Beer	0	1954
ceremonies			
	Discussing the Woman	0	1943
	Apuny	0	1959
Ceremony to			
impose a curse	Cursing a Thief	0	1942
on a thief			

etogo is operative only during ceremonies, and only on ceremonial occasions is a man's *etogo* affiliation of importance.

Most *etogo* ceremonies are either funerary ceremonies or ceremonies that are meant to maintain and restore relations with the dead. Only one *etogo* ceremony serves neither of these purposes: the ceremony called "Cursing a Thief" (*gato akwo*). Table IV lists the eleven *etogo* ceremonies known to the people of Obanya Kura; most of these are falling into disuse. The table indicates the principal function of each ceremony and also gives some idea of the current usage of each ceremony by denoting how often it was performed during the period of study (or, if not performed then, when it was last performed).

IDEAS CONCERNING THE DEAD

Of the eleven *etogo* ceremonies listed in Table IV, ten are related to death, being either funerary ceremonies or ceremonies directed at maintaining relations with the dead. We cannot understand *etogo* ceremonies unless we first consider Lango ideas about death, funerals, and relations with the dead.

There is no actual ancestor worship in Lango, and the dead are of interest to the living only for the harm they may bring. Shades (*tipu*) of the dead can cause death, illness, barrenness, and impotence, and they may be responsible for quarreling and conflict among kinsmen, which may lead to segmentation. Every living person possesses a shade, which accompanies him during the course of his life. In the daytime, the shade can be seen moving along the ground at its owner's feet. In the evening, the shade is not seen; it may choose to enter its owner's head if it is in need of rest, or it may wander about visiting other shades. The shade is of little concern to its owner, for it does not generally affect his health or personal affairs. It is true that the shade has some human attributes: a voracious appetite, sexual longing, and a love of music and dance. Something of a theory of personality is embodied in shade beliefs, for a person's selfishness and greed are often attributed to the assertiveness of his shade. Shades have few likable qualities; indeed, they resemble real people only by virtue of their desires. The real nature of the shade of a living person is an abstract question, however, for shades assume importance in human affairs only after their owners have died. The belief in shades operates as a theory of personality only in a very abstract sense, because the relation between a man's personality and his shade is vague and uncertain, and a man's derelictions can never be excused on the grounds that his shade is exerting control over him.[3]

The shade of a living person can be described in terms of Freud's concept of the id; it represents unbridled desires, or a drive for sexual and alimentary satisfaction. By extension, the shade also represents a human drive which is responsible for greed and competitiveness. I know of no instance in which the actions or the personality of a particular person were explained as being caused by the person's shade. Rather than accounting for the behavior of particular individuals, the belief in shades offers a philosophical explanation of differences among human

---

3. In this regard Lango beliefs in shades are not unlike those of the Nyakusa, who, according to Monica Wilson (1971:29), exhibit marked ambivalence toward shades.

beings. Some people are weak, others are strong. Some men are able to acquire several wives and many cows, and regularly come out ahead of their fellow men in social transactions. This state of affairs is due to differences in the strengths of shades.

It stands to reason that this theory is also related to general beliefs about the differences between categories of people: men and women, adults and children, the old and the young. Men are believed to have more powerful shades than women, and this difference is said to account for the control that men have over women in social life. Men frequently victimize women because their innate drives, or shades, are more powerful. Children are weaker than adults because their shades have not yet begun to express themselves fully; that is, shades do not impel children to the same degree that they impel adults. In general, the shade of a person becomes more active as the person matures, and this explains why older men are frequently more greedy than younger men and are able to control more resources.

In the final analysis, Langi say, social differentiation depends on more than the relative strengths of shades. Some persons who have weak shades are physically or intellectually capable of directing the energy of their shades in such a way that they come out ahead of their fellows. Others become successful not because they have strong shades but because of strength of character and the ability to get along well with people. The belief in shades is but one aspect of a theory of social differentiation, and no attempt is made to analyze the shades of particular persons. The shades of living persons are not really a matter for consideration, because the shade does not become important until a person dies. The most significant feature of the ontology of shades is the way in which it attempts to account for two of the most elementary differences between persons: sex differences and ego differences.

Theoretically the belief in shades also applies to living things other than human beings. That is, every living thing has a shade, and the shade becomes important when its owner dies. This idea is a theoretical refinement which is not even held by all Langi. Several adepts informed me that every living thing has a shade, but most people displayed a singular lack of concern when questioned on the matter. They generally conceded that it is probably true of domesticated animals, notably the dog, which owes its greedy nature to its shade. No one, adept or otherwise, was able to develop this idea to the point of discussing shades of dead dogs and how they affect the living. Indeed, the topic provoked laughter, so far is it from human concern.

The shade remains with its owner until shortly after death. As the corpse is lowered into the grave, the shade flees and takes refuge in the bush not far from the house of its owner. The period immediately following death is especially critical because death suddenly separates the shade from its resting place in the head of its owner. This separation accounts for the practice of burying the corpse as soon as possible. The shade is in a highly agitated state immediately after the death, and it lingers close to the corpse. Some say that the shade buzzes about the head like a fly, and it is desirable to separate the shade from the body by burying the corpse, hoping that the shade will wander into the bush. After burial the shade begins to wander through the bush in the area surrounding the house of its owner—an area about 250 yards in diameter. As it wanders through this area, it seeks out a permanent resting place, such as the crotch of a tree or the burrow of a small animal. The shade continues to be restless during this period of wandering, for it is in a transitional state between its former abode and its permanent abode.[4] The shade is believed to remain in the bush for eternity, although no one is much concerned with the shades of ancestors beyond the preceding one or two generations. Shades of earlier ancestors are forgotten, for they do not interfere with people. As soon as a dead ancestor passes from the memory of the living, his shade ceases to be important. The shade of a recently deceased ancestor, however, exerts its selfish nature over men. It becomes annoyed at the conduct of a living kinsman, and it either possesses the kinsman directly or sends a spirit emissary to trouble the victim with spirit possession. Spirit possession and its treatment by adepts will be considered in Chapter V; for the present it is sufficient to

---

4. The ancestral-spirit beliefs and funerary practices of the LoDagaa of West Africa provide a striking parallel. A long mourning period lasts from the death of a LoDagaa until the last of the funerary ceremonies has been performed. "During this liminal period the status of the dead man is in transition. He has as yet no permanent shrine, nor is he considered one of the ancestors; he is a . . . visible ghost, rather than . . . a true ancestral spirit" (Goody 1962:236).

point out that *etogo* ceremonies and spirit-possession activities
are the only things that make the belief in shades socially significant. *Etogo* ceremonies are largely preventive measures designed to assure that shades will not attack the living. Spirit-
possession dances are curative: they help people to rid themselves
of shades after they have become possessed. At present, *etogo*
ceremonies are not considered very effective against shades, and
most people are inclined not to think much about shades unless
it has been shown that a person has been possessed by a shade.

THE ETOGO AND THE SHADES

The *etogo* exercise a minimal degree of control over the shades,
and they also affect relations between the shade of a dead man
and his living kinsmen. The *etogo* is responsible for conducting
funerary ceremonies that help to maintain social relations which
might be damaged by the death of a person. The most important
such ceremony is the one that formalizes the remarriage of a
widow in a leviratic arrangement. If the ceremonies are not performed properly, the shade of the dead man is likely to bring
misfortune on his living kinsmen. Shades are vengeful, and dissatisfaction with the funeral arrangements is the most common
reason for disrupting human affairs that is attributed to shades.
The relation between the funerary ceremonies and the shades
is indirect but important. The ceremonies are largely secular
affairs, unconcerned with spirits. A funeral is a gathering of the
kinsmen and neighbors of the deceased when beer and food
should be exchanged. The shades take note of these activities,
and if they are carried out, the shades will probably be satisfied,
but ultimately one cannot be certain, for shades are capricious
and they often act arbitrarily. The relation between the *etogo*
and the shades has been expressed differently by Hayley, who
wrote, "Control over the *tipu* [shade] of a dead man is exercised
by his *etogo* group" (1947:111). This statement should be modified, for the point of the belief in shades as a causal explanation
of disease and other misfortunes is that no one really exercises
control over them. Precautions can be taken, but no one can be
certain of the moods or motivations of shades.

THE FUNERAL CEREMONIES

Cung Lyel *("Standing on the Grave")*

When a person dies, the burial is to take place as soon as possible, but it must be carried out during daylight. Thus a person who dies during the night will be buried early the next morning. This practice has social consequences, for it means that many kinsmen will not be able to attend the burial, and only a few of the *etogo* elders will attend. Further, unless a kinsman or a neighbor happens to have a supply of beer on hand, there will not be enough beer to serve a large number of guests. Since it takes about three weeks to prepare beer, one cannot count on finding beer when attending a burial. Kinsmen and *etogo* elders who live outside the vicinage must be informed of the death, and people who live more than two miles away will not receive word in time to attend. Any delay in the burial might arouse the anger of the shade, for the shade is said to be in a highly excitable state during the period between the death of its owner and the burial of the body. This does not mean that the shade is dangerous to the point of attacking people at that time; rather, it is easily offended and must not be displeased. After it has withdrawn to the bush, it may take revenge upon its owner's descendants for delaying the burial, so a hasty burial is a precautionary measure.

A second precaution dictates the place of burial. A person must be buried adjacent to his own house or near the house of a close agnatic kinsman. Most commonly, the grave is dug at the edge of the clearing that contained the person's house. The important point is that the grave be near the residence of the person's agnatic kinsmen in case the shade should ever trouble them. A persistently troublesome shade can be subdued by an *etogo* ritual in which the corpse is exhumed and burned. This ritual, to be described later, affects the choice of a burial site. If a person should die while working in Lira, for example, an effort will be made to bring the body back to his home for burial. The problem arises when someone dies at the Lira Hospital or in one of the other government medical facilities. The hospital procedure is to place the corpse in a morgue and arrange for a burial.

This type of burial is particularly disturbing to a shade, because shades do not enjoy the company of other shades and are repelled by the stench of death. As an additional reason for burying the body close to the home of the agnatic kinsmen, some informants say that a shade will be much happier where it can observe the affairs of its kinsmen close at hand. The shade becomes lonely when the body is buried in a distant area and consequently is more apt to be provoked.

The Standing on the Grave is concerned primarily with the burial. Immediately after learning of the death, the women of the household begin to wail while standing with arms raised and hands clasped and resting against the back of the neck. The sound of the wailing attracts people from neighboring homesteads, and these people will make up the audience at the burial. Several young married men are recruited to dig the grave. Meanwhile the women sit together in a group, wailing intermittently and reviewing the circumstances of the death among themselves. Two or three close female kinsmen wash the body while the grave is being dug, and they shave the head and wrap the body in a cloth. If time permits, a new cloth of muslin may be purchased; if not, the body may be dressed in ordinary clothing. The preparation of the body takes place inside the house, and women who do not participate in the task remain outside, perhaps sipping beer if any is available. The number of people attending is not more than twenty, all drawn from the deceased's household and neighboring households.

Driberg gives a good description of burial procedures during the 1917 period.

> The burial position is for a woman on her left side and for a man on his right; the legs are bent and knees are drawn upright towards the chest . . . the arms are bent at the elbows . . . the eyes are closed, and the ears are sealed with the leaves of the *ocogo* tree to prevent earth from entering. If this last precaution is omitted, the deceased will haunt the heir till he dies. The head of the deceased is shaved, and the hair, together with his wooden pillow is thrown into the grave (1923:166–167).

Several of these customs are no longer practiced. The body is laid not on its side but flat on its back, the same position being used for both sexes. This means that the body is not flexed, and the arms are either placed flat against the sides or flexed across the chest with the hands clasped and resting on the chest. I was not able to learn of any explanation for these changes. Because the mode of burial has come to resemble the Christian practice, it may be associated with missionary activities, although the funerals I attended did not contain any other Christian elements, such as the cross. The extended burial position may also be related to the introduction of the metal hoe, which facilitates the digging of a large grave.

The practice of burying the hair clippings and personal objects with the body is still adhered to. The personal objects include all of a man's clothing and his hoe, his spear, and any other metal items he habitually used, such as a knife. The same rule applies to women, and it is also important to bury a woman's beads with her. Lango women wear strands of small beads (*tigo*) around the waist, and these are removed from the body after death and are placed on top of the corpse with the other personal possessions.

It is believed that a corpse can shift position in its grave if its shade should become aroused. To prevent any such movement, pieces of stone are placed on top of the corpse and along its sides. The stones are fragments of the household grinding block, a large piece of volcanic rock, which is smashed into pieces during the burial.

The entire burial procedure takes about three hours, and after the grave has been filled the visitors disperse. If beer is provided, a group of kinsmen remain to drink and to discuss the circumstances and probable cause of the death. Throughout all the burial activities, the visible role of the *etogo* is minimal, and, to the observer, the Standing on the Grave hardly deserves to be classified as an *etogo* ceremony. The role of the *etogo* in the ceremony lies more in the realm of belief than in that of activity. The *etogo* is expected to assist in the maintenance of relations with the dead; therefore an *etogo* elder should be present at the burial to see that the grave is properly dug, the body bathed, and the stones placed on the body. One *etogo* elder was present at each burial I attended, but I never saw an elder act in a supervisory capacity. At one funeral, an *etogo* elder offered two suggestions pertaining to the digging of the hole; at another funeral, an *etogo* elder was asked what kind of cloth the corpse should be buried in. In no instance did the *etogo* elder receive any special consideration or deference by virtue of his *etogo* identity. When an *etogo* elder offered advice or made suggestions, he did so informally, and in several instances the same sort of advice was proffered by men in attendance who were not members of the *etogo*. In other words, the *etogo* elders were simply there, and that in itself is considered to be necessary and sufficient for conducting a proper burial.

This was not always true. Until a few years ago, the *etogo* was more active in the burial. Elders of the *etogo* of the deceased were expected to slaughter a sheep near the grave. The sheep was provided by a brother or a clansman of the deceased. Clansmen of the deceased were not allowed to eat the meat; it was eaten by other men of the *etogo*. The reason for this interdiction is the belief that the shade of a dead man attacks only the members of the man's lineage and the women who have married into that lineage. Men of other lineages can consider themselves secure from attack. Hence, *etogo* elders who are not in the clan of the deceased can eat the meat of the animal sacrificed to appease the shade.

Another funerary custom that has been discontinued is the practice of serving a special pot of beer called *kongo tipu* ("beer of the shade"). A small pot of beer was brought to the burial by an *etogo* elder, and all the elders would drink from this pot immediately after the grave was filled. If beer was to be served to the other mourners, it would not be served until the *etogo* had finished their pot.

These two examples of discontinued practices indicate that in the past *etogo* participation in funerals was more extensive. An effort was always made to have *etogo* elders present who represented several clans, but this is no longer true. In three of the five burials I attended, the *etogo* members who were present were all clansmen of the same generation as the head of the household. In two of the five, the *etogo* members belonged to clans other than that of the household head. In all five, the visiting *etogo* elders lived close by.

Yabo Lyel ("*Grave Opening*")

Ideally, the burial should be followed by a larger ceremony called *yabo lyel* ("grave opening"). This occasion provides the opportunity for the immediate family of the deceased to invite neighbors and kinsmen to mourn with them, since the brevity of the burial ceremony does not allow time to prepare for a large number of guests. The logistics of preparing beer enter into the ceremonial pattern, since (as we have said) it is not always possible to serve beer at the burial itself. As an assurance that there will not be a scarcity of beer at the Grave Opening, the celebration is always scheduled for the season when beer is most plentiful. Millet and sorghum, the two main ingredients of beer, are harvested in October and November, and beer is most abundant during the dry months of December and January. These months are also the least demanding period of the yearly round of labor, because the crops have been harvested and work in the fields does not begin until the ground can be cultivated—at the onset of the rains, in late March. Hence, the dry months offer the best opportunity for holding ceremonies.

It is desirable to hold the Grave Opening in the second dry season after the death, but there is latitude in the timing of the ceremony. Thus, if a man dies in March, just at the beginning of the rainy season, it might be considered appropriate to hold the Grave Opening in the next dry season. The only rule is that the Grave Opening should be held during a dry season but no sooner than nine months after the death. This means that kinsmen have flexibility in postponing the ceremony, and if it is delayed beyond the second dry season, the obligation will be dismissed, and the Grave Opening may never be held.

Traditionally, the primary function of the Grave Opening was to assure the shade of the deceased that living kinsmen were concerned with its well-being; in other words, it was a commemorative celebration. Shades are thought to have a keen insight into human affairs and a great need for attention. They seek revenge when human beings fail to honor them; the Grave Opening is one of the principal means of placating the shade. An allied function of the Grave Opening was more sociological than spiritual: to allow *etogo* elders to decide on a suitable husband for the widows of a dead man. This is one reason that Grave Opening ceremonies were more common for married men than for any other persons. Agreeing on a new husband is an important matter and should be done within a year after a man dies. Widow remarriage is leviratic, the widow being remarried to a classificatory brother of her deceased husband. The question of remarriage is discussed by lineage members, and, at present, the lineage members reach a decision among themselves. Traditionally, the decision did not rest solely in the hands of the lineage; lineage members discussed the matter, but the final decision was announced at the Grave Opening feast by the *etogo* elders.

Another traditional feature of the Grave Opening that is no longer observed was the ceremony Mixing the Funeral Beer, to be described later. On the day before the feast, the men of the *etogo* gathered at the site to mix the beer that would be served at the feast. For the mixing, they divided themselves into three groups called "meat groups."

At all *etogo* feasts the men seat themselves in three meat groups. These groups separate themselves from one another and drink beer from different pots, and if an animal has been slaughtered for the occasion they eat different cuts of meat. The groups have the same names throughout Lango. The names are *Ikore* ("chest"), *Aboi* ("stomach"), and *Oguru* ("backbone"). The distribution of meat does not follow these names exactly but proceeds as follows:

> *Ikore*—Cuts from the thighs, the flanks, and the sides of the rib cage
>
> *Aboi*—The intestines and cuts from the front part of the rib cage
>
> *Oguru*—Cuts from the shoulders and from along the backbone

The head is given to one person, most often the head of the household where the feast is being held, or the person who provided the animal for the feast. The other cuts of meat are then served to the *etogo* elders according to their membership in the meat groups. Any remaining meat is given to visitors who are present, but visitors are not allowed to sit with the *etogo* elders in their meat circles.

Membership in a meat group is for life. A man is assigned to a meat group when he begins to attend *etogo* feasts, at the age of fifteen or so, and he is not permitted to change his meat-group affiliation even if he migrates to a new area and attaches himself to a different *etogo*. To change from one meat group to another or to attend an *etogo* feast and eat a cut of meat belonging to another meat group are both said to be capital offenses, although I was never able to learn of anyone who was killed for such a transgression. A man is allowed to eat any cut of meat when the feast is not an *etogo* event, but if the rule is violated at an *etogo* feast, the offender is said to be committing an act of greed. Moreover, this rule illustrates one of the few clear relations of the *etogo* to the spiritual world, for this particular act of greed is an offense that insults the Creator (Jok), who requires that other elders of the *etogo* administer the penalty of death.

In addition to the division into meat groups, another organization principle affects the physical arrangement of persons at an *etogo* feast. This is a separation into boys (*awobi*), whose fathers are alive, and elders (*adongi*), whose fathers are dead. This separation causes a further split within each meat group, so that the physical arrangement of one *etogo* feast held in 1904, as described by an informant, can be diagrammed as in Figure 4. Each of the smaller circles represents a cluster of males sitting around a beer pot.

On this occasion, a large amount of beer was prepared, and there was enough to serve everyone. If there happens to be a

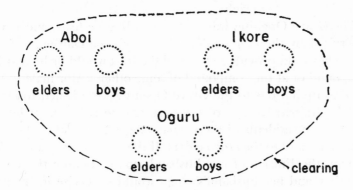

Figure 4: Physical Arrangement of Guests at an *Etogo* Ceremony

shortage of beer, however, the boys will not be served, although individual boys might be invited from time to time during the evening to sit at the beer pot of the elders. Similarly, when meat is served, the elders place the cuts of meat in the center of their own circle, and toss portions of meat to the boys' circle. This gesture takes on an added significance when one considers that in any other context it is an insult to toss food to a person.

Throughout the activities of the *etogo*, there are expressions of the opposition between generations and of the inferior social position of the younger men. The boys must assist the elders by fetching paraphernalia for them and carrying out other minor tasks. Young men are expected to observe the ritual activities but are not permitted to direct the rituals themselves. During much of the ritual, the young men arrange themselves behind the elders, where they simply watch what is going on or respond in unison to prayers led by the elders.

The division into three meat groups seems to have little to do with antagonisms between the generations, but it is effective as a means of ensuring that no single clan comes to dominate an *etogo* ceremony. The meat group cuts across clan ties because most members of a man's meat group do not belong to his clan. The rule that dictates which meat group a man will belong to ensures that he will interact with members of other families and other lineages at *etogo* ceremonies. A firstborn son is assigned to the meat group after his father's in the sequence *Aboi-Ikore-Oguru*. The second son is assigned to the meat group after that, and so on. Figure 5 illustrates the principle; in the figure, birth order is from left to right.

The Grave Opening was primarily a lineage feast, and it was supervised by the *etogo* elders. A senior male clansman of the deceased would provide a cow, and the feast would be held at his compound or at the compound of some other senior male in the lineage. Invitations to the Grave Opening were issued to members of the patrilineage of the deceased, to a few matrilateral kinsmen, to residents of the vicinage regardless of their kinship affiliations, and to the *etogo* elders. If the deceased was a married woman, the lineage of her husband would sponsor the Grave Opening, and her husband's *etogo* would supervise it. The ac-

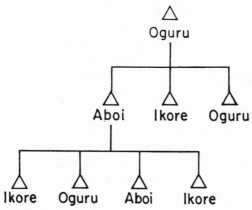

Figure 5: Membership in Meat Groups

tivities of the *etogo* elders at the feast were to mix the beer, to slaughter the cow, and to distribute portions of the meat among the three meat groups and among the guests. The presence of the *etogo* elders at the Grave Opening feast was considered essential in preventing the shade from taking action against the survivors.

Langi are losing interest in the Grave Opening, and it is acceptable for surviving kinsmen to plead that they cannot afford to hold the ceremony. Ideally, the Grave Opening should be held for every person who dies, except children who have not been weaned. The ideal was never met, for a selective process always operated which meant that the higher the status of the deceased, the more likely it was that a Grave Opening would be held. In reality, the ceremony is almost exclusively held to mourn the death of an adult male, or an older woman who has had several children; it is rarely held for a child or even a grown daughter.

By subscribing to the ideal that a Grave Opening should be held for everyone, Langi allow themselves to take advantage of such situations as an unusually plentiful harvest and to make themselves the sponsors of large feasts to which many kinsmen and neighbors are invited. As might be expected, a man who holds such feasts enhances his own status and improves relations with his peers. The Grave Opening is nevertheless falling into disuse among the cultivators of Obanya Kura.

However, the ceremony has undergone an interesting adaptation[5], for it is carried out enthusiastically by wage earners who are employed by the government and find themselves living at jobs some distance from their family homes. A man in this situation who wishes to maintain kinship relations with a large number of kinsmen in the rural area can return to his home during the dry season and sponsor a Grave Opening feast for a lineage member who has recently died. Similarly, the funerary ceremonies that follow the death of a Lango white-collar government official include an elaborate Grave Opening commemoration. There is ample time to make arrangements, and important guests arrive in automobiles from Lira. The feast provides an opportunity for prosperous men to translate their status into terms that are recognizable and familiar to their rural kinsmen. This sort of Grave Opening is primarily a social gathering; it lacks the *etogo* activities which were the basis of the traditional Grave Opening. In the modern form, the *etogo* members are not called on, nor is much attention paid to the problem of maintaining relations with the shade of the deceased. Rather, the emphasis is on sociability, strengthening ties between cultivators and townsmen, and the personal aggrandizement of the sponsor.

Rubo Moko Lyel (*"Mixing the Funeral Beer"*)

The traditional mixing of the beer on the day before the Grave Opening was called *rubo moko lyel* ("mixing the funeral beer"). In the yard where the Grave Opening feast was to be held, the men of the *etogo* divided themselves into the three meat groups. Each group formed a circle, and the members of each group selected one young man from that group. The three young men approached the heap of *moko* (a dry, fermented mixture of sorghum and millet), which had been placed directly in front of the door of the house. The head of the household then presented them with containers that held *bilo*, which, like *moko*, is a dry, mealy material that has already been fermented. The young men received the *bilo* and mixed it into the *moko*. They ar-

5. For comparative material on the funerary practices of African peoples see Jack Goody (1962) on the LoDagaa of West Africa and Wyatt MacGaffey (1970) on peoples of the lower Congo.

ranged the *moko* into three piles of equal size, and each pile was said to be beer of a particular meat group. The young men put the *moko* in pots and added water to permit the final twenty-four-hour fermentation to take place. Each pot was stored inside a different house around the compound, and would be removed on the following day and served by a member of the appropriate meat group.

Ngolo Dako (*"Discussing the Woman"*)

In addition to mixing the beer, the *etogo* elders sometimes perform another task on the day before the Grave Opening: deciding on a suitable partner for the widow in remarriage. There is considerable disagreement among older informants on the role of the *etogo* in this matter. All agree that the *etogo* announces the decision, but only one informant thought that the actual choice of a husband was up to the *etogo*. The most commonly stated view is that the widow herself decides which man of her husband's clan she will marry, in consultation with senior members of the lineage whose advice she should heed. If she is an older woman with adolescent sons, she will be strongly influenced by her sons' opinions, because her choice will be crucial for the sons in their effort to obtain cattle for bridewealth. A widow who has remarried is quick to point out that she chose the remarriage husband by herself with the aid of the lineage of the deceased husband, and that *etogo* members had little to do with the decision.

It is unlikely that *etogo* elders were ever fully entrusted with the responsibility of selecting husbands for widows. Nevertheless, the *etogo* of the deceased husband does have a ritual responsibility to fulfill when a widow is remarried. This is carried out on the day before the Grave Opening, i.e., on the same day as the *rubo moko lyel.* The event is called *ngolo dako* ("discussing the woman"). *Etogo* elders, after mixing the beer, are served beer in the widow's yard, and an *etogo* elder stands and announces the name of the husband. The announcement rarely comes as a surprise to anyone, and usually the husband has prepared himself by bringing a goat to be sacrificed and eaten by the *etogo* elders present. The widow and her new husband stand in the doorway of their house, and one of the *etogo* members slits the animal's throat. The animal is then butchered by the young men of the *etogo*, and the cuts of meat are distributed properly among the three meat groups. The meat is roasted, and the husband eats in his meat group with the elders, who honor him by presenting him with the head of the animal and one of the front legs. A strip of skin about two inches wide is cut from the neck of the goat in such a way that it forms a ring. It is dried to form a strap (*del me ngolo gola*, "strap for discussing matters in the front yard"), which is placed around the neck of the woman. She wears it for several hours, until she retires that night. This occasion formalizes the remarriage of the widow; it is essentially a marriage ceremony.

The goat must be sacrificed or the woman will be afflicted with illness and misfortune by the shade of her former husband. Shades are extremely sensitive, and a shade may become jealous of the new husband. Normally he does not, since most male shades are said to grieve over the loneliness of their wives during the first few months of widowhood and are happy to learn that their wives will be provided for in remarriage. Moreover, if the wife is still of childbearing age, the shade should be pleased by the possibility that the woman can bear children who will belong to the lineage of the deceased husband. Chances are good that the shade will not object to the remarriage, but one can never be certain of the mood or motivation of the shade; hence the goat is sacrificed in its name, since all shades are particularly fond of meat. The *etogo* elders eat the goat meat in the name of the shade, for they are responsible for maintaining good relations with the dead. The strap of skin worn by the widow has an explicit meaning and is a feature that recurs in several Lango ceremonies. The strap signifies a woman's incorporation into the lineage of her husband, and, in this ceremony, is used to reassure the shade that his widow remains married in his descent group and that the contractual agreement of marriage is still intact. The widow remarriage that is contracted in the Discussing the Woman is considered a fitting beginning for the feasting that accompanies a Grave Opening. It is entirely possible, however, that a husband cannot be found for a widow before the Grave Opening, or that the remarriage must be postponed for some reason. This is acceptable, and the Discussing the Woman may be held independent of the Grave Opening.

Relations among the Funerary Ceremonies

We have considered four funerary ceremonies. The two most important, the Standing on the Grave (burial) and the Grave Opening, are separated by at least nine months. The other two ceremonies, Mixing the Funeral Beer and Discussing the Woman, are usually held near the time of the Grave Opening, but either of them may be held long after the Grave Opening.

There is ambiguity about when the mourning period ends in Lango. Later we shall discuss another *etogo* ceremony, the *Apuny*, which is described as the formal end of the mourning period. However, the *Apuny* is no longer held, and the mourning period effectively ends at the time of the Grave Opening or either of the two ceremonies associated with it. The Grave Opening ceremonies have always marked the time when a widow was free to remarry, and after any of these ceremonies she was allowed to grow her hair back (a woman cuts her hair when her husband dies). My interpretation of this situation is that the Grave Opening and the two associated ceremonies marked the end of a seclusion period, whereas the *Apuny* marked the end of a period of general condolence.

There is an interesting parallel between the restoration of social relations after a death and the activities of the shade of the deceased. During the interval between the burial and the Grave Opening, the shade wanders in the bush near the residence of the deceased looking for a permanent resting place; during this period the shade is said to be restless and is clearly in a state of transition. This state of transition ends at the time of the Grave Opening, which is also the time when a widow ends her seclusion. The Grave Opening, then, marks the end of a transitional period which is both spiritual and social. In the spiritual domain, the shade has found a permanent resting place, and in the social domain, the widow is free to remarry. If we focus exclusively on the spiritual domain we can see that the activities of the shade replicate the pattern of rites of passage, outlined by Van Gennep (1960). The pattern consists of three phases: separation (leaving the head of the deceased), isolation (wandering in the bush looking for a resting place), and reincorporation (settling into a permanent resting place from which to oversee human affairs).

The three phases are not so clearly outlined in the social domain, but can be discerned in the social roles of the survivors— particularly widows. The Standing on the Grave marks the separation of the widow from both her husband and her household, for the latter has been drastically disrupted by the death of its nominal head. After the Standing on the Grave, the widow has an indeterminate status until she remarries in a leviratic arrangement. During this period she is structurally isolated from the clan of her husband. Her remarriage at the time of the Discussing the Woman restores the woman's position as a wife in a household and reincorporates her into her dead husband's clan.

Golo Cogo *("Exhuming the Bones")*

One other *etogo* activity is directed toward the problem of maintaining relations with the shade of a dead person. In mentioning shade possession we noted that shades can cause trouble to people, particularly women and children, and that an adept is summoned to explain the cause of the condition and to cure it. One procedure is more closely associated with *etogo* elders than with the performance of an adept. This procedure, called *golo cogo* ("exhuming the bones"), is an attempt to mollify a troublesome shade.

An adept has at hand several methods for handling spirit possession. Sometimes those methods fail, and she may recommend that the patient seek the help of others. If an adept has failed at several attempts to cure a person, the failure can be explained as a result of an especially strong spirit which is causing the trouble. Repeated failures will lead an adept to reevaluate the patient's problems, and the adept may decide that the shade is unhappy because of the location of its owner's grave. The shade may have a peculiar temperament that demands separation from living people, in which case the adept may state that a poor choice was made when the shade was buried so close to the compound of its kinsmen. The adept then prescribes that several elders from the *etogo* of the deceased meet to exhume the remains and then burn them. This is easily done by two or three elders with the aid of some young men. The only difficulty in this procedure is the problem of deciding where the bones should be removed to. Shades and other spirits frequent swampy areas, and any tract of low, moist land is suitable for the burning and relocation of the bones. A pyre of dried grass and firewood is prepared, the bones are placed thereon, and the fire is fed for about an hour and a half until the bones have virtually disintegrated.

Langi customarily offer two explanations for the efficacy of burning and relocating the bones. One is that the shade becomes disoriented when the body is relocated, and it cannot properly observe and intercede in the affairs of its living kinsmen. The fire adds to the confusion of the shade, because the smoke and heat permanently blind it, so that it is unable to find its victims. The second explanation is that the water of the swamp prevents the shade from carrying out its activities. Water is a more dense medium than air, and the shade cannot extricate itself from its new resting place. Driberg noted that a similar explanation prevailed during the time of his study (1923:168).

A third explanation was invoked in an incident in Agweng. The shade of a woman had been causing impotence in her grandson, with the result that his wife had not conceived, and their marriage was in jeopardy. When the bones of the woman were exhumed and burned, the kinsmen said that they had "killed" the shade, and that it would cause no more trouble. The destruction of the shade is accomplished only if the shade is exposed to a very hot fire for a long time. The shade continued to cause trouble, and the adept declared that the three *etogo* elders who had burned the bones had not allowed the fire to get hot enough, and that they had only succeeded in arousing the ire of the shade.

It might be asked why an adept would entrust the burning to *etogo* elders when she might burn the bones herself and perhaps command a fee for the service. One adept explained this as an aspect of the division of labor between adepts and *etogo* elders: *Etogo* elders bury people; that is their responsibility; it is logical, therefore, to ask them to exhume bones. They are more familiar with the problems of burial than adepts are, for the latter are curers, and they cure primarily by dancing.

Apuny

The *Apuny* (*punyo*: "to end the period of mourning") is concerned with a collectivity of dead persons rather than with an
individual. At the time of my study it had last been celebrated in
Obanya Kura in 1959, but traditionally it was held once each
year. Since there are three *etogo* groups in Obanya Kura, each
set of *etogo* elders held their feast every third year. At present
etogo elders are concerned over the lack of interest in the *Apuny*
and fear that it will never be performed again, since few young
men have witnessed the *Apuny* and most are unable to describe
the ceremony or say what it means.

The traditional *Apuny* ceremony was described by Hayley
(1947:64–66), who pointed out that the goal of the *Apuny* is to
placate the shades so that they will not trouble people by causing drought. The *Apuny* was held in the dry season, usually in
December, and Langi did not expect the ceremony to bring rain
immediately. They viewed it as a means of ensuring that plentiful rains would fall in March and April. If the onset of the rainy
season was late, so that a drought appeared imminent, the ritual
response would be not an *Apuny* but a specific rain dance (*myelo
kot*).

The rainmaking aspect of the *Apuny* places the ceremony in
a complicated set of rainmaking rituals in Lango. Rainmaking
was described by Driberg (1923:249–263) and by Hayley (1947:
64), and is worthy of comment because it was the only form of
ritual activity in Lango that was centralized and under the strict
control of a single clan. Judging from Driberg's and Hayley's
descriptions, rainmaking activities were in the hands of the
Jo Iromo clan until the 1920s, when the Banya clan took control.
The chief reason for the shift seems to have been the prominence
of a man named Lingo, born of a Madi father and a Lango mother and adopted into the Lango clan called Banya. Lingo lived
near Aduku, about twenty miles south of Lira. He trained some
young men of the Banya clan to perform the rain dance (*myelo
kot*) in different parts of the district. These men were directly
responsible to Lingo and could carry out the rain dance only
after he had ordered them to do so.

A similar arrangement prevailed for the *Apuny*. *Etogo* could perform the ceremony only after they had been given permission by a member of the Banya clan. In the Aloi area, a man named Igwar was described as a rainmaker from the Banya clan, although he had not been active since the last *Apuny*, in 1959.

Igwar explained that the chief rainmaker and nominal head of the Banya clan residing in Aduku would perform a divination sometime in November to ascertain the proper time for the *Apuny*. He would direct one of the etogo in the Aduku area to perform an *Apuny*, and it would do so. Then he would direct some of the *etogo* about eight miles from Aduku to hold their *Apuny*; more distant *etogo* would follow until *Apuny* ceremonies had been held all over Lango. Thus *Apuny* would spread from Aduku in a pattern like the emanation of concentric rings from the point at which a stone is dropped into water. The series of *Apuny* occurred every year, but not all *etogo* participated every year. The decline of the *Apuny* relates to causes external to developments in Obanya Kura and cannot be accounted for here.

Langi cannot explain clearly the relations between the rainmaking function of the *Apuny* and its role in placating the shades. Although the word *Apuny* denotes the end of the mourning period, it is difficult to see what relation the ceremony had to funerary activities. It did not betoken any change in the situation of the mourners, and we have already noted that the real end of the period of seclusion comes at the time of the Grave Opening ceremony. Most informants see the *Apuny* as a means of preventing illness in the community by pacifying the shades of especially powerful men, which are capable of inflicting harm on the living. Shades vary in their ability to inflict illness, and the power of a shade generally depends on the strength and personality of its owner during his lifetime. Shades that are especially powerful are not only able to cause illness, but possess an ill-defined power over natural phenomena, such as wind, rain, and the abundance of game animals. This belief explains why the *Apuny* is significant in a rain ceremony: the shades involved in an *Apuny* are so powerful that they must be addressed.

When a group of *etogo* elders have been advised by an elder of the Banya clan that they should consider having an *Apuny*, the men of the *etogo* assemble a list of all the men of that *etogo*

who have died since the previous *Apuny*. Only adult males are
considered, and usually only adult males who have achieved
prominence in their lifetimes as (for example) the father of
many children, or as a man who amassed numerous cattle, or
as a man who excelled in warfare or hunting. If it happens that
no prominent man has died in the three or four years since the
previous *Apuny*, the ceremony will be postponed until the next
time the Banya clan makes the suggestion. But it is generally possible to find two or three deceased men to honor, even if they are
not of high status.

Having decided which shades shall be honored, the *etogo* elders visit the household head in each of the lineages being honored. A kinsman is expected to provide a bull for sacrifice at the
Apuny. Two clear rules are used to determine which person is
asked: (1) if the widow of the man being honored has remarried
in a leviratic arrangement (*olako*), her new husband must provide the bull; (2) if the widow has not remarried, the male heir
of the deceased, i.e., the man who inherited his cattle, must
provide it. The latter rule places the obligation on the eldest
son of the deceased, or, lacking one, on the deceased's eldest
brother. When the *etogo* elders make this request they stand in
a line and announce to the man that a bull is expected of him.
Each *etogo* elder carries a stick from the *epobo* tree (*Sambucus
nigra*), a tree which symbolizes the power of the *etogo* and which
has the power to render a person sterile. If the man refuses to
offer a bull for sacrifice, the *etogo* elders "beat" him into sub-
mission with the *epobo* sticks (the beating is not intended to injure him physically) or they take the more drastic action of drop-
ping their sticks in unison. If they do the latter, it is believed,
the man will die within a year. The severity of this punishment
indicates that such a refusal is taken as a grave insult to the dead
man whose shade the *Apuny* is to honor and to the *etogo* itself. I
was told of one incident in which this curse was carried out, and
the victim was said to have died several months later. Hayley
(1947:64) recounted an incident in which the victim was beaten
and was not seriously injured.

Each *etogo* has a special site where its *Apuny* ceremonies are
held. The generic term for the site is *lwala* ("red soil"), and it

must be near a stream bed, because streams provide access to the resting places of shades.

The men of the *etogo* collect the bulls early on the morning of the *Apuny* and take them to the *lwala*. Women and children are prohibited from attending. It would be dangerous for them, since *etogo* elders summon the shades, and the shades approach the men and share meat with them. The shades may become irritated and attack those present, and women and children are especially vulnerable to such attacks. A man takes certain precautions, however, and all the men keep their *epobo* sticks and their spears close at hand for the duration of the ceremony. Some *etogo* elders observed that on the last occasions when the *Apuny* was performed in Obanya Kura, women and children followed the men to the feast but remained at a discreet distance from the men and out of their sight. They were brought portions of meat but did not participate in any other way.

The young men of the *etogo* slaughter the bulls, distribute the meat, and roast it over three fires, one for each meat group. The men of each meat group line up according to age to receive their servings, the oldest one being the first. Those men whose fathers have not yet died sit off to the side of the elders of their meat group, and portions of meat are thrown to them. Each man who donated a bull for the *Apuny* is given the uncooked head of his bull to take home and one of the cooked forequarters.

After the meat is consumed, all the men form a line facing the fire, with their backs to the stream bed. An older man is designated as the prayer leader (*aduong a gato*) for the ceremony. He faces the line of men and leads a prayer which is meant to be a final statement to the shades, telling them that they have not been forgotten by the living. The prayer leader recites each line of the prayer by himself, and the chorus of men repeats the line in response:

Wiye dong i wil.	You are not forgotten.
Olelo pacowa; olelo.	We are happy at home; we are happy.
Pacowa okwe.	Our home is peaceful.
Ibuto i opukeni.	Sleep in your burrows.
Opukeni dong okwe.	Your burrows are now at peace.

Opule omin omic.   All the burrows are sealed.
Wang dong omiye gin   We have given you what you wanted.
ayam imito.

The word *opukeni* offers a clue to the meaning of this prayer.
It is used here to mean "your grave" and comes from the root
opuk ("burrow"). The common Lango word for grave is *lyel*;
opuk refers to a small hole or tunnel formed by a small burrow-
ing animal such as the edible rat, which tunnels into anthills.
Such a hole can be blocked and smoke driven into it to trap the
animal. The word *opuk* likens the resting place of a shade to
the lair of a small animal. The shade can move in and out of its
resting place to circulate among the living and bring trouble
to them. It would be desirable to seal the holes to keep the shades
in their proper places, and that is one of the purposes of the
Apuny. The shades are kept in their places, and the community
is made safer by the performance of the *Apuny*.

While the prayer is recited, each man holds his *epobo* stick in
one hand and his spear in the other, because both of these are
necessary for his protection. After the prayer is completed, the
period of danger is past, and each man discards his *epobo* stick
in the fire. This marks the end of the *Apuny* ceremony, and people leave the site to return to their homes.

Curing Ceremonies

In a sense, all the funerary ceremonies performed by the *etogo*
are concerned with the health of the living, for they serve to
maintain good relations with the shades, thereby lessening the
probability of spirit possession. The only funeral ceremony concerned with curing particular cases of illness rather than maintaining the health of the community in general is the reburial
ceremony (*golo cogo*), which is sometimes prescribed by an adept
as part of the course of treatment for a particular sick person.
The *golo cogo* is therefore both a funerary and a curing
ceremony.

Three other *etogo* ceremonies can be prescribed by an adept:
the *gato twor* ("blessing the sick"), the *lamo twor* ("praying for
the sick"), and the *gato bwoc* ("blessing the impotent"). The first
two can be used to cure almost any sickness attributed to spirit

possession. The last is held only for men who are impotent. All three ceremonies are still performed, and they are the most important *etogo* activities at present. They are not performed so frequently as they were in the past, however, and they are now supervised by only a few *etogo* elders, since it is becoming increasingly difficult to find men capable of conducting these ceremonies. Comparison of Hayley's descriptions of the curing ceremonies with those I observed shows that the form of the ceremonies has been simplified since 1938. During my field work, the Blessing the Sick was performed four times in Obanya Kura, the Praying for the Sick three times, and the Blessing the Impotent twice (see Table IV). (I observed additional performances of the ceremonies in neighboring vicinages.)

I shall also describe two *etogo* ceremonies that are concerned with the health of the community at large and are not prescribed by adepts. These are the *gato kot* ("rain blessing") and the *gato akwo* ("cursing a thief"). The former is believed to protect people from lightning, and the latter is designed to banish a known thief from the community. Both ceremonies are prescribed and carried out by the *etogo elders*.

GATO TWOR *("Blessing the Sick")* This is the most commonly performed *etogo* ceremony; it is considered particularly effective in curing protracted illness due to spirit possession or unknown causes. In two instances that occurred during my field work, the Blessing the Sick was not supervised by *etogo* elders but was performed by female adepts, since no *etogo* elders could be found to take part. It is likely that the ceremony will be taken over entirely by adepts in several years, if the *etogo* continues to disintegrate at its present rate.

A Blessing the Sick was held in Obanya Kura in 1965 for a man sixty-five years of age, who had been suffering from dysentery for months and had not received effective treatment at the local dispensary. He consulted an adept, who told him that she was unable to determine whether he was possessed by a spirit and suggested that it would not be worth the trouble and expense for him to go through the usual treatments for exorcising a spirit. Nor could she direct him to take medicines, since he had already taken medicines and had not responded. She suggested that he ask members of his *etogo* to hold a Blessing the Sick, since his ailment seemed to be a general one. He informed some kinsmen about the decision of the adept, and they agreed to assist him in seeking out the *etogo* elders and also to obtain a sheep to be sacrificed at the ceremony.

It took some doing to find a clansman willing to donate a sheep, but after three days the son of the patient's brother finally acceded to the request. Two *etogo* elders, one an older brother of the patient, agreed to direct the ceremony, and the patient's wife prepared two pots of beer.

On the morning of the ceremony, the two *etogo* elders went to the bush to collect sprigs of *olam* (*Ficus glumosa*) and *okutagwe* (*Acacia camplyacantha*). They made two small bundles of *olam* sprigs and tied them onto the sacrificial sheep—one on the back of the animal and the other on its belly. The bundles were tied on with a cord made from sprigs of *okutagwe*. Both plants have magical properties: the *olam* is associated with blessing (from *lamo*: "to consecrate or bless"), and the tree itself is a favorite resting spot of shades after they leave the grave. *Etogo* men often meet under the *olam* tree, and a sprig of *olam* is considered to be a means of bringing a person closer to the world of spirits and shades. I am unaware of the symbolism associated with the *okutagwe*, except that the plant is frequently used as a cure for constipation and other intestinal disorders. Its therapeutic value appears to be magical, for it is not taken internally or applied topically but is used as one of the ritual elements in curing ceremonies.

The two front legs of the sheep were tied together with strings of *okutagwe*, and the two hind legs similarly tied. One *etogo* elder grasped the animal by its hind legs and dragged it counterclockwise once around the patient's house. The other *etogo* elder and all others present were inside the house. They responded to the prayer led by the elder dragging the sheep around the house:

Leader: *Oryemo jo otoo.*   The dead have been driven away.
Response: *Oryemo.*   Driven away.
Leader: *Olucu jo acon.*   The ancestors have been driven away.
Response: *Olucu.*   Driven away.
Leader: *Ka wiye wil ci ber.*   The ancestors have been discouraged.

Response: *Ci ber.*	Have been discouraged.
Leader: *Paco dong oyot.*	If it is all forgotten it will be good.
Response: *Dong oyot.*	It will be good.
Leader: *Oyara paco.*	Our home shall still be healthy.
Response: *Oyara.*	Still be healthy.
Leader: *Icur i man ingit.*	May our village multiply.
Response: *Icur.*	May it multiply.
Leader: *Olelo paco.*	We are happy at home.
Response: *Olelo.*	We are happy.
Leader: *Idwar man ingit.*	When the children are hunting.
Response: *Idwar.*	Are hunting.
Leader: *Olelo a man ingit.*	When the children are happy.
Response: *Olelo.*	Are happy.

As the elder dragged the sheep around the house, he held his spear in his right hand, and after reciting each line of the prayer he jabbed his spear against the wall of the house while those in the house responded to his words. They jabbed their spears in unison against the inside wall of the house each time the leader began to recite.

The most likely interpretation of the prayer and the thrusting of spears is that the acts are a symbolic representation of the perpetual conflict between the living and the dead. The two *etogo* elders who participated in the ceremony corroborated this interpretation, although they were not certain whether the living were represented by those inside the house or by the elder dragging the sheep outside.

After the sheep had circled the house, it was taken to the bush and killed there by several young men, who slit its throat and butchered the animal. The meat on this occasion was not distributed according to meat-group procedures, but was divided among those present, the donor of the sheep being given the head. The meat-group rules were not followed because not enough *etogo* members were present to form three meat groups. The two elders removed the skin of the sheep before the butchering and burned it in a small fire in the bush. They were concerned not so much with destroying the skin as with destroying the wool. The sheep was contaminated through contact with the plants fastened to it. If any of the wool had been left around, it could have caused further illness at the home of the patient, for it has a polluting effect on anyone who touches it. The meat itself was not allowed to be brought back to the house of the patient, for the same reason. Some of the meat was immediately roasted over the fire, and other portions were left uncooked and were suspended from trees to be taken home by the guests when they left. The patient and his family were permitted to eat meat with the others, but not to take any back to their house, for fear of contamination. Similar rules pertain to the disposal of the viscera and bones of the sheep, which must be taken away by one of the elders and deposited in a secret place.

After the meat was roasted, the ritual was over, and people retired to the house of the patient, where they drank beer prepared for the occasion. Traditionally the *etogo* elders secluded themselves inside the house, drinking a separate pot of beer, while all others sat in the yard. That was not done in this particular ceremony, presumably because not enough *etogo* men were present to warrant seclusion. One ritual element during the beer drinking was rigidly maintained, however: the provision of two different-sized pots for the *etogo* members. They are first served beer in a large pot, and when they have finished that, they are given a small pot of beer. The larger pot symbolizes the relation of the *etogo* to the world of shades. The shades are numerous because they represent all dead ancestors, and they must be served in a large pot. The world of living men is less populous and can therefore be symbolized by a smaller pot. The duality implicit in this symbol expresses the ritual position of the *etogo* in the Lango belief system. To use Victor Turner's phrase, they are "betwixt and between" in that they serve as intermediaries between the world of men and the world of shades. The Blessing the Sick would appear to be a statement of this liminal quality of the *etogo*—its ability to mediate between the two worlds. The therapeutic value of the ceremony arises not from any specific treatment administered to the patient but rather from the fact of mediation itself, which is accomplished through the symbols we have described.

LAMO TWOR *("Praying for the Sick")*   The circumstances of Praying for the Sick are similar to those of the Blessing the Sick: it is likely to be prescribed by an adept to cure a person who has been suffering from some generalized ailment for a long time. The role of the adept is considerably greater in the Praying for the Sick than in other *etogo* ceremonies, for she not only prescribes the ceremony but gives detailed instructions as to how it is to be conducted. Through divination, the adept discerns which three species of plants should be used and in which direction the operator (the *etogo* elder who performs the ceremony) should walk. The ceremony takes little more than thirty minutes, and although *etogo* members are notified of the day and location, the *lamo twor* is not likely to attract more than two or three *etogo* elders and perhaps half a dozen kinsmen of the patient. The operator should not be in the clan of the patient but should be in his *etogo*, although in some instances during the last few years the operator was not even in the patient's *etogo*, and this caused little concern.

On the morning of the ceremony, the operator goes into the bush near the patient's home and gathers sprigs of three species of plants. In earlier consultations with the adept, the patient has been told which three species of plants are to be used, and the operator now obtains them. The *okutagwe* tree is usually prescribed, but the adept may choose any three species from a large number of plants with a wide range of medicinal and symbolic properties. After the sprigs of the three plants have been collected, they are tied into a bundle together with a newly hatched chick and a lizard.

The patient is seated in the doorway of his house, facing outward. The operator approaches him, carrying the bundle in his left hand and his spear in his right hand. He dips the bundle into a pan of water and sprinkles the patient on the chest, and then sprinkles the roof of the house. The dipping and sprinkling are performed three times, and at each sprinkling of the patient, the operator says this prayer:

O may yin.	We have defeated you.
Yin jo acen.	You ancestors.
Ikelo wi paco pingo?	Why do you bring your heads back home?
Wan okweri.	We refuse you.

Yin yam otoo.	You have been dead for a long time.
Kare pingo dok ilelo kop kan?	Why should you bring trouble back here?
Tin abwoti dong idoki ka kare.	Today I refuse you, so get back to where you belong.

After the prayer has been recited three times, the operator walks away from the house and into the bush, heading in the direction in which the adept told him to proceed. After walking about 100 yards, he lays the bundle on the ground, trying to conceal it behind a tree or an anthill so it cannot be easily found, for if it is picked up and brought back to the house of the patient it can bring further illness to him or his family. Furthermore, the bundle must be placed on the ground in such a way that the stems of the sprigs point toward the patient's house and the tips point away; and the heads of the lizard and the chick must point away from the patient's house.

I could obtain no exegesis regarding the symbolic meaning of the elements that make up the bundle, except that the bundle itself acquires spiritual power. This power endangers the operator; hence he must hold his spear throughout the ceremony, and he must dispose of the bundle properly. The power of the bundle seems to arise from the unusual juxtaposition of three different plants with the chick and lizard, for none of these elements in itself has spiritual power. The spiritual power of the bundle is said to enter through the tips of the branches and through the heads of the lizard and the chick (all these point in the same direction). It is to be expected that the power would leave by the same route by which it entered; hence the tips of the springs point away from the patient and his house.

The Praying for the Sick is similar to the Blessing the Sick in many respects, although the two rituals differ in symbolic content, the former employing a medicine bundle and the latter relying on the sacrifice of a sheep. They are similar in that the curative power of each derives from the ability of the symbolic objects to attract spiritual power, which emanates from the shades, to bring the patient close to this power, and to protect him from the power by concealing the symbolic object at the conclusion of the ceremony.

GATO BWOC *("Blessing the Impotent")* Unlike the *etogo* ceremonies described so far, the Blessing the Impotent is meant to cure only one condition. Impotence is caused by shades that are dissatisfied with the treatmtnt they have been accorded by the living. This dissatisfaction can result from some offense committed during the life of the shade's owner or from insufficient homage paid to the shade at funerary ceremonies. One case of impotence in Obanya Kura was caused by the shade of a twin. Only one of the twins had died, and its shade felt that unequal treatment had caused the death. The shade took revenge by rendering the father impotent. Another frequent cause of impotence is incest, for this act arouses the wrath of the shades (or of one particular shade) and drives them (or it) to punish the offender or a close kinsman of the offender.

The Blessing the Impotent, like other *etogo* curing ceremonies, is prescribed by an adept. The patient consults an adept to determine the cause of impotence, and if the adept decides that the patient cannot be cured with medicines, she recommends that a Blessing the Impotent be held. An *etogo* elder in the patient's *etogo* but not in the patient's clan will be asked to supervise the ceremony, and other *etogo* elders will be invited.

In 1966, a young man in Obanya Kura became impotent after he slept with the sister of his brother's wife, and an adept prescribed a Blessing the Impotent for him. Six *etogo* elders gathered for the ceremony, bringing sheaves of a grass called *onini*. This grass grows only on hilltops. Because shades and associated spirits often dwell on hilltops, the grass has had contact with shades, and therefore it has a vaguely defined spiritual power. A frame was built in the patient's yard and thatched with sticks to form a small temporary house. The patient sat in the doorway of the house with his back against the door.

In a house nearby, beer prepared by the patient's mother was stored in two special pots. One was a black pot and the other was a double-mouthed pot *(adog aryo)*. Such pots are used only for ritual purposes. The double-mouthed pot is used in funerary ceremonies for twins, and on those occasions the two mouths are associated with the twins' shades. The symbolism of these two types of pots is not clear, and informants offer little help in explaining their meaning. The only statement I obtained on the matter was that the double-mouthed pot is associated with fertility, and that a barren woman may be directed to drink from such a pot.

Beer was scooped out of the black pot into a small calabash, and the operator (the elder in charge of the ceremony) added a little water to the calabash and struck the patient lightly on the chest, so that some of the mixture of beer and water spilled on him. The calabash was then passed behind him—that is, waved between the doorway of the small house and the patient's back. The operator next carried the calabash of beer counterclockwise around the house and gave the calabash to the patient, who drank the rest of its contents. The procedure was repeated with beer poured from the double-mouthed pot. The patient rose, and the *etogo* elders finished the beer in the double-mouthed pot and then the beer in the black pot. Beer in two ordinary pots was served to the other guests, and the *gato bwoc* ended quietly when the beer was gone.

GATO KOT *("Rain Blessing")* One other *etogo* ceremony, the Rain Blessing, is performed to treat a particular condition. The Rain Blessing is held if any of the following things has happened: (1) a person has been struck by lightning, whether or not the accident caused injury; (2) a homestead has been struck by lightning, whether or not the accident caused physical damage; and (3) a person has been struck or nearly struck by lightning several times in the past and is considered prone to lightning attack (then a Rain Blessing should be performed at the beginning of the rainy season).

Unlike some other *etogo* curing ceremonies, the Rain Blessing is still performed often. Two Rain Blessings were held during my study, although the ceremony, to be effective, calls for considerable effort from members of the patient's household and requires the services of about six *etogo* elders. Interest in lightning and in the Rain Blessing is more a result of Lango cosmology than of concern with the physical damage wrought by lightning. Lightning is a manifestation of supernatural power and is an indication that there is discord in the world of the shades. Lightning causes concern not only for the damage it causes, but as an omen of greater trouble to come.

In February 1966, a Rain Blessing took place in Obanya Kura after an old woman was seriously injured by lightning. The woman lived with her oldest son, Okello, and his family, and it was decided to hold a Rain Blessing to protect the household from attack in the future. No adept was consulted, since the lightning itself was a forceful statement on the need to have the ceremony. Okello, as the head of the household, invited the *etogo* elders, and six elders came at midmorning on the appointed day. Two of the elders were close neighbors of Okello, and the others came from about three miles away. About thirty people from Okello's lineage were present, all of them from Obanya Kura, and about fifty neighbors and affinal kinsmen came to watch the activities.

The *etogo* elders brought bundles of the grass *onini*, which they had picked on the previous day. (This is the grass used to build the temporary house in the Blessing the Impotent. Because the grass grows on hilltops, it is considered to have come in contact with shades.) After the elders arrived, they twined the grass into ropes, making about eighty feet. They strung the ropes around the yard, using trees and poles as supports. They consulted Okello on the direction of the lightning, for the rope was supposed to demarcate the path of the lightning bolt.

The six elders then formed a tight circle and squatted on the ground, each holding his spear in his right hand. They extended their right hands into the center of the circle so that the six spears touched. The shafts of the spears were vertical, and the points rested on the ground. One of the elders led a prayer and the remaining five responded in unison:

Leader: *Owilo we acen.*	We made the ancestors forget.
Response: *Owilo.*	We made them forget.
Leader: *Owilo wi kot.*	We made the rain forget.
Response: *Owilo.*	We made it forget.
Leader: *Oloo wi kot.*	We defeated the rain.
Response: *Oloo.*	We defeated it.

Leader: *Oriemo jo acen,*   We have driven away the ancestors.
   ka abutu ci ber.   If they lie down, it will be good.
Response: *Oriemo, ci oriemo.* We have driven them away.

After the prayer, five of the *etogo* elders arose. The leader, Ongolo, remained squatting on the ground. With the point of his spear, he dug a hole about four inches deep in the ground; he planted a shoot of the tree *ibur Kaa* in the hole. This tree is symbolically associated with lightning, because its white sap stings the eyes and causes temporary blindness, like a flash of lightning. A large saucepan containing salt and onions was placed beside the shoot, but the symbolism of these foods is unclear.[6]

The next set of activities consisted of dragging a sheep around the house while members of Okello's lineage remained inside the house with the *etogo* elders. (The other guests stayed in the yard.) This procedure varied slightly from a similar episode already described in connection with the Blessing the Sick. After the sheep had been dragged around the house, the elder approached the door of the house and told the people inside to follow him down to a stream about one-half mile from Okello's house. He held a spear in his right hand and led the sheep with his left hand. The lineage members followed him in single file —women and children first, followed by the men. Two of the *etogo* elders walked in front of the men of the lineage, separating them from the women, who had married in, and two other *etogo* elders walked at the rear of the procession. As they proceeded toward the stream, a member of Okello's lineage beat a slow, steady drumbeat to inform the shades that the people were coming to visit them and to sacrifice a sheep and some chickens in their honor.

The destination of this procession was the part of the stream bed designated as *lwala* ("red soil"). This is the same site on which the *Apuny* is held, and it is ritually significant because it is believed to be a sacred spot—i.e., land inhabited by shades. In the Rain Blessing, this strip of red soil served as the site for

---

6. Both salt and onions are relatively new to Lango, having been introduced shortly after the first European contact. Before, salt was prepared by leaching the ashes of cooking fires.

a sacrifice directed to the shades to discourage them from sending
any more lightning to the homes of men. As the *etogo* elders gathered at the *lwala*, they situated themselves on the center of the
strip of red soil, thus bringing themselves into close contact with
the shades. The people of Okello's lineage were directed to stand
away from the *lwala* lest they be endangered by proximity to the
shades. The men stood in a line in front of the women and children to shield them from the power of the shades.

The elder who led the sheep to the stream bed killed the
animal hastily by spearing it through the heart. He took two
chickens from another *etogo* elder, and cut off the head of one
with his spear. He buried the body of the chicken in the ground,
with its feet pointing toward the surface, and placed the head
on the ground nearby in such a way that the beak pointed toward
the sky. The second chicken was not killed but was presented to
one of the *etogo* elders, who upon receiving the gift left the ceremony immediately to go home. Both chickens were said to have
a special relation to shades: lightning is believed to have the
appearance of the head of a chicken which strikes out at men
with its beak. In placing the chicken's head on the ground, the
etogo elder was returning lightning to the control of shades and
protecting men. The chicken that was presented to the *etogo*
elder was dangerous because of its relation to shades; therefore
it could not be returned to Okello's homestead and had to be
guarded by an *etogo* elder.

After the chickens were disposed of, the drumming began
again, and the leader led the people back to Okello's house for
the conclusion of the ceremony. Two *etogo* elders remained behind to butcher the sacrificial sheep. They kept all the meat for
themselves except one front leg, which they put in the saucepan
of salt and onions. The saucepan and its contents were left as an
offering for the shade of Okello's father, which was believed to
have been the cause of the lightning attack on Okello's house.
After the two elders butchered the sheep and left the sacrifice,
they too left immediately for their homes, taking care not to
follow the path that led back to Okello's house, lest the meat of
the sheep, through them, contaminate the people of the household and cause more trouble there.

The ceremony ended in Okello's yard, because the *etogo* elders were members of Okello's lineage. The elders drank beer from black pots and double-mouthed pots, each person taking his turn, while the leader stood and gave a lengthy discourse on the elders' success in restoring relations between Okello's family and the shade of Okello's father and in healing Okello's mother of the injuries she had sustained in the lightning attack. The speech and ritualized beer drinking concluded the *etogo* activities, and the rest of the afternoon was spent in the usual social drinking of four large pots of beer, which had been prepared by Okello's mother.

Gato Akwo (*"Cursing a Thief"*)

The Cursing a Thief has not been carried out in Obanya Kura since 1951. It differs markedly from other *etogo* ceremonies in its purpose: it is unrelated to funeral activities; it is not curative; it has little to do with relations between living people and shades. The Cursing a Thief is a ritual means of detecting and punishing thieves within the community. As such, it is the only juridical activity of the *etogo*, for the *etogo* elders are not concerned with the settlement of disputes or with litigation. Only in cases of theft do they have the authority to decide the guilt or innocence of a wrongdoer and the appropriate punishment.

The authority of the *etogo* in cases of theft is limited: not all types of theft can be handled through the Cursing a Thief. The ceremony applies to thefts of food, crops, or tools or other household items, but not to thefts of livestock. One informant indicated that not all *etogo* had the authority to perform the ceremony; in the past only one *etogo* in the Aloi area had this authority, and it protected all residents of the area regardless of their *etogo* affiliation. Other informants were uncertain whether the ceremony could be performed by one or all *etogo*, but all agreed that it was an *etogo* ceremony, for it could not be carried out in any context other than that of the *etogo*.

The procedure of the Cursing a Thief is simple; it includes less symbolism than we have noted in other *etogo* ceremonies. If a person has had something stolen from him he has the right to go to the *etogo* and request the ceremony. He will be obliged to provide beer or a gift of perhaps a chicken—or both—to each *etogo* elder who participates in the ceremony; consequently, a person is not likely to invoke the assistance of the *etogo* unless the thievery has been going on for a long time.

If the *etogo* elders agree to perform the Cursing a Thief, they meet at the house where the object has been stolen and attempt to establish the identity of the thief by divination. They go to an intersection of two paths[7] close to the house and dig two holes about one foot deep. The elders sit in a circle around the holes, and the leader cuts the heads off two chickens and places one head in each hole. The heads are placed in such a way that their eyes are looking up and they are supposedly able to see the thief if he should return.

After the heads are buried, the *etogo* leader directs this curse:

Leader: *Ka akwo otoo, ci ber.*	If this thief should die, that would be good.
Response: *Ci ber.*	That would be good.
Leader: *Ka ongi.*	Let him cry.
Response: *Ongi.*	Let him cry.
Leader: *Ka cadu ocelo, ci ber.*	If he should suffer from diarrhea that would be good.
Response: *Ci ber.*	That would be good.
Leader: *Ka okok "wui."*	If he should cry *"wui"* [a cry of pain].
Response: *Wui.*	*Wui.*
Leader: *Ka dyeb omako, ka otoo, ci ber.*	If he is attacked with dysentery, if he should die, that would be good.
Response: *Ci ber.*	That would be good.
Leader: *Ka iwinyo ni otoo, wan olelo ni ber.*	If you hear that he has died, we shall rejoice.

At the conclusion of the curse, the elders rise simultaneously and wail the same lament that is heard at funerals. The threats contained in the curse are greatly intensified by the wailing, and it is believed that the curse is an effective sanction against thieves.

7. Beidelman discusses the symbolic significance of crossroads in his study of the Kaguru of Tanzania (1971:34). Beidelman suggests that crossroads are symbolically important in many cultures because they are a statement of liminality: an intersection, being a meeting of two opposing forces, implies a conjunction of opposites.

Many thieves died after the curse had been imposed upon them, and others became so fearful after the curse had been carried out that they went to the *etogo* elders, confessed their guilt, and asked the elders to revoke the curse.

This happened in Obanya Kura in the 1940s when a woman stole a pot from another woman. The *etogo* was called in to perform a Cursing a Thief, which took place in midmorning. In midafternoon of the same day, the thief broke out in a rash and became feverish, whereupon her husband went to the *etogo* elders and told them what had happened to his wife. The elders went to the house of the sick woman and were able to cure her by sprinkling water on her and saying a prayer for her health. As soon as she recovered, she returned the pot and offered a chicken in reparation to the woman from whom she had stolen the pot.

In another case, a chicken was stolen from a man. Unable to ascertain the identity of the thief, he asked some *etogo* elders to hold the ceremony. After the curse, the man's wife became ill, and she died the next morning. A great deal of ill will resulted from the incident, for the *etogo* elders returned and accused the man of having virtually murdered his own wife. They said that he should have investigated the theft more carefully before calling the *etogo*, for a man has no right to take such drastic action against his wife. After all, wives are prone to commit such petty crimes around the household. No action other than this censure was taken against the man, but the example illustrates the seriousness with which Langi traditionally viewed the Cursing a Thief.

THE CHANGING NATURE OF THE ETOGO AND ITS CEREMONIES

Etogo ceremonies are performed infrequently, and interest in some if not all of the ceremonies is declining. The Blessing the Sick continues to be viable and is often prescribed by adepts and performed by the *etogo*. The funerary ceremonies continue to be associated with the *etogo*, although the elders no longer play so vital a role as they once did. The least viable of the *etogo* ceremonies are the *Apuny* and the Cursing a Thief. These two ceremonies were not performed during my research, and the descriptions presented here are based on the testimony of older men who had witnessed them in recent years.

In addition to the statements of men in Obanya Kura, many of whom lamented the infrequency of *etogo* ceremonies, other evidence supports the view that the *etogo* is less important in Lango life than it once was.

First, *etogo* activities are difficult to organize. Often a man who is advised to hold an *etogo* ceremony is unable to arouse the interest of the *etogo* elders, and because of social inertia the ceremony is not held. Even for the Blessing the Sick, the statistics on the frequency of occurrence are deceptive. Although this ceremony was held more often during my field work than other *etogo* ceremonies, its form was much simpler than in the past, when seven or eight elders attended and it included more ritual than I have described. Moreover, when the Blessing the Sick, the Praying for the Sick, and the Blessing the Impotent have been held in recent years they have been attended by no more than four *etogo* elders—usually by only two or three. As a result, these three ceremonies are coming more under the control of adepts. An adept has been present whenever these ceremonies have been performed in recent years in Obanya Kura. Generally, the adept plays no role in the ceremony other than that of a guest. But in two performances I observed, the Blessing the Sick was held with no *etogo* elders present and was supervised entirely by adepts, and its form was modified from that of the ceremony as carried out by *etogo* elders.

The difficulty of mobilizing elders is only one reason for the decline of interest in *etogo* ceremonies. The matter is compounded by the failure of men under the age of fifty to take more than a passing interest in the *etogo*. Their attitude can be described as indifference rather than hostility. Most of these men are aware of the meaning and the general nature of the *etogo* and are able to discuss the affiliation of their own clans in an *etogo* network with other clans. Few of them can describe the ceremonies, however, and the elders claim that there are no young men living today who will be able to perform the *etogo* ceremonies a generation hence. My observations confirmed this speculation by the elders. I never saw young men sit near the elders during a ceremony to observe and learn the procedure.

Yet observing ceremonies is the only way to learn the role of an *etogo* elder, for young men have never been systematically trained in the performance of the rituals.

For funerary ceremonies, as for curing ceremonies, the statistics on frequency are deceptive. The *Apuny* is seldom celebrated, and, judging by the lack of interest in it, we can predict that the ceremony will be virtually unknown in ten years. The Grave Opening, though still observed, is now used almost exclusively as a means of paying honor to a man who has achieved high status outside village life. The burial ceremony would appear to be the most persistent *etogo* ceremony, if we consider frequency alone. Yet we have seen that the burial ceremony is not actually controlled by the *etogo*. Kinsmen of the deceased may invite an *etogo* elder to the burial, or an elder may feel obliged to attend without being asked, but once he is present the elder has no voice in the matter of disposing of the corpse and is treated only as an honored guest. The burial ceremony is performed more frequently than any other, because the dead must be buried. The frequency of the ceremony does not in itself attest to the vitality and persistence of the *etogo*.

If few elders remain interested in the *etogo* and if young men are apathetic, what are the attitudes of Lango women? Women are marginal to *etogo* activities: they are excluded from participation in the ceremonies except when they are object of the ceremonies, as when a woman is being cured in a Blessing the Sick. When they are allowed to attend, they are relegated to the background, and they are enjoined from eating with the men of the *etogo* and from drinking beer from pots set aside for the men. Women do not feel discriminated against, and most of them believe that *etogo* activities are an important means of preventing attacks by shades and in curing victims of such attacks. Older women are especially concerned about the decline of the *etogo* as an institution, because, like older men, they believe that the decline is one of the main reasons that shades have attacked the living so frequently in recent years.

Lango women say that *etogo* curing ceremonies do not help women as effectively as they help men. Women see the *etogo* as an institution designed primarily to serve the needs of their husbands' patrilineal descent groups. A woman, as an outsider

who has married into her husband's descent group, does not
assume that the *etogo* is as beneficial to her as to her husband.
She sees her husband's *etogo* activities as remote from and partly
alien to her own interests. The *etogo* exists to serve men, and all
its members are men; hence she can never participate in its
activities except in a minimal way. For this reason, women are
less concerned than elders over the decreasing importance of the
etogo.

If we consider the relation of the *etogo* to other aspects of
Lango society, we can see that the decline of the *etogo* is not a
fortuitous development.

Political Change

As a religious institution, of course, the *etogo* provides Langi
with a means of relating to the supernatural world and of controlling that world through the ability to establish contact with
the shades. The *etogo* is also a network of men bound to one
another only partly on the principle of descent. In a society whose
basic mode of organization is the principle of patrilineality, the
etogo serves to cut across lines of clanship and facilitate the co-
habitation of members of clans that are bound together in *etogo*
networks. There are other means of cutting across clan lines—
most notably exogamy and the establishment of affinal ties, but
also the communal work group. The *etogo* networks derive their
importance from their religious role in the community, because
Langi believe that *etogo* ceremonies are necessary for maintaining the health and material welfare of the community, by protecting the living from the shades.

The significance of the *etogo* as an organization that cuts across
lines of clanship can be seen in some rules of warfare in precontact Lango. Folklore, song, and everyday conversation contain
many references to warfare and probably exaggerate the significance of warfare in the precolonial period. Warfare took the
form of raids to exact revenge or to obtain cattle or food. In a
raid, a party of fifteen to twenty men would attack a settlement
just before dawn. Many raids resulted in injuries or even fa-
talities. It is difficult to ascertain how often raids occurred, but
the villages in the Aloi area seem to have been involved in such
skirmishes on an average of once every four years. One lineage

moved into Opele *wang tic* in the 1920s after their village had been attacked three times and several of their members had been killed.

During the precolonial period, Langi did not live in dispersed homesteads but occupied village settlements, presumably to fortify themselves against attack. Driberg described the villages as follows:

The Langi live in villages which vary considerably in size from ten to one hundred and fifty huts. In pre-administration days, when war was the natural condition of things and peace an interlude, villages were larger than in these more settled times, as the larger the village the greater the security on the one hand, and the more extensive their opportunities for plunder, on the other (1923:71).

There are numerous accounts of attacks made on villages by other villages. What is significant about intervillage warfare with regard to the *etogo* is that every *etogo* included men from several villages, and ideally, of course, *etogo* ties extended throughout the entire district. In an attack, a man was not permitted to fight any member of his own *etogo*. A man who wounded or killed a member of his own *etogo* was banned from all ceremonial activities until a cleansing rite was performed for him. There are even accounts of two villages' forming an alliance because large numbers of men in both villages belonged to the same *etogo*. These features of Lango warfare and alliance suggest that, in the precolonial period, the *etogo* served to make intervillage raids less frequent and to minimize injury when they did occur (Tarantino 1949*b*:230–234).

Warfare came to a gradual halt after 1914, when colonial rule was established in Lango (Ingham 1955). In the late 1920s, the settlement pattern began to alter, largely as a result of the *Pax Britannica* imposed on Lango District by the new government. It became less important to have an organization that cut across clan lines and reduced conflict between descent groups. The political function of the *etogo* was taken over by the colonial government, and the *etogo* began to decline.

Economic Change

To establish an administrative government was one of the two basic goals of the colonial agents in Lango. The other was to institute a system whereby the Langi would become part of the economic life of Uganda as suppliers of agricultural products to the world market. To this end, the colonial administration introduced cotton in 1914, along with a requirement that every adult male pay an annual poll tax of fourteen shillings. These two innovations went hand in hand: every Lango man was obliged to grow cotton for the cash to pay his poll tax. Having established this initial nexus between the Lango cultivator and the world market, the colonial administration introduced other crops, such as cassava, potatoes, groundnuts, and citrus fruits.[8] The importance of these new crops was not merely that they varied the Lango diet, but also that they afforded protection against famine. This was particularly true of potatoes and cassava, which are more resistant to drought than the traditional Lango staples of millet and sorghum. The introduction of money and of weekly markets facilitated the exchange of foodstuffs, helping cultivators whose food crops were less successful in any particular year than their cotton. These innovations gave the Langi considerable protection from famine by reducing their dependence on wild foods. This was especially important because the rinderpest epizootic of 1890 had killed almost all the cattle in Lango, and the wild-game supply had begun to dwindle in the 1890s.

A result of the colonial administration's innovations was that the individual cultivator became less dependent on the support of kinsmen for his food, and the sharing of food among kinsmen became less important. Another result was that internal migration became less frequent, and it was therefore not so essential for men to extend their alliances to members of other descent groups, as they did in an *etogo* network.

It is to be expected that the changing ecology of Lango and the greater independence of the individual cultivator would have had their effects on the *etogo*. From the sociological point of view, the *etogo* was a network of men which not only bound them to assist one another ceremonially but which interrelated individuals and lineages in a way that facilitated the exchange of foodstuffs and other forms of assistance. From the point of view

8. The colonial history of Lango bears especially close resemblances to that of the Lugbara of northern Uganda. See Middleton (1971:21).

of the individual Lango *etogo* member, the functions of the *etogo* were to improve relations with the shades and to ensure the abundance of crops through ensuring adequate rainfall. As the cultivator became less dependent on others and less subject to the forces of the environment, his interest in the *etogo* decreased.

Other economic conditions made people less willing to participate in *etogo* ceremonies. For example, all *etogo* ceremonies except the *Apuny* and the Cursing a Thief require the preparation of large amounts of beer. Holding an *etogo* ceremony calls for a considerable expenditure of both labor and food resources. At present the people of Obanya Kura are reluctant to prepare beer for *etogo* feasts when they can sell the beer in the marketplace. They prefer to convert the beer into money to purchase items that they feel are more important to them than the goodwill of the *etogo*.

As another example, the *Apuny* calls for a donation of a bull from the descendants of the shades that are being honored. There is now a cattle market in Lango which meets monthly; men sell their cattle to agents who ship the livestock to the meat markets of Kampala. A man can sell a bull for about 200 shillings at market, and he is not unaware of this fact when *etogo* elders ask for a donation of a bull for the shades. The elders themselves say that this is the reason there have been no *Apuny* ceremonies in Obanya Kura since 1959. The men of the area are reluctant to give bulls.

In the final analysis, however, religious change cannot be reduced to an epiphenomenon of political change and material maximization. As we shall see for the *kwer* ceremonies, Langi are willing to make heavy expenditures when the ceremonies are ideologically or personally satisfying to them. The *Etogo* ceremonies are no longer satisfying enough. The fellowship that the *etogo* offered to Lango men can now be had at beer gatherings in the marketplace, where a man can select a group of drinking partners and enjoy an afternoon with them. It is clear that young men derive greater satisfaction from this sort of sociability than from the *etogo*. Moreover, in a beer-drinking group in the marketplace a man is not accorded a lower status if his father happens to be alive, a point that leads young men to look with disfavor on the *etogo*.

Competing Techniques of Curing

Alternative techniques of curing compete with the curing activities of the *etogo*. Government clinics provide medical services at no cost to the Langi. These clinics are staffed by medical assistants who diagnose and treat a wide range of ailments and injuries. Cases that they cannot handle are referred to the Lira Hospital, and patients are transferred there by ambulance. Although these medical services are deficient compared with those available in Kampala, their success in treating infectious diseases, fractures, snakebites, and pediatric conditions is startling. Chronic illnesses that the clinics cannot cure are regarded as manifestations of spirit possession and as such fall into the province of the adepts. The curative function of the *etogo* is performed by other agencies, and this change, like the political and economic ones, has diminished interest in the ceremonies of the *etogo*.

IV

Kwer: *Ceremonies of Incorporation*

In this chapter we shall discuss the second of the three ceremonial complexes in Lango. The eight *kwer* ceremonies are performed for married women at different stages in their careers as wives and mothers. We have seen that female participation in the *etogo* ceremonies is minimal. In contrast, the *kwer* ceremonies are very much concerned with women. It can be said that the *kwer* ceremonies are "about" women, just as *etogo* ceremonies are "about" relations with the shades. Not only do both sexes participate in the *kwer* ceremonies, but the ceremonies honor women and celebrate their place in Lango society. We shall demonstrate that, in addition to honoring women, *kwer* ceremonies are ritual statements of the ambiguity surrounding womanhood in Lango society.

The declared purpose of the *kwer* ceremonies is to restore the good health of a woman and her children and to ensure that they remain healthy. Langi do not think of *kwer* ceremonies as healing ceremonies intended to cure a particular patient of a particular ailment. Although some *kwer* ceremonies are occasioned by illness, the ceremonies are regarded as general restorative measures which are particularly valuable in warding off future ailments. Furthermore, the protection afforded a woman by the *kwer* ceremonies is cumulative, so that a woman who has had all eight ceremonies performed for her is said to be stronger and thus better protected against disease than a woman who has not.

The present chapter will (1) consider the overall relation between the *kwer* ceremonial complex and Lango social organization, (2) describe the ceremonies, and (3) discuss why the *kwer* ceremonies continue to be practiced and why they remain more popular than the ceremonies of the elders.

THE KWER CEREMONIES IN LANGO SOCIAL ORGANIZATION

The word *kwer* comes from the verb *kwero* ("to refuse"), which is used to denote the observance of clan prohibitions. For example, the clan name "Okwerocuga" refers to the clan's principal food prohibition, that of a type of ant called *cuga*; the name is translated literally as "the people who will not eat the *cuga* ant." The noun *kwer* refers to a type of ceremony, but its basic meaning pertains to the food taboos and other prohibitions associated with clanship. Etymologically, then, there is a relation between the *kwer* ceremonies and the clan prohibitions, and this relation is borne out by the symbolism employed in the *kwer* ceremonies.

The eight *kwer* ceremonies differ greatly in details, but all share one important feature: In each *kwer* ceremony, a pot of beer is set aside and designated as "beer for ritual purification" (*kongo me lwoko kwer*). Serving this beer is a central part of the ceremony, and is related to the significance of the *kwer* ceremonies in Lango social organization. The beer does not differ physically from ordinary Lango beer, but a symbolic meaning is attached to it: it is said to express the obligation of a woman to drink beer with the members of her husband's clan and to obey the prohibitions of that clan.

The "beer for ritual purification" is prepared by the mother of the woman being honored at the ceremony. Before the beer is served, the outside of the pot containing the beer is ritually washed by the women who have married into the clan of the husband of the woman being honored. The act of washing the pot is also charged with symbolic meaning, for it expresses (1) co-operation among the women who are classified together as co-wives (that is, the woman whom the ceremony honors and the women of her generation who have married into her husband's clan), (2) the like qualities of these women as seen in their common obligation to observe the same clan prohibitions, and (3) the social fact that ultimately these women are "outsiders," as seen

in their common task of washing a pot that belongs to the consanguineal kinsmen of one of them.

The theme expressed in the use of the "beer for ritual purification" and in many other symbols in the *kwer* ceremonies is that
of incorporating a woman into the clan of her husband while
paying heed to the principal tenet of patrilineal descent: that a
woman belongs to the clan of her father. We discussed in Chapter
II the ambiguous status of the Lango married woman in the context of family organization and household economics. The *kwer*
ceremonies introduce the problem of incorporation once again,
for we observe in these ceremonies the gathering of the two descent groups that have some claim over a woman: the descent
group of her husband and that of her father. In the course of
the ceremonies we observe the symbolic expression of these competing claims.

It is significant that the *kwer* ceremonies are associated with
motherhood, which is the principal determinant of a woman's
status within her husband's lineage. The first *kwer* ceremony
celebrates childbirth, and most of the others honor a woman's
status as a mother. The final *kwer* ceremony, for example, held
when it is believed that a woman has stopped bearing children,
is seen as a conclusion to her childbearing career.

A woman gains greater respect from her affinal kinsmen and
enhances her own position with her husband as she bears children. With this in mind, we might consider the conditions in
which a woman is likely to have a *kwer* ceremony performed for
her. The ceremonies are of three types: (1) two ceremonies celebrate the birth of a child; (2) five are held in response to recurrent sickness of the woman or her children, perhaps accompanied
by the death of one or more children; and (3) one general ceremony is held in honor of a woman and her children. In this last
instance the *kwer* ceremony is not signaled by any physical event,
and the circumstances that occasion it are somewhat vague.

For most of the eight *kwer* ceremonies, it is the responsibility
of the woman's consanguineal kinsmen to sponsor the ceremony.
If a woman's affinal kinsmen think the woman is not fulfilling
her role as a bearer of children for her husband's lineage, they
may urge her consanguineal kinsmen to sponsor a ceremony. Her
affinal kinsmen do not necessarily see her failure to fulfill the role

as her fault; they might recognize that sickness or the death of her children has worked against her. And when a woman is healthy and is meeting the expectations of her husband's lineage as a bearer of children, her kinsmen are likely to hold a *kwer* for her to celebrate her fecundity. Thus a woman's kinsmen are called on to show support for her when her status in her husband's lineage is either being enhanced by childbirth or being jeopardized by her failure to bear children.

Ideally, a woman should have all eight *kwer* ceremonies performed for her in a specified sequence, each ceremony being held at a certain point in her career as a mother. In fact, however, there is no strict obligation for the parents or parents-in-law of a woman to hold *kwer* ceremonies for her, and because the ceremonies are costly, these kinsmen often reluctant to hold them. Of the women in Obanya Kura old enough to have had all the ceremonies performed for them, only 4 percent had done so. Women do not believe that *kwer* ceremonies are particularly efficacious medically, and when they are confronted with sick children or barrenness, they are likely to seek strictly medical cures before considering a *kwer* ceremony. It is significant in this regard that the impetus for a *kwer* ceremony usually derives from the concern of the woman's husband and the women of his lineage. When they perceive that she is losing her children or has not borne more children, they are likely to approach her consanguineal kinsmen and request a *kwer* ceremony. The woman's affines regard compliance with the request as a sign that her consanguines are interested in her well-being and are anxious for her to be a satisfactory wife and mother.

The example of Alicia Akello shows how a *kwer* ceremony might come to be performed. Alicia had two children, aged eleven and nine, and had shown no sign of pregnancy since the birth of her second child. Two *kwer* ceremonies had been held for her while her children were infants; none had been performed since. Her husband became concerned over her failure to bear more children, and he began talking about taking a second wife. Alicia's mother-in-law had begun to quarrel with her and had made reference to the small number of children she had borne. Alicia visited her mother's house and described the deteriorating relations with her husband's kinsmen, attributing her problem to her failure to bear more children. During the next few months her mother saved up some money and collected millet for beer. She made some beer herself and bought some, and organized a *kwer* ceremony for Alicia. Neither Alicia or her mother expected the ceremony to bring on another pregnancy, but they both asserted that the ceremony would "help."

The relation between the *kwer* ceremonies and Lango social organization can best be understood after the ceremonies have been described. Table V introduces the description by listing the eight *kwer* ceremonies and some of their features. (We shall use the word "patient" to denote the woman for whom a *kwer* ceremony is held. The term is not entirely satisfactory, since *kwer* ceremonies are not strictly curing ceremonies, but it seems to be the most appropriate English term.)

KWER A DAKO NYWAL ("KWER FOR A WOMAN WHO HAS GIVEN BIRTH")

The first two *kwer* ceremonies differ from the others in that it is obvious whether and when they should be held. They are occasioned by the dramatic biological event of childbirth, and it is clear to the woman's kinsmen, both consanguineal and affinal, that the two childbirth *kwer* should be held for her. The sometimes difficult process of deciding whether a *kwer* should be held is not a feature of the childbirth *kwer*—and it is more difficult for a woman's consanguineal kinsmen to evade their responsibilities to her.

The first *kwer* ceremony is called *kwer a dako nywal* ("*kwer* for a woman who has given birth") or sometimes *kwer atin* ("*kwer* for the child"). When a woman gives birth, her husband should see that her parents are informed as soon as possible. The woman's parents should have anticipated the birth by preparing the dry components of beer well before hand, so that they will be ready to serve beer three or four days after the birth.

Lango women follow a rule of postpartum seclusion.[1] Immediately after a woman gives birth, her mother-in-law cuts branches from the *omeng* tree (*Combretum Gueinzii*) and lays

---

1. Driberg's description (1923:139–140) of postpartum seclusion during his field work differs in several minor details from the seclusions I observed.

Kwer Ceremonies and Some of Their Features

Lango term	English translation	Stated purpose	When held	Where held	Who provides the beer
Kwer a dako nyval	Kwer for a Woman Who Has Given Birth	To celebrate childbirth and ending of postpartum seclusion	Shortly after childbirth	Patient's married residence	Patient's consanguines
Yeyo kongo me abena	Bringing Beer for the Carrying Strap	To present carrying strap to patient	5–6 weeks after birth of first child	Patient's married residence	Patient's consanguines
Kiro wang	Sprinkling the Eyes	To protect eyes; to allow patient to re-enter houses of consanguines	Indefinite	Patient's natal residence	Patient's affines and consanguines
Tongo keno	Cutting the Hearth	To instruct patient in building a hearth	Indefinite	Patient's natal residence	Patient's consanguines
Tweyo lao	Tying the Strap	To tie a strap on patient	After patient has born several children	Patient's married residence	Patient's affines
Kayo cogo	Biting the Bone	To ensure health of patient and her children	When oldest child is 7–9 years old or at illness	Patient's natal residence	Patient's consanguines
Lako we	Cleaning the Chyme	To counteract one feature of Biting the Bone	After Biting the Bone	Patient's married residence	Patient's affines
Yeyo moko me agara	Bringing Beer for the Ankle Bells	To celebrate patient's full status as a mother; to protect youngest child from illness	When oldest child is 10–13 years old	Residence of person providing bridewealth to patient's husband	Patient's affines and consanguines

them on the ground to form a circular enclosure in front of the young mother's house. The diameter of the enclosure is about twelve feet, and the doorway of the house opens directly on the enclosure. The mother, with her infant, must remain in the house and the enclosure; she may rest in the shade or do light work. She is permitted to leave the enclosure only to urinate or defecate, and the only people permitted to visit her in the enclosure or the house are women who have married into her husband's clan. She is not allowed to prepare food for herself; food and water are brought to her by other women. While in seclusion she may not eat meat or butter or drink milk, since these foods are thought to reduce her future fertility. She must also avoid cowpeas and any food that contains salt. Because salt is added to most Lango foods during cooking, this last avoidance rule requires the preparation of special salt-free foods for women in seclusion. Such food, described as "tasteless" (*abobot*), is generally prepared by the mother-in-law. One particular dish, *nyuka*, a thick gruel of ground millet and water, is not ordinarily eaten by Langi but is considered especially appropriate for the delicate condition of a woman in seclusion. During seclusion a woman is also expected to follow the food prohibitions of her husband's clan, under the supervision of her mother-in-law.

While in seclusion, the young mother must take certain precautions in handling her child. In particular, she must not touch the child's genitals. To do so would cause a male child to be impotent in later life or a female child to be barren.

The period of seclusion lasts for four days after the birth of a boy and three days after the birth of a girl. (The number four symbolizes males, and the number three symbolizes females.) The *Kwer* for a Woman Who Has Given Birth marks the end of seclusion. The parents of the young mother, having been notified of the birth, should be present on the day seclusion ends. They should arrive in midmorning at the home of their daughter bearing two pots of beer and another pot containing millet, meat, cowpeas, and some shea-butternut oil. The beer pots are set up in the yard of the young mother, and just before people begin to drink, she breaks her seclusion by removing the branches that had formed the enclosure in her yard. The completion of the seclusion is called *donyo* ("to enter") and is said to be a reentrance into social life marked by the mother's drinking beer with both her consanguineal and her affinal kinsmen. During the seclusion itself the woman is said to be "untied" or "separated."

One of the two pots of beer prepared by the young woman's mother is designated as "beer for ritual purification" and is kept apart from the other pot. After the woman has broken her seclusion, her classificatory co-wives wash the outside of the pot containing the "beer for ritual purification," and they drink the beer with the young mother. Meanwhile, her parents sit in a nearby house drinking beer from the other pot with the parents of her husband. (It is necessary to isolate her parents in a house because of the rule of mother-in-law avoidance.) The young woman's husband drinks beer in the yard with a few clansmen and invited neighbors; this group drinks from a small pot into which some of the ordinary beer has been poured.

Aside from washing the pot and drinking the "beer for ritual purification," the only ritual in the *Kwer* for a Woman Who Has Given Birth occurs after the senior kinsmen have finished their beer, late in the afternoon. The grandparents of the newborn child, remaining inside the house where they have been drinking beer, anoint each other with the shea-butternut oil which the young mother's parents brought. First the two grandfathers dip their hands into the oil and face each other. Then each reaches over the other man's shoulders, placing his hands on the shoulder blades. Simultaneously they rub their hands up over each other's shoulders and down the front of the chest as far as the lower end of the sternum. As they spread oil onto each other's shoulders, they say, in turn, "You are my close friend. May you be healthy" ("*Yin bedo dyera. Komi bedo oyot*"). The two women then anoint each other in the same manner, reciting the same salutation.

After the anointing, the visitors return to their homes. The patient's parents leave the two pots at the patient's home. A few weeks later, the patient's mother-in-law, accompanied by the patient and one or two other women, must make a return visit to the patient's parents; she will fill the pots with prepared dry beer or money (about five shillings) and return them to the patient's parents.

YEYO MOKO ME ABENA ("BRINGING BEER FOR THE CARRYING STRAP")

Five or six weeks after the birth of a woman's first child, her consanguineal kinsmen are expected to provide the woman with an animal hide which she will cut to make an *abena*, a rectangular piece of hide with a strap at each corner. The *abena* is used to carry an infant on its mother's back and is secured by means of the four straps, which the mother pulls around her and ties against her chest. Not all animal skins are suitable for an *abena*: the women of a clan must use the skin of the species of animal that their clan prescribes.

A real or classificatory brother of the patient—preferably the brother who is cattle-linked to her—is responsible for hunting the animal, skinning it, and tanning the hide. A small group of consanguineal kinsmen brings the hide to the patient at her husband's house, and this visit constitutes the Bringing Beer for the Carrying Strap. The patient's mother must prepare two pots of beer, which are brought with the skin. Very little ceremonial activity accompanies this *kwer*: the *abena* is presented to the patient, and a small portion of beer, again designated as "beer for ritual purification," is set aside in a separate pot to be served only to women who have married into the lineage of the patient's husband. This group is made up of five or six women who live nearby—the patient's mother-in-law, the patient's co-wives, and the patient's husband's brothers' wives. The remainder of the beer is served in one or two pots to the other people present.

The Bringing Beer for the Carrying Strap is not an important *kwer* ceremony, and since only a small amount of beer is prepared, it is attended by only about twenty-five persons. As an example, the kinship composition of those present at one such *kwer* ceremony that I attended is shown in Figure 6. In addition to this small group of kinsmen, eight non-kinsmen from the patient's neighborhood were present. The visit lasts about five hours, the wife's kinsmen returning to their homes late in the afternoon.

About 50 percent of the women in Alebtong have had the Bringing Beer for the Carrying Strap. A woman who has not had the ceremony either made her own *abena* without the ceremony,

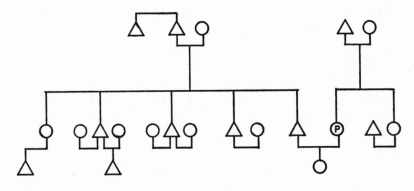

⊙ patient

Figure 6: Kinsmen Who Attended a Bringing Beer for the Carrying Strap

asking her husband to kill the appropriate animal[2], or obtained an *abena* from a real or classificatory sister who had an extra *abena* not in use. For many women, the ceremony is not held after the birth of the first child, but is delayed until the birth of the second child or even the third.

The symbolic meaning of this ceremony centers on the species of animal which is killed and whose skin is made into a carrying strap. This species is not necessarily a species that the clan treats in a special way in connection with food prohibitions and other clan observances. One reason is that not all the animals treated in clan observances can provide a suitable hide for a carrying strap. For example, members of the Okwerocuga clan have a number of interdictions concerning the avoidance of *cuga* ants but make their carrying straps from the hides of bushbucks. However, there is a vague mystical relation between the members of a clan and the species of animal from which they make their carrying straps. This relation cannot be interpreted as a totemic relation. It is one in which the members of a clan recognize a particular species of animal as their favorite hunting animal. Each clan is believed to be especially skilled at hunting its species, and I was told that in the past men had used magical substances

2. From what I can tell, this is a lapse from correct procedure, and several in-formants felt that it was impermissible for a woman to obtain a carrying strap from her husband even if he did hunt the correct species of animal.

to enable them to hunt this species more effectively. This species was said to be the property of the clan, and older men referred to the species as "our animals" or "the animals of our clan." In speaking of this relation the members of a clan implied that they owned the species and enjoyed a particular kind of control over it—namely, the ability to hunt animals of that species with special proficiency. Other clans were free to hunt animals of that species, but they would probably not be so successful in the hunt as that clan would.

I believe that the use of these particular animal species in the *kwer* ceremony makes an important symbolic statement about the relationship of the young mother to her natal clan. Her brothers hunt the animal that they "own" and "control," and present their sister with its hide, which she will use to make a carrying strap for her child. In doing so, they are symbolizing their relationship to their sister—which is also a matter of "ownership" and "control." Consider some of the metaphors expressing the differences between men and women. Men are said to "hunt" women when they court; men are seen as being sedentary, whereas women migrate from the homes of their fathers to the homes of their husbands "like animals of the bush"; women are said to be "wild" by nature and to have to be subdued. In another vein, women are "wealth" or "property" (*lim*); men "own" their wives; and a man "buys" his wife from her father when he pays bridewealth. It is quite logical that this symbolic statement of ownership and control should be made shortly after a young woman has borne a child, for it is an assertion of the relationship of the child to its matrilateral kinsmen and a reminder that the child's patriclan does not have exclusive rights over the child.

KIRO WANG ("SPRINKLING THE EYES")

There is less agreement on the timing of the Sprinkling the Eyes than for the two aforementioned *kwer* ceremonies. In the past, the ideal was to hold the Sprinkling the Eyes six to nine months after the birth of each child. Langi now agree that this is not necessary but that a woman should have a Sprinkling the Eyes performed for her during her lifetime, preferably between the births of her first and second children. In actuality, however, many women neglect to have the Sprinkling the Eyes performed at all, and only 35 percent of the women in Obanya Kura who would have been eligible for this *kwer* had undergone the ceremony. The Sprinkling the Eyes is prophylactic in its aim: its purpose is to protect the eyes of a woman or her children from disease. A woman is not supposed to request this *kwer* unless eye trouble afflicts her or her children, but a minor eye irritation or a headache can be interpreted as an eye ailment and used as a pretext for holding the ceremony.

A strong incentive for holding a Sprinkling the Eyes is that after giving birth a woman may not enter any house in the compound of her natal family until she has had the ceremony performed for her. Lango believe that, if she or her children should enter the house of her mother (for example) before the ceremony has been held, they are likely to be stricken with an eye ailment. A woman who frequently visits her natal home might be inconvenienced by this rule until she has the Sprinkling the Eyes performed for her. She should not sleep overnight when she visits her parents. Any threat of leaving her husband is weakened because her husband is aware that she should not sleep at the home of her parents, and some women stated that this rule effectively reduces a woman's bargaining power with her husband. Her parents, in turn, may encourage her to have the Sprinkling the Eyes because they find it useful to have their married daughter visit them for periods of a week or ten days at times when her labor would be welcomed. She may be called upon to cook, look after children, or help to make beer when there is a shortage of female labor in her parents' home.

I recorded one incident in which a young woman who had not had a Sprinkling the Eyes performed for her went to visit at her natal home. She neglected the interdiction against staying overnight at her mother's home and remained with her mother for five days. About three months later her child developed symptoms which appeared to be malarial but which were interpreted as a consequence of her protracted visit to her natal home. She complained to her co-wives and to her husband, saying that a Sprinkling the Eyes should be performed for her, but the child recovered, and the matter was forgotten shortly.

The distance between a women's natal residence and her mar-

ried residence is important in deciding whether and when the
Sprinkling the Eyes should be held. As in most other *kwer* ceremonies, the disposition of the ceremony reflects the general pattern of exogamy in Lango. If a marriage occurs between a man
and a woman of the same neighborhood, there will not be so
much pressure on the woman to hold the Sprinkling the Eyes,
because she can make frequent visits to her parents' home and
return to her husband's home on the same day. She will not be
greatly inconvenienced by the fact that she has not had a Sprinkling the Eyes performed for her, except that her bargaining
power with her husband will be reduced. If, on the other hand,
her natal homestead is more than about sixteen miles away—that
is, farther than a woman can walk conveniently in a day carrying
a baby on her back—she is not likely to visit her parents except on
some important occasion. She will be effectively lost to her parents as a source of assistance when special tasks need to be done.
The need for a Sprinkling the Eyes will not be great, since the
daughter would not be able to return home anyway. Most often,
however, the distance between married residence and natal home
is about six miles. The woman can be counted on to assist her
consanguineal relatives from time to time, yet it will be more
convenient for her to stay overnight, and a Sprinkling the Eyes
is desirable.

What follows is a description of a Sprinkling the Eyes which
was held for a woman named Klusti, who was about thirty-four
years old. Klusti had a six-year-old child and a three-month-old
infant. Neither Klusti nor her children seemed ill, but her father
visited her one day and suggested that a Sprinkling the Eyes be
held for her. We should note that Klusti's father had planted
more millet than usual in the previous season, and his granaries
were said to be full.

Klusti's mother-in-law was informed that the Sprinkling the
Eyes was to be held, and she prepared a gallon of beer to bring to
the ceremony. Meanwhile, Klusti's mother prepared approximately twenty gallons of beer. On the appointed day Klusti, her
two children, and some affinal kinsmen set out early in the morning to walk four miles to the home of her parents. The group is
diagrammed in Figure 7.

When the party arrived at the home of Klusti's mother, Klusti

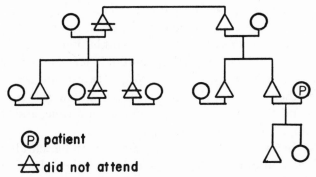

Ⓟ **patient**

⚠ **did not attend**

Figure 7: Patient and Her Affinal Kinsmen Who Attended a Sprinkling
the Eyes

presented her mother with a calabash of beer which she had
brought from the home of her husband. Klusti's mother accepted
the calabash and brought it inside the house to store until the
following day, after the guests had gone, when she drank the beer
with her husband. After the guests had given their greetings they
remained standing in the yard. Klusti's mother brought a calabash full of water and a sprig of leaves of the *alwak* plant and
presented them to Klusti's classificatory mother-in-law. (The first
woman to accept the water and the sprig should be a classificatory
mother-in-law, and the last should be the actual mother-in-law.)

Klusti then stood in the yard about ten feet from her mother's
sleeping house and faced the doorway. Her classificatory mother-
in-law held the calabash with her left hand, dipped the sprig of
alwak leaves into the water, and shook the sprig first into Klusti's
eyes and then into the eyes of the two children, beginning with
the older. When she had finished sprinkling, she proclaimed:

Wun dong kom wu bed oyot,	Now you will stay well,
Pien dong otieko kiro	Because we have finished
wanguwu oko tunga neawu.	sprinkling your eyes at the
	home of your mother's
	brothers.

She handed the calabash and the sprig of leaves to Klusti's
actual mother-in-law, who sprinkled Klusti and the children in
the same way and recited the same blessing. (If several classifi-

catory mothers-in-law of the patient attend the ceremony, each
one should sprinkle the patient and her children, and the patient's actual mother-in-law should sprinkle them last.)

Klusti and her children then entered her mother's house.
Klusti stood inside the doorway, facing outward, and her classificatory mother-in-law and her actual mother-in-law each sprinkled
her eyes and the eyes of her children a second time, and recited
the blessing.

Klusti then walked throughout the area with her children and
visited the houses of her brothers and her father's brother. She
and her children stood in the doorway of each house and were
sprinkled by her actual mother-in-law. She entered the houses
where her clansmen slept, but none of the kitchens or outbuild-
ings. The group did not follow any particular sequence as they
moved from house to house, and the recitation was not repeated
after the initial sprinklings at the doorway of Klusti's mother's
house.

While Klusti, her children, and her mother-in-law were walking from one house to another, her parents sat in the mother's
yard with the other visitors. Klusti's husband waited with his
brother and his father's brother's son, but they had seated themselves inside the house of Klusti's brother because of the rule of
mother-in-law avoidance. Klusti's mother had set aside a pot of
beer designated as "beer for ritual purification." The outside of
the pot was washed by Klusti's husband's brother's wife and
classificatory husband's brother's wives (the wives of Klusti's
husband's father's brother's sons), and then a gourdful of undi-
luted beer was scooped from the top and set aside. This portion
of the beer is termed the "head." It is thick and grainy and is
considered to be especially good food for women, the sick, and
the aged because it gives more strength than ordinary beer.

The beer in the pot was then diluted with water, and a second
gourdful, called "beer for blessing" (*kongo a gwelo*), was scooped
off the top. Klusti's classificatory mother-in-law (the woman who
had been the first to sprinkle Klusti and her children) took the
gourd. With the index finger of her right hand she dabbed beer
on Klusti's forehead, sternum, right shoulder, left shoulder, right
knee, and left knee, dipping her finger into the gourd each time.
She followed the same procedure with each of Klusti's children.

The gourd was then passed to Klusti's actual mother-in-law, who blessed Klusti and her children in the same way.

After the blessing (*gwelo*), the visiting women (except Klusti's mother-in-law) drank together in the ordinary fashion from the pot of "beer for ritual purification." Klusti's mother-in-law and father-in-law were brought inside a house, where they drank beer with Klusti's parents. The rest of the men seated themselves near the edge of the yard, where beer was served to them. After the visiting women had finished drinking the "beer for ritual purification," they passed around the gourd containing the "head" of the beer. Then Klusti's mother joined the women in the yard, and the visiting women divided themselves into two groups: those in Klusti's generation and those in the generation of her mother-in-law. A different pot of beer was brought to each group. Drinking continued all night, and people began to dance in the early evening and continued intermittently until dawn.

Several symbols are employed in the Sprinkling the Eyes, and these symbols offer some clues to the meaning of the ceremony. The *alwak* plant is associated with birth and fecundity. It grows wild in Lango District and is readily found. It is said to have been planted by Jok, the Creater, so that people would use it for blessing women. The plant is not said to have any particular medicinal properties, but it is associated with women and childbirth.

The act of sprinkling water on someone with a sprig of *alwak* leaves is associated with welcoming the person into the home of his consanguineal kinsmen, and it connotes a restoration of relations between children and parents. It is sometimes done when a person who has been living outside Lango District for many years returns home. I saw it performed for a man who had been on bad terms with his father and mother for eight years but was being welcomed back into the household.

The meaning of the frothy head of beer which is dabbed on the patient's body is slightly more complicated. The head of beer is said to contain all the valuable properties of beer in a condensed form: it is nutritive and life-giving, and its consumption joins people together in communality as they drink it. From the exegetical statements I was able to obtain, it appears that the most important characteristic of the head is its conjunctive property— its ability to join elements together. It is in this sense that the head is used in the Sprinkling the Eyes. It is applied on key parts of the patient's body to symbolize the wholeness of the patient—to make the statement that she is indeed one.

The general form of the Sprinkling the Eyes is similar to that of the other *kwer* ceremonies. We can observe opposition between the consanguineal and affinal kinsmen of the patient; her dependence on her affines for her ability to reproduce (the sprinkling and blessing are done by her mothers-in-law); and her relationship with her parents and her brothers as she stands in the doorways of their houses. The patient is importantly involved in both kinship groups. She stands inside the houses of her mother and her brothers looking outward as her mothers-in-law sprinkle her. At the conclusion, the patient is made whole when she is blessed with the frothy head of beer, which joins the key segments of her body into one. Not only does the patient belong to both kinship groups, but she and her children join the two groups together.

TONGO KENO ("CUTTING THE HEARTH")

This *kwer* includes very little ritual and involves only a small group of consanguineal and affinal kinsmen. Only six of the women in Obanya Kura have had this ceremony performed for them, and few of the younger women have ever seen the Cutting the Hearth or know anything of its nature or purpose. No Cutting the Hearth was performed in *Obanya Kura* during my field work, and I was able to obtain little information on the ceremony.

Any woman who has borne two or three children may request that a Cutting the Hearth be held for her at the home of her parents. Although the avowed purpose of the ceremony is to instruct a woman on how to build a hearth, it cannot be considered a true technique of instruction. A Lango hearth requires no special knowledge to construct: it consists of three large volcanic stones—one in the back and one on each side. The only difficulty in building the hearth is in transporting the stones to the site of the hearth, since they may weigh as much as sixty pounds each. A woman asks her husband to collect these stones shortly after she takes up residence in her husband's home. She will have been using her own hearth for several years when the ceremony is held.

The beer for Cutting the Hearth is made by the patient's mother, and consists of one small pot of beer set aside as the "beer for ritual purification" and one or two other small pots. On the morning of the ceremony, the patient leaves her husband's home with some of her classificatory co-wives, her children, and any other of her husband's kinsmen who wish to come along, and they walk to the home of the patient's mother.

Before the patient enters her mother's yard she is sprinkled with water by a senior member of her father's family. The sprinkling is similar to that done in the Sprinkling the Eyes, except that the water is directed only at the woman's sternum, not at her face. The sprinkling has the same symbolic significance, that of accepting the woman at the home of her parents.

After the patient is sprinkled, she and her classificatory co-wives wash the pot containing the "beer for ritual purification." The patient scoops a calabash of beer from the top of the pot, drinks from it, and then puts it aside until the other beer is finished. Because so few people attend this ceremony, the beer is served in one pot at a time to a single circle of people, both affines and consanguines of the patient.

The final part of the Cutting the Hearth comes when the beer is finished. The patient stands inside her mother's house with one of her classificatory co-wives. A hoe is handed to the patient, and she and the other woman grasp the handle together. The patient holds the hoe loosely, and the other woman guides it. They dig three small holes in the dirt floor of the house. The holes are about two inches deep, and they are laid out in a triangular pattern to represent the foundation of three hearthstones. While the two women dig the holes, the other women say, "We are teaching you how to make your hearth" ("*En dong onyuti tongo kenoni*").

There is little else to the ceremony. The three holes are not meant to be used as the foundation of a hearth; no stones are placed on them, and they are soon forgotten. The visitors depart shortly after the holes are dug. The patient may follow up the Cutting the Hearth by presenting some millet, beer, or other gift of food to her mother a few weeks after the feast.

The hearth is the symbol of the domesticity of a married woman and her position as the principal woman in her household. She uses the hearth to prepare food. The place of the hearth in Lango speech and folklore is reminiscent of the symbol of the hearth in European peasant culture. The Cutting the Hearth points out the relation of a woman to her mother's household. It is there that she "learns" how to make the foundation for a hearth, and it is there that she learns the techniques necessary for domestic life. At the same time, she is involved in a cooperative effort with her classificatory co-wives, one of whom guides the handle of the hoe as she digs the three small foundation holes. Three holes are dug because the number three is symbolically associated with females. The hoe has no symbolic significance; it is the principal digging tool in Lango.

TWEYO LAO ("TYING THE STRAP")

The *tweyo lao* ("tying the strap") should be held after the Sprinkling the Eyes and before the Biting the Bone, but, beyond that, there is little agreement among informants on when it should take place. The decision to hold the Tying the Strap is made by a woman's mother-in-law and father-in-law and by other elders in her husband's local lineage.

Once it has been decided to hold a *tweyo lao*, the patient's mother-in-law, her co-wives, and her classificatory co-wives begin to prepare beer. The mother-in-law prepares three large pots; the others prepare an additional three pots. The patient herself does not make beer nor carry out any of the other preparations for the Tying the Strap. Young married women, usually the patient's classificatory co-wives, carry out such tasks as gathering grass to make *odolo* (rings of grass about eight inches in diameter on which the beer pots are placed). They go out in a group to gather the grass and then walk to a nearby stream to collect two sticks called *icac*, cut from the *kwomo* plant. Two plants are uprooted and stripped of their twigs and leaves, and the stem of each plant (the *icac*), about three to four feet long, is used in the ceremony.

The term *tweyo lao* refers to tying on the *lao*, a strap of leather about twenty-four inches long and three inches wide. One end is fastened to a woman's waistband and the other hangs down behind her. Driberg (1923:65) noted that a man would give a *lao* to a woman after she bore him a child. Driberg did not describe the *tweyo lao* as a ceremony, nor did he state the circumstances in which a woman wore a *lao*. These omissions make it difficult to ascertain whether the *lao* had the same social usage in Driberg's day as it now does. At present, the *lao* is worn only during the *tweyo lao* ceremony, with the result that the *lao* itself is becoming rare; sometimes one must be made specially for the ceremony. The sole symbolic significance of the *lao* comes from its relation to the ceremony. Langi say only that the *lao* denotes that a woman is the mother of children who actually belong to the clan of her husband. In providing his wife with a *lao*, the husband is symbolically claiming the children for his lineage. The symbolic significance of the *lao* is expressed in the way the husband acquires a *lao* to present to his wife on the day of the ceremony. He must borrow a *lao* from a woman who has married into his lineage. To do this, he must visit the household of a woman who has married a member of his patrilineage in his own generation—that is, his brother's or classificatory brother's wife. Each local lineage possesses a *lao*, which is used by each household of the lineage when its time comes for a *tweyo lao* to be held. The *lao* represents the incorporation of women and their children into the lineage as well as the unity of all the lineage members.

I describe here a Tying the Strap that took place in early 1967. The patient had three children, aged nine, five, and one. Her mother-in-law decided to hold the ceremony for her on the grounds that the daughter-in-law had been "staying well" with the people of her husband's lineage. The patient had borne children without any particular difficulties and had the reputation of being a hardworking and trustworthy woman.

Early on the morning when the ceremony was to take place, the wife of one of the patient's husband's brothers spread a cowhide on the ground in front of the house belonging to the patient's mother-in-law. While this was being done, the patient stood at the edge of the yard and one of her husband's brothers removed her clothing. The husband's brother's wife who had spread the cowhide then tied around the patient's waist the *lao* and a *cip*, a leather cord with fringe hanging down to cover the genitals. The patient then walked toward the doorway of the house and seated herself on the hide with her back toward the doorway and her legs extended in front of her. The two *icac* sticks were placed at her sides in such a way that one end of each stick rested on the ground, close to the patient's thigh, and the other end rested on her shoulder.

Women who had married into her husband's clan then anointed her with shea-butternut oil. Each woman dipped the fingers of both hands into a gourd containing the oil and, kneeling before the patient, reached over the patient's shoulders, placed both hands on the shoulder blades, and drew the hands up over the patient's shoulders and down onto the breasts. As in the Sprinkling the Eyes, a classificatory mother-in-law of the patient was first and the actual mother-in-law was last. When the patient had been anointed by each woman present, all her children and her husband's sister's son were anointed in the same manner.

After the anointing, a classificatory mother-in-law of the patient held the index finger of the patient's right hand, and the patient stood as if she were being pulled up by the older woman. The two women ran from the doorway of the house to the edge of the yard, a distance of perhaps thirty-five feet, while ululating and pretending to brandish spears at each other.

The women next entered the house of the patient's mother-in-law, where the pots of beer were stored. The pot containing the "beer for ritual purification" was washed by the women who had married into the lineage of the patient's husband (except the patient). Then, as in the other *kwer* ceremonies, some beer was scooped from the top of this pot in a calabash and was designated as the "head" (*wi kongo me lwoko kwer*). The patient, her children, and her husband's sister's son all took a sip of beer from the calabash, and the rest of the beer in the calabash was set aside to be drunk later.

The three pots of beer prepared by the mother-in-law were the first portions of beer to be served. One pot was given to the older men, one pot was given to the younger men, and a third was to be shared among the women. The women remained inside the house of the patient's mother-in-law, and the men arranged themselves in the two age groups in a nearby house. After the first beer was finished, some of the women in the patient's generation prepared a meal of cowpeas and millet bread. Before it was served, one of the younger women performed the blessing (*gwelo*). She dipped both hands into the cowpeas and dabbed some on the patient, then on the patient's children, and finally on the patient's husband's sister's son. When the food had been consumed, the three pots of beer that had been prepared by the women of the patient's generation were served. These were divided in the same way as the first serving of beer.

The beer lasted well into the night, and the company dispersed around midnight. The patient, however, remained in the house of her mother-in-law and slept there with her children and her mother-in-law.

On the morning following the ceremony, the patient's mother-in-law removed the *lao* and the *cip* from the patient and returned them to the woman who had loaned them for the occasion. The items belonged to the wife of one of the patient's husband's brothers.

This particular Tying the Strap ceremony differed little from others I observed. The only significant difference was that the patient spent the night of the ceremony sleeping in the house of her mother-in-law; that is not usually done.

We have noted the meaning of the *lao* itself. Several other elements in the ceremony call for comment. The patient is undressed by a brother of her husband just before the *lao* and the *cip* are tied around her waist. The relationship between a Lango woman and her husband's brother is marked by a special familiarity. It is similar to some of the "joking relationships" discussed by Radcliffe-Brown (1952:90–116). The two frequently tease each other and engage in sexual joking to a degree that is not normally present in other dyadic relationships in Lango. A man may take food from his brother's wife and may make demands on her for minor services. Langi say that this behavior is logical because when a woman takes a husband, she "marries" her husband's brother. They point out that a man may have sexual rights to his brother's wife after his brother dies (although these rights will become activated only if the relationship between the two parties is formalized into a widow remarriage). A woman's ties to her husband's brother are derived from marriage and are an important part of her association with her husband's lineage. The participation of the husband's brother in the Tying the Strap confirms this point.

The mock battle is the abbreviated form of a ritual in which two groups of people simulate opposition toward each other. The members of a lineage align themselves on one side of a yard, and all the women who have married into that lineage oppose them, standing on the other side. At a signal, each group charges the other, singing songs of contempt. Hayley (1947:83–87) gave a detailed description of this kind of Tying the Strap ceremony and reported that it was performed often in Lango District. Although the Tying the Strap ceremonies Hayley observed were substantially similar to those I observed, they differed in some important respects. Most significant, the ceremony as described by Hayley contained much more ritualized abuse between mother-in-law and daughter-in-law than it now does. The element of conflict between the patient and her husband's kinsmen is still present but is far less dramatic. The present ritual, like the earlier form, expresses the difficulty of maintaining lineage solidarity when it is necessary to rely on women outside one's clan to ensure the continuation of the lineage. The threat that these women represent to the integrity of the lineage is portrayed by the shouting and the gestures of mock hostility.

KAYO COGO ("BITING THE BONE") AND LAKO WE ("CLEANING THE CHYME")

These two ceremonies take place on separate occasions, but they must be considered together because the Cleaning the Chyme is a sequel to the Biting the Bone. When a woman has a Biting the Bone performed for her, members of her husband's lineage believe, the ceremony is incomplete unless it is followed by a Cleaning the Chyme. The latter is never performed by itself, for the only reason to perform it is to counteract one feature of the Biting the Bone. Occasionally the Biting the Bone is not followed by a Cleaning the Chyme[3]; some other event or circumstance might intervene or the lineage of the woman's husband might be unable to provide beer. From the point of view of the

3. Of thirty-eight Biting the Bone ceremonies I was told about, seven were not followed by the cleaning the chyme.

husband and his lineage, this situation is undesirable, since it means that the Biting the Bone remains incomplete. We shall return to this point when describing the ceremonies.

A woman has these ceremonies performed for her when her oldest child is about seven to nine years old. The woman's father-in-law decides when the Biting the Bone is to be held. If a man sees that his son's children have been chronically ill with a disorder which does not respond to medical treatment or to the ministrations of an adept, he may conclude that a *kwer* ceremony should be undertaken. If his son's oldest child is within the age range for a Biting the Bone, and if a Tying the Strap has already been held, he may further conclude that the Biting the Bone is the most appropriate *kwer* ceremony. He should make a preliminary visit to his son's wife's father, suggest a date to him, and ask him to donate a bull for the ceremony. His wife and several of his classificatory wives should accompany him on this visit. The parents of the patient, having been notified of the visit in advance, are expected to have prepared beer and food for the guests. The patient's father-in-law is brought to the kraal of the patient's father, where he inspects the cattle and selects a bull to be killed for the Biting the Bone. If the patient's father has no suitable bull, he is expected to buy one or obtain one from his kinsmen. After selecting a bull, the two men set a date for the ceremony, and the patient's father-in-law returns home.

On the appointed day, a party of about ten persons walks from the house of the patient to the house of her parents.[4] The patient walks ahead of the others and carries a large, empty calabash, which will be used for carrying meat on the return trip. When the group of visitors arrives, all enter the yard of the patient's mother, with the exception of the patient herself, who remains standing at the edge of the yard, holding the empty calabash. The patient's mother approaches her and sprinkles her with water to welcome her home. As in the Cutting the Hearth, a sprig of the *alwak* plant is dipped into a calabash of water, and the water is sprinkled on the sternums of the patient and her children. The patient's mother bites the stem of the branch, chews the mouthful, and spits the chewed substance on her daughter's chest. Then

4. Driberg's description (1923:145) of the Biting the Bone as it was performed in his day differs in several minor details from the ceremonies I observed.

she says, "May your body remain cool" ("*Komi dong dwer*").

The patient's father, assisted by his sons, then brings the bull from the kraal to the edge of the yard. The men who have brought the bull call out to the men in the lineage of the patient's husband and ask them to accept the bull. At this moment the bull is transferred from one lineage to another: the visiting men seize the bull and lead it to the doorway of the patient's mother's house. The animal is forced to lie on the ground and is held down. The patient seats herself astride the bull. Her children and one or two of her classificatory cowives also seat themselves on the bull. The bull's nose is covered with the carrying strap that the patient used to carry her children. The men in the clan of the patient's husband tie the bull's front legs together and its hind legs together, and one of these men kills the bull by clubbing it on the head with a pestle. The women and children rise from the bull as soon as it is dead and withdraw to the edge of the yard to wait while the men skin and butcher the animal.

The meat is carefully divided, and most of it is distributed among the clan of the patient's husband. The distribution of meat is as follows:

Patient's mother: head, right front leg, one lobe of the liver, anterior half of the intestine, anterior half of the stomach, right half of the hipbone, right half of the ribs

Patient's mother-in-law: left half of the hipbone, left half of the ribs, posterior half of the stomach

Patient's classificatory mothers-in-law: posterior part of the intestine, remaining lobes of the liver

Patient's husband's sister (the sister whose bridewealth cattle went toward the bridewealth of the patient's husband): left front leg

Patient's husband's sister's oldest son: backbone and rump

Patient's father-in-law: right rear leg

Patient's classificatory fathers-in-law: left rear leg

A section called the *atoro* ("sternum") is also cut from the bull. It includes the skin from the underside of the animal together with the sternum and the muscles of the abdominal wall that remain attached to the skin as it is stripped from the animal. A hole about twelve inches across is cut out of the center of the *atoro*.

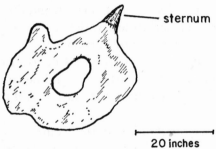

sternum

20 inches

Figure 8: The *Atoro*

During the butchering, the large intestine is removed and cut open. The brothers and classificatory brothers of the patient step forward, and each takes a handful of chyme from the large intestine. They rub the chyme on the chests of the patient and her children while reciting: "We are rubbing this chyme on your chest so that your body may remain healthy."

The butchering should be completed by midafternoon, and beer is then served. One pot of beer is designated as "beer for ritual purification." The patient carries out the customary *kwer* procedure of scooping a gourdful of beer from the top of this pot, drinking it with her children, and setting aside the beer that remains in the pot until the feast is almost over. One pot of beer is served to the men who butchered the animal. The rest of the beer is served in four pots to four groups: senior men, senior women, younger men, and younger women.

Late in the afternoon, the visitors prepare to return home, carrying their shares of the meat. Some of the meat is wrapped in banana leaves; some is carried in the calabash that the patient brought; and some is carried in smaller calabashes, which the visitors brought. After the visitors leave, they walk a short distance from the house of the patient's mother. This distance should be no more than about one-half mile, and it may be as little as sixty yards. The visitors build a fire and cook the left ribs, which had been allocated to the patient's mother-in-law. They eat the meat, and the mother-in-law keeps the rib bones and takes them home with her.

Just before they set out again, the patient slips the *atoro* around her neck. Her head goes through the hole in the center of the skin, the sternum hangs against her chest, and the large section of skin lies against her back. Ideally, the *atoro* should be worn for the duration of the homeward journey and then removed when the patient approaches her married residence. In practice, however, women find the *atoro* distasteful and heavy, and they wear it for only a short while during the journey and then carry it the rest of the way.

When the party arrives home, the women withdraw to their separate houses, taking their shares of meat and the shares belonging to the men in their households. On the following morning, the patient's mother-in-law boils the *atoro* in a large pot with the meat that she brought. When the *atoro* has been boiled for hours, a senior woman who married into the lineage of the patient's husband removes it from the pot and presents it to the patient, who holds the sternum to her mouth and bites it (*kayo cogo*: "biting the bone").The meat that was boiled in the pot is served to members of the husband's local lineage.

The patient's mother-in-law keeps the left rib bones and the left half of the hip bone. She places these in the ceiling of her house, inserting them between the wooden frame of the roof and the grass thatching. The patient's mother places the right rib bones and the right half of the hip bone in the ceiling of her house in the same way. Each woman is expected to keep the bones in her ceiling concealed and see that they are not stolen by sorcerers who wish to harm the patient and her children. The bones remain in the ceiling until the house is to be destroyed or abandoned. Then the woman who is responsible for looking after them buries them secretly in the bush.

Some informants say that the patient's husband should repay her parents for the bull they killed at the ceremony. A few years after the Biting the Bone, the husband should bring a "bull for the bone" (*dyang me cogo*) as repayment to his father-in-law. This may have been done in the past, but my research, including questions on herds and the transfer of cattle, yielded no record of any bull's ever being transferred as repayment for a *kwer*.

To be effective, the Biting the Bone must be followed by a Cleaning the Chyme about two months later. The purpose of the Cleaning the Chyme is to counteract one of the principal ritual elements of the Biting the Bone: the smearing of chyme on the body of the patient and her children by her brothers and classificatory brothers. The chyme is believed to have magical properties which protect the patient and her children from illness. By smearing the chyme and thus conferring the benefits of its magical properties on the patient, her brothers are expressing their own control over her, and, equally important, over her children. The act symbolizes the relationship that a woman has with members of her lineage in general and with her brothers in particular, and therefore expresses the problem that is central to all *kwer* ceremonies: the matter of control over a woman and her reproductive powers, or the incorporation of a woman and children into the husband's lineage.

The Cleaning the Chyme is organized by the clan of the patient's husband. The patient's mother-in-law and some of her classificatory co-wives prepare a small amount of beer, and a sauce of simsim (sesame) and simsim bread, both of which are savored as accompaniments to goat meat. On the morning of the Cleaning the Chyme, members of the husband's local lineage assemble, and the husband's brother kills a goat provided by a senior member of the local lineage. While the goat is being butchered, strips of skin (*del*) are cut from its neck. Each strip is about fourteen inches long and one inch wide. A slit about twelve inches long is made down the middle of the strip. A person puts his head through the slit and wears the strip around his neck until it decays and falls off. Enough strips are cut to provide one for the patient and one for each of her children. The strip of goatskin is believed to prevent illness from attacking the wearer, but to be more efficacious for children than for adults.

After the goat has been butchered, the intestines are cut open and the chyme is removed. The husband's brothers and the husband each take a handful of chyme and rub it first on the chest of the patient and then on the chests of her children. As they rub the chyme in the same manner as the patient's own brothers and classificatory brothers did in Biting the Bone, the husband and his brothers say nothing. The ritual element of rubbing the chyme is the most important part of the ceremony, for in rubbing the chyme on the patient, her husband's brothers believe that they are purifying her. The chyme that they rub on her and her children is seen as an antidote to the chyme used in the Biting the Bone. Langi believe that the husband's lineage must apply to the woman a powerful substance which will counteract the substance placed on her by the people of her natal lineage. If the Biting the Bone were not followed by a Cleaning the Chyme, a woman not only would be inadequately protected, but would be under the control of her natal lineage until she was purified by chyme from an animal belonging to the lineage of her husband.

In the final part of the Cleaning the Chyme, the members of the husband's local lineage and a few neighbors seat themselves around beer pots and drink the beer prepared by the women in the lineage. The goat is roasted, and the meat is served only to the men and to a few old women, for many women believe that goat meat causes infertility. The food prepared by the classificatory co-wives of the patient is served with the goat meat, and more beer is served after the meal. Sometimes a pot of beer is set aside as "beer for ritual purification," but this is not an essential part of the Cleaning the Chyme, as it is in other *kwer* ceremonies. For this reason it could be argued that the Cleaning the Chyme does not stand by itself as a *kwer* ceremony but should be classified as the conclusion of the Biting the Bone. That is why I have described both ceremonies together.

Having described the form of the Biting the Bone and the Cleaning the Chyme, I turn to an interpretation of some of the outstanding symbols used in the ceremonies.

Slaughtering the Bull

The bull is clubbed on the head with a pestle while the patient and her children straddle its back. The choice of clubbing the animal over killing it with a spear is a statement of the relation between the two lineages that are joined by marriage. Langi say explicitly that these two ways of slaughtering a sacrificial animal differ in two important respects. First, if the animal is speared its blood is shed, and shedding blood is associated with violence and with warfare or feuding. Second, the spear is a symbol of masculinity because it is associated with two exclusively male activities: warfare and hunting. A spear may never be pointed at a woman (Driberg 1923:193, 207), nor is a woman allowed to carry a spear. The pestle is considered the female equivalent of the spear. It is regarded as "the women's weapon," and occasionally women do use it as a weapon. The pestle is used in the Biting the Bone because it dramatizes the ideal relation between the two sets of affines—a relation that is free of bloodshed.

Smearing the Chyme

The use of chyme for ritual purposes has been noted in several studies of Nilotic religion, and Lango ideas about chyme are similar to those held by other Nilotes. Among the Shilluk, the chyme of a murdered man is smeared on himself and his murderer in the hope that a feud will not break out. According to Oyler (1920:299), the Shilluk believe that chyme is a symbol of unity, for an animal eats many types of food but they all become one when they enter the stomach. Lienhardt (1961:206) reports that the Dinka word *wei* means "chyme" but also means "life" or "breath." "Wei is something which living beings have and which is the source of their animation." Finally, among the Nuer "chyme (*wau*) is what makes the flesh and maintains the life of the beast . . . [and it is] smeared on a Dinka at his adoption into a Nuer lineage" (Evans-Pritchard 1956:214).

In Lango, the word *we* means "chyme," and it is etymologically related to the verb *yuweyo* ("to breathe"). *We* also means "breath," and, in a metaphorical usage, it refers to a life-force which enters a person at birth and is transmitted through the patrilineage. Breath is said to emanate from the stomach, whch is the vital center of the body.

Lango statements on the meaning of chyme, examined in the light of other studies of Nilotic religion, help us understand the use of chyme in these two ceremonies. In the Biting the Bone, the patient's brothers smear chyme on the patient to symbolize that her life (breath or chyme) comes from her patrilineal kinsmen. Later, in the Cleaning the Chyme, the patient's husband's brothers counteract the application of chyme to the patient by applying their own, thus nullifying her ties to her patrilineage.

The Atoro (*Sternum*)

When the patient walks away from the house of her parents she places around her neck the *atoro*, a piece of the hide of the slaughtered bull. The skin itself is not important except to hold the bull's sternum (*atoro*) so that it will lie flat against hers. The sternum is said to be a point of strength in the bodies of animals and men. It is the keystone in the skeletal structure, and if it is broken or removed, the body collapses. The Lango conception of the sternum recalls our comments on chyme, which represents, among other things, a life-force. The sternum does not represent life-force, but, being a pivotal point in the skeletal structure of the body, it is as important as chyme.

I could not obtain an explanation of why the sternum of the bull is hung around the patient's neck, except that the practice is said to demonstrate how close the woman is to her father's cattle. Along these lines, we can note several other details of the ceremony that physically or symbolically juxtapose the patient and her children with the slaughtered bull: her children's carrying strap is tied around the snout of the bull; she and her children sit on the animal while it is being clubbed; and she is smeared with its chyme. The woman is being symbolically merged with the bull belonging to her father's patrilineage, just as she is joined by descent to that patrilineage. After the ceremony, she removes the sternum of the bull from her chest and bites it to represent severing her ties to her patrilineage. In the meantime, her husband's kinsmen eat the bull, and they will later cleanse her of the chyme. Like much of the symbolism in *kwer* ceremonies, the various uses of the bull in the Biting the Bone and the Cleaning the Chyme strongly suggest that the basic issue in these ceremonies is the ambiguity of a married woman's descent-group affiliation.

YEYO MOKO ME AGARA ("BRINGING BEER FOR THE ANKLE BELLS")

The Bringing Beer for the Ankle Bells is the most important *kwer* ceremony. It is the most frequently performed; it has the largest number of participants; and a woman regards it as the *kwer* ceremony that is most essential to her status as wife and mother. Of the sixty-five women in Obanya Kura who had been eligible for the ceremony, forty-three had had it performed for them. The Bringing Beer for the Ankle Bells is the final ceremony in the *kwer* series. It is held when a woman's oldest child is about ten to thirteen. Langi believe that, after the onset of puberty, children are less subject to the control of their mothers, and the Bringing Beer for the Ankle Bells should be held while a woman's children are still living with her and while she still has control over them.

The decision to hold the ceremony is made by the patient's consanguineal kinsmen, and the heaviest expense falls on them. The patient's father should visit the patient and announce to her husband and her husband's father that he would like to make preparations for a Bringing Beer for the Ankle Bells. He should also advise the husband's kinsmen when the feast will be held and what preparations they should make. The location for the feast is easily chosen, since the feast should be held at the home of the person who helped the patient's husband pay the bridewealth; typically this is the patient's father-in-law. The discussions are likely to last for several hours, because the patient's affinal kinsmen are expected to make a large quantity of beer, and if they are short of millet or manpower they may plead that the feast would present hardships and ask that it be postponed.

In December 1966 I attended a Bringing Beer for the Ankle Bells at the home of Peter Okello. The ceremony was held for Justina, the wife of Okello's son. Justina was the mother of four children, aged seven to fourteen. Justina had shown no sign of pregnancy since the birth of her youngest child, and it was presumed that she would not bear any more children. Justina's mother had visited her in September, and they had talked about having a Bringing Beer for the Ankle Bells several months later. Justina's father and mother discussed the matter with Justina's husband, Tomasi, and they agreed that the ceremony should be held in the yard of Tomasi's father, which was a short distance from Justina's house.

Justina's mother set about preparing the beer for the ceremony and requested the help of her co-wife and classificatory co-wives. Two of her classificatory co-wives and her actual co-wife helped her. The four women first prepared two large sacks, (about 150 pounds) of *moko*, a dry, mealy mixture of fermented sorghum and millet which represents the final stage in beer making before water is added. Beer is prepared from this dry mixture by adding water and allowing the final fermentation to proceed for twenty-four hours. Ten days before the ceremony, Justina's parents and three young men of Justina's lineage carried the two sacks of

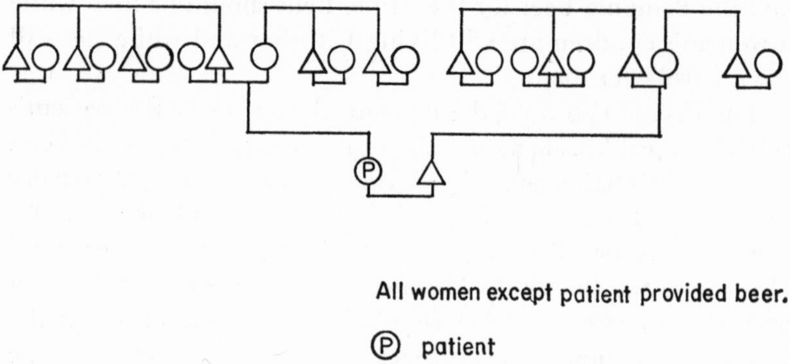

All women except patient provided beer.

Ⓟ patient

Figure 9: Kinsmen Who Provided Beer for a Bringing Beer for the Ankle Bells

moko to Peter Okello's compound. Justina's mother-in-law put the *moko* inside Justina's house to store until the day of the ceremony. At the feast this *moko* would be given to the men in Justina's husband's lineage.

In the meantime, Justina's mother and her mother's co-wife and classificatory co-wives prepared twenty more pots of beer to be served at the ceremony. Justina's mother-in-law and three of her mother-in-law's classificatory co-wives set to work preparing about the same amount of beer. A wide range of kinsmen were called on to provide beer for the occasion (see Figure 9). Women who had married into the patrilineage of Justina's mother were asked to provide two pots of beer each, and they did so. A woman who had married into the patrilineage of Justina's mother-in-law also provided two pots. Justina's mother had the heaviest obligation; in addition to the two sacks of *moko*, she provided seven pots of beer.

Justina's parents also had the responsibility of collecting the following objects for the ceremony.

1) The *agara*, a small sheet of metal folded into a crude sphere, containing a metal ball. The *agara* is worn around one ankle and resembles a sleigh bell in sound and appearance.
2) About five *agita*, sheets of metal about one inch long. The sheet is flat and wedge-shaped; one end is rolled so that the *agita* can be strung on a cord to wear around the waist.

3) About five *lyeta*, ordinary squares of sheet metal rolled to form tubes about three-eighths inch in diameter and one-half inch long. *Lyeta*, like *agita*, are strung and worn around the waist.

4) The hide of a bushbuck (*akal*).

5) One *abena*, a piece of hide fitted with straps and used for carrying a baby.

6) One *icac*, a stick about four feet long cut from the *kwomo*, a bush that grows near streams.

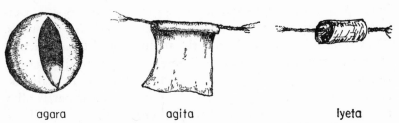

agara   agita   lyeta

Figure 10: Artifacts Used in the Bringing Beer for the Ankle Bells

A few days before the feast, the hosts—that is, members of the lineage that had provided cattle for Justina's bridewealth—gathered material for the ceremony and built special structures. Women gathered grass and twined it into rings on which beer pots would be set. Justina was excused from these tasks, and most of the work was distributed among her classificatory co-wives. The men of her husband's lineage canvassed the neighborhood to borrow chairs. While doing so, they issued formal invitations to the ceremony to all neighbors living within a radius of about one mile. The hosts also issued invitations to select kinsmen living well outside their neighborhood. It is especially desirable that representatives of different branches of the hosts' lineage attend the Bringing Beer for the Ankle Bells. A few senior members of the *jo doggola* traveled from twelve to fifteen miles away to represent their groups.

The hosts were also responsible for constructing two special structures (*bola*), to be used only during the ceremony. A work party of eight men was needed to gather the material and construct the buildings in two days. All but one member of the work party belonged to the patrilineage of Justina's husband, Tomasi. Five were sons of Tomasi's brothers; two were Tomasi's brothers; and one young man, not a kinsman, was hired for two shillings.

Each building was ten feet wide, twenty feet long, and seven feet high, and was divided into two rooms of equal size. The buildings were situated in the grass just outside the area where the feast was to be held. They were for the exclusive use of Justina's agnatic kinsmen. One was for the use of people in the generation of Justina's parents or above.

A young man from the lineage of Justina's husband was appointed to serve as steward for the feast. He was to carry the heavy pots of beer and see that guests were served properly. Certain characteristics are sought in the steward and his assistants. They should be men who have the reputation of temperateness at beer parties and of politeness. These requirements spring from the hosts' anxiety that arguments might arise as a result of drunkenness and that fighting might break out. The hosts partly allay this anxiety by building special quarters for the guests: if the members of the patient's lineage are isolated in a separate house, a quarrel between the two lineages is less likely. Another reason for isolating the guests is that the patient's husband and his classificatory brothers can more easily avoid their mothers-in-law.

On the day of the feast, the members of Justina's lineage set out from their home in a large group, planning to arrive at the site of the feast late in the afternoon. Justina's mother carried a basket containing the ceremonial objects, and young men of the lineage carried twenty large pots of beer. The party stopped three times to rest on the side of the path, because Justina's last-born child was a girl. If it had been a boy they would have made four rest stops.

Early in the afternoon, while the hosts were awaiting the guests, Justina's husband dug two rows of shallow holes in front of Justina's house with a hoe. The holes were dug about six inches wide and two feet apart so that beer pots could be set in them. The beer prepared by Tomasi's lineage was kept inside Justina's house so that it would not be visible to the guests as they entered the yard.

The arrival of the guests, when they present their beer pots, is always a sensitive moment, for the patient's agnatic kinsmen are expected to provide approximately the same amount of beer as her affinal kinsmen. Everyone notes the number of pots, but it is impolite for anyone in either group to comment on the amount of beer provided by the other. The pots brought by the guests were set in the holes in front of Justina's house for display. The guests, however, relied on guesswork to determine how much beer their hosts had provided. That beer was kept inside Justina's house, away from view, and was served one pot at a time.

A small pot of the guests' beer was designated as the "beer for ritual purification" and was brought inside Justina's house, where the women who had married into the lineage of Justina's husband washed the outside of the pot. First Justina poured water onto the pot and rubbed it with her hands; then the other women did likewise. Justina scooped the "head" of the beer from the pot, using a calabash; she and her children drank from the calabash, followed by the other women. The women remained inside the house drinking until they had finished the pot of "beer for ritual purification."

While the women were drinking inside the house, the *moko*, which had been prepared by the guests and delivered earlier, was brought out of Justina's house, where it had been stored. It was in small sacks, each containing about ten pounds, and the sacks were distributed among the men in the lineage of Justina's husband. The men formed a line, and each man was given one sack. About fifteen sacks were distributed in this way, and as each man received his sack, he made a donation of about fifteen shillings, which is roughly one-half the market value of the *moko*. The amount of the donation is not fixed, but each recipient is bound by the rules of reciprocity to make some monetary payment. One member of Justina's husband's lineage was responsible for distributing the *moko*. He was also responsible for writing down the name of each recipient and the amount of money that the recipient donated. This clerk later gave all the money to Justina's father as a partial repayment of the expenditure that the father's lineage had made.

Shortly after the guests arrived, they were seated inside the specially built houses, where they were served beer prepared by the hosts' lineage. Members of the hosts' lineage, neighbors, and other visitors were seated in the yard in several large circles, and they were served pots of the beer that had been brought by the guests. At one point in the evening, Justina's father-in-law passed a hat among the people drinking in the yard and asked them to donate money to Justina's father to help pay for the beer.

The ritual that constituted the ceremony centered on the objects carried to the feast by Justina's mother: the *agara*, the bushbuck hide, the *agita*, the *lyeta*, the *abena*, and the *icac* stick. The basket also contained enough *moko* to make one pot of beer and some shea-butternut oil. Shortly after Justina's mother arrived, she added water to the *moko* to make a pot of beer, which was served on the following morning to Justina's classificatory co-wives.

Toward nightfall, Justina seated herself in front of her house with her back against the doorway and her legs extended in front of her. One of her classificatory co-wives sat in front of her, about three feet away, and held the *agara*, the *agita*, and the *lyeta*. Using an underhand motion, she threw all the objects at once to Justina, who tried to catch them in a calabash. Justina threw them back in the same way to the other woman, who also tried to catch them in a calabash. The objects were thrown back and forth three times, because Justina's last-born child was a girl. If the child had been a boy, the women would have thrown the objects four times.

Justina's mother-in-law then anointed the metal objects with shea-butternut oil. She also anointed Justina, rubbing the oil over her head and shoulders. She anointed Justina's children in the same way. Then the co-wife and classificatory co-wives of Justina's mother-in-law took their turns anointing Justina and the children. After the anointing, one of Justina's classificatory mothers-in-law seized Justina by the hand, and the two women ran to the edge of the yard while ululating in loud, shrill voices and feigning anger. As they turned to come back to the center of the yard, they waved their arms as if brandishing spears. The mock anger was not directed at each other; the women were acting as if they were about to attack Justina's house.

The *agara*, *agita*, and *lyeta* were then handed to Justina, who seated herself on the bushbuck hide beside her children. She strung the *agita* and *lyeta* onto a cord long enough to tie around a child's waist. She strung three *agita* and three *lyeta*, because her last-born child was a girl. The objects were strung so that the *agita* alternated with the *lyeta*. She fastened the *agara* to a leather cord which could be worn around the ankle. Justina then tied the *agara* and the waistband onto her oldest child. The child sat in the center of the bushbuck hide, and he was then anointed with oil by one of Justina's classificatory mothers-in-law. The child removed the *agara* and the waistband, and Justina attached them to her next-oldest child, who was likewise anointed. This procedure was followed with all of Justina's children, but the youngest child did not remove the *agara* and waistband after she was anointed. The youngest child is supposed to wear the *agara* until the mother gives birth again or, if the mother does not give birth, for two or three years. The waistband is not so important as the *agara*, because the *lyeta* and *agita*, which are attached to the waistband, are not considered so effective as the *agara* in preventing illness. The *agara*, because of the noise it makes, is believed to frighten spirits away from the wearer. The *lyeta* and *agita* are only supplemental to the *agara*. The *agita* are believed to cut a spirit that attacks the wearer, and the *lyeta* to burn the spirit.

After the *agara* was tied to the youngest child, Justina's mother presented the *icac* stick to Justina. Once the stick was handed to her, no one was allowed to touch it, for there is a belief that a person who touches an *icac* stick that does not belong to him will become blind. The power of the *icac* stick comes from the *kwomo* plant, from which the *icac* stick is taken. The plant grows in thick clusters near streams and serves as a kind of barrier between mankind and the spirits that dwell in the streams. Spirits trying to leave streams to bring harm to men often find that their way is blocked by the *kwomo* plant. The *icac* stick, accordingly, is a talisman which protects its owner from being attacked by spirits. Women carry the *icac* stick when they are going on long journeys or when they are visiting areas that they do not know well—in other words, on occasions when they are most likely to be attacked by spirits.

The bushbuck hide was also presented to Justina, but she gave it to her husband's young married sister, who used it as a ground-cloth. Justina kept the *abena*. She later bore another child and used the *abena* to carry the infant on her back. (The patient is not expected to bear another child, however; the presentation of the *abena* is a symbol honoring her past procreative achievements.)

The presentation of these objects took place around nightfall.

The participants were Justina, her children, her classificatory mothers, and a group of women who had married into her husband's clan. While this group was seated in front of Justina's house, the rest of the company remained in the buildings and in the yard.

Food was served to everyone shortly after dark, and the beer pots were replenished throughout the night.

CONCLUSION

We are now in a better position to understand the meaning of the *kwer* ceremonies and, in particular, the relation of the ceremonies to the problem of the incorporation of a woman and her children into her husband's descent group (Leach 1961:21). In Chapter II we saw that the combination of patrilineal descent and virilocal residence presents a twofold problem to a married woman. She is physically separated from her consanguineal kinsmen and no longer interacts with them daily, as she did before marriage. And she acquires a new set of people with whom she must regularly interact—her affinal kinsmen and the other residents of the neighborhood that she moves into. The situation of the young married woman is exacerbated by the demands placed on her by her mother-in-law and her husband. Finally, the woman is expected to show signs of pregnancy within a year after her marriage, and she must continue to bear children if she is to earn respect in the eyes of her affinal kinsmen.

The *kwer* ceremonies facilitate the incorporation of a woman into her husband's lineage and neighborhood by celebrating those occasions which are critical in determining her status as a wife and mother. Two of the ceremonies—the *Kwer* for a Woman Who Has Given Birth and the Bringing Beer for the Carrying Strap—are occasioned by the event of childbirth. The others—with the exception of the Cutting the Hearth—are held on those occasions when a woman's status is seriously jeopardized by the possibility that her children will die.

Children figure importantly in several of the *kwer* ceremonies. The place of children in the ceremonies is related to the problem of "complementary filiation," a concept developed by Meyer Fortes in his studies of the Tallensi and Ashanti (1949:35). Fortes states that although the Tallensi follow a patrilineal rule of descent they recognize that biologically a child is related to both parents. Leach (1961:10) argues convincingly that we cannot infer from the Tallensi example that the recognition of complementary filiation is a cultural universal, but the fact remains that the selection of a unilineal rule of descent entails a choice whereby membership in a descent group is determined either matrilineally or patrilineally (Fox 1967:41–49). The unilineal rule of descent serves the sociological function of recruiting people into descent groups in such a way that the membership of each descent group is relatively unambiguous. In asserting that a child is "descended" from only one parent, however, a society with a unilineal rule of descent neglects the fact that "filiation in all societies is bilateral—a child is the descendant of his *pater* and *mater*, social father and mother" (Buchler and Selby 1968:69). The *kwer* ceremonies employ symbols that attempt to resolve the ambiguity of "complementary filiation" by demonstrating that, although a child is affiliated with both the mother's side and the father's side, a choice must be made between the two sides, and the Lango child is more closely tied to the father's side.

But if the purpose of the *kwer* ceremonies is to incorporate a woman and her children into her husband's lineage, why should the woman's consanguineal kinsmen play such an important part in the ceremonies? Two of the ceremonies are held at the home of her parents, and in all the ceremonies her parents are expected to participate. Nor do all the ceremonies equally stress the relationship of a woman to her affinal kinsmen; the Sprinkling the Eyes and the Biting the Bone emphasize a woman's obligations to her parents and other consanguineal kinsmen.

Figure 11 illustrates this point diagrammatically by classifying the *kwer* ceremonies according to whether they emphasize the affinal kinsmen's control over a woman or the consanguineal kinsmen's.

The figure classifies each *kwer* ceremony on the basis of whether it was held at the patient's parents' house or at her husband's house and what sort of ritual took place during the ceremony. The classification is not definitive; it represents only one way of interpreting the ceremonies. Two ceremonies—the Cutting the Hearth and the Bringing Beer for the Ankle Bells—seem to em-

Emphasis on woman's relationship to affines		*Emphasis on woman's relationship to consanguines*
Kwer for a Woman Who Has Given Birth		
Bringing Beer for the Carrying Strap		
		Sprinkling the Eyes
	Cutting the Hearth	
Tying the Strap		
		Biting the Bone
Cleaning the Chyme		
	Bringing Beer for the Ankle Bells	

Figure 11: Classification of *Kwer* Ceremonies According to Emphasis on Affinal or Consanguineal Relationships

phasize consanguineal and affinal ties equally. For that reason, I have placed them in the center of the diagram. It is clear that the Sprinkling the Eyes and the Biting the Bone are ceremonies in which the woman's consanguineal kin group shows its control over her. The Biting the Bone, in fact, emphasizes the relationship between a woman and her natal family to such an extent that it must be canceled out, as it were, by a Cleaning the Chyme held later by her affinal kinsmen.

The *kwer* ceremonies, then, do not necessarily resolve the problem of incorporating the woman into her husband's descent group, for as long as it is recognized that she is a member of her father's patrilineal descent group, the problem defies resolution. This series of ceremonies serves as a symbolic representation of the fact that a woman is related to both groups: the ceremonies alternate between her husband's house and her parents' house.

The *kwer* are a ceremonial expression of certain Lango ideals on the relation between men and women. The Lango word for "woman" is *dako*, from the verb *dag* ("to migrate, to wander").

In discussing this term, Langi explain that a man remains stationary, whereas a woman is destined to move from one household to another: first from the household of her father to that of her husband, and, in the event of divorce and remarriage, from one husband's household to another's. The migratory nature of a woman is touched on in those *kwer* ceremonies in which she walks to the residence of her parents with her classificatory co-wives and mothers-in-law.

There are other reasons why the woman's consanguineal kinsmen figure importantly in *kwer* ceremonies. In every *kwer* except the Cutting the Hearth, a woman's parents and brothers express their support for her on some occasion when her status as a wife and mother is being either enhanced or jeopardized. Moreover, the *kwer* ceremonies offer the opportunity for exchanges to be carried out between two lineages joined by marriage. In the Biting the Bone, for example, the patient's father is obliged to offer a bull for the ceremony, because he incurred an obligation to his daughter's husband's lineage when he received cattle from them at her marriage. The *kwer* ceremonies are the only occasions other than marriage arrangements when institutionalized group visiting takes place between the two lineages. The reciprocal nature of the visiting-and-exchange relation would be lost if the *kwer* ceremonies were held exclusively at the house of the patient's husband, for the *kwer* ceremonies would then become one-sided. As they are carried out, the *kwer* ceremonies affirm the relation between the two lineages and allow them to work jointly toward a resolution of the ambiguous status of women.

At present, the *kwer* ceremonies thrive in Lango. I estimate that during the period of my field work twenty-six *kwer* ceremonies, forty spirit-possession ceremonies, and five *etogo* ceremonies took place in Obanya Kura. *Kwer* ceremonies have been affected far less by social change than *etogo* ceremonies or spirit-possession ceremonies have. All *kwer* ceremonies but one continue to be carried out, even though some compete with spirit-possession activities. If a woman is sick, she can adopt one of several alternatives—including a *kwer* ceremony and a spirit-possession dance. As the spirit-possession dance is becoming more popular, there may actually be a slight tendency for women not to have a *kwer* ceremony in situations that in the past would definitely have called for one. However, it is impossible to collect data on the incidence of *kwer* ceremonies in the past for a comparison. What can be said is that young women are still aware of the ceremonies, they attend them enthusiastically, and they feel that their kinsmen are obliged to hold some if not all of the ceremonies for them. The only *kwer* ceremony that appears to have been virtually forgotten is the Cutting the Hearth; few women under thirty are even aware that such a *kwer* ceremony ever existed.

Langi continue to sponsor the ceremonies even though they are sometimes costly (although the expense is the reason most commonly offered by someone who refuses to sponsor a ceremony). The least expensive *kwer* I observed was a *Kwer* for a Woman Who Has Given Birth that cost the parents of the patient's husband three shillings. The most expensive was a Bringing Beer for the Ankle Bells that cost the patient's affinal kinsmen about 180 shillings and the patient's agnatic kinsmen about 160 shillings. In this respect the *kwer* ceremonies stand in sharp contrast to the *etogo* ceremonies, for people are no longer motivated to pay the expense of inviting the *etogo* kinsmen and holding a ceremony. It is clear that the *kwer* ceremonies have persisted because, unlike the *etogo*, they are related to problems that are still significant to Lango people: the ambiguous status of women in a patrilineal, virilocal society; the incorporation of a woman into her husband's kin group; and the relation between lineages that are bound my marriage.

V

The Adept and the Spirit World

Of the three ceremonial complexes that compose the public aspect of Lango religion, spirit-possession activities are the most prominent at present. Virtually every Lango vicinage has a woman who has been initiated as an adept and is thereby qualified to perform the curing ceremonies. Similarly, at any given time a vicinage is likely to have a woman, or possibly a man, who is suffering from spirit possession and is undergoing treatment or is considering doing so. About once every three weeks one can hear the steady drumming that lasts all night and signals to the people of the vicinage that a spirit-possession dance is taking place. Spirit possession looms large as a topic of conversation, and women are ready to compare experiences and offer opinions about spirits and possession.

In this chapter we shall consider the question why spirit possession has become increasingly prominent in the last fifty years, while *etogo* and *kwer* activities have declined. We shall consider the roles of the adept and the patient and describe the performance of the adept.

The essential features of the spirit-possession complex are as follows: A person who is chronically ill and has not been helped by treatment at the government clinic or by Lango medicines is likely to consult an adept to learn whether the illness is caused by spirit possession. An adept can offer a diagnosis, sometimes using a technique of divination, and can tell the patient (typically a woman) whether she is possessed and what kind of spirit is causing the trouble. The adept can suggest a technique for exorcising the spirit. The most elaborate and expensive technique is the possession dance. If the patient is not rid of the spirit after several attempts, the adept may conclude that the patient is possessed by a spirit which is unwilling to leave, and that the patient is being summoned to become an adept herself. If the patient can afford the training fee and the initiation dance, she may decide to become an adept, thus transforming the spirit within her from a troublesome force into a force that can be used to cure others.

THE HISTORY OF SPIRIT POSSESSION IN LANGO

The ethnographic reports of Driberg and Hayley suggest some conclusions about the introduction of spirit-possession beliefs into Lango and the subsequent development of the possession complex. Driberg (1923:234–240) described the adepts' activities, which were more varied than they are now. According to Driberg, occasionally a shade would cause trouble to the members of a lineage or to an entire village. If the shade could not be driven away, a shrine was built for it, and the shade then served as an oracle for the members of the lineage or village. Questions about the proper day for a hunt, the selection of a site for a new village, or the advisability of attacking a village were asked of the oracle, the adept serving as a medium. The adept was believed to be able to interpret the will of the shade, and was called an *ajoka* ("person of Jok"). In addition to serving as a medium, the adept had a wide knowledge of medicines and could perform simple cures. Driberg saw spirit possession as an epileptic seizure (1923: 238) but said that the Langi explained it as the visitation of a particular spirit named "Jok Nam." He implied that spirit possession was a recent phenomenon and attempted to trace its introduction into Lango. Driberg argued that belief in the spirit Jok Nam was not an indigenous Lango belief but "a modern manifestation of Jok, dating back to 1897, the year when Kabarega escaped from Bunyoro. As the name suggests, this *Jok* is a direct outcome of Bantu influence. His cult is now defunct, except for the phenomenon of possession and its treatment, and he is said to speak Paluo and Bunyoro" (1923:220). Driberg presented some linguistic evidence in the names of plants used to cure spirit possession. He concluded that "demoniacal possession is a complaint of recent origin, or largely increased in its incidence since about 1897" (1923:221).

Further support for the view that spirit possession entered Lango from some other area may lie in the term *Jok Nam*, the name of the possessing spirit. This can be translated "lake spirit," denoting a spirit from the other side of Lake Kioga, most likely from Nyoro. This suggestion would be tenuous were it not that the Lango name for the Nyoro people is *Jo Nam*, "People from the Lake."[1] *Nam* usually refers to Lake Kioga, and is frequently extended to refer to people or things from Nyoro. The term *Jok Nam* is no longer used, nor is the term *abanwa*, which was used in the early part of the century to refer to a member of the special class of adepts who treated spirit possession. The origin of the word *abanwa* is clear, for in the Nyoro language, the word *kubandwa* means "to be divinely possessed" (Driberg 1923:237; Beattie 1957:150).

Driberg said further that "In the days before *Jok Nam* was recognized one so possessed was simply flogged to the accompaniment of drums and singing till the seizure passed, and at the present time if a person becomes possessed while on a journey, he is often merely trounced with the spear-shaft of his comrade" (1928:238). (Since Driberg confused spirit possession with epileptic seizure, we cannot be certain whether he was describing epilepsy or spirit possession.) He went on to say that, at the time of his stay in Lango, a ceremony to cure spirit possession was becoming popular. This ceremony, as he described it (1923:239), seems to have been a simpler version of the ceremony now performed.

Driberg's argument that spirit possession diffused from Nyoro gains credence when we consider the history of contact between Nyoro and Lango. The contact became intensified in the late nineteenth century, when the Nyoro sent messengers to Lango, asking the Langi to assist the forces of Kamurasi, who was engaged in a dispute with his brother over the throne of Nyoro. The Langi complied, and Kamurasi was successful. In 1897, when his son, Kabarega, assumed the throne and became involved in warfare against the Baganda, he too sent for and received Lango

1. The term *Jo Nam* is also used to refer to the riverine Alur, but it is most commonly used to refer to the Nyoro people.

military assistance. Thus, by the turn of the century there had been two periods of direct contact between Lango and Nyoro. The contact resumed in another form in 1910, when the colonial administration assigned Nyoro agents to Lango District in its attempt to establish colonial rule there (Tarantino 1949b:233–234; Ingham 1955:156–168).

Hayley visited Lango in 1935 and 1936. Judging by his account (1947:153–157), several changes had taken place in the spirit-possession complex since Driberg's time. Hayley did not say how prevalent spirit possession was, nor did he describe its social setting. The term *Jok Nam* was still in currency, but evidently the Nyoro term *abanwa* was not used to refer to an adept who cured spirit possession.[2] Hayley (1947:154) reported that Langi referred to an adept as *ajwaka* ("one who has control over Jok power"). It seems that spirit possession had become incorporated into Lango religion by 1935, that there was no special class of adepts who treated spirit possession exclusively, as there was in Driberg's time, and that the possession dance, characterized by both the adept's and the patient's going into dissociated states, was fairly widespread. The only "foreign" aspect of the possession complex was the use of the term *Jok Nam*, which indicated the Bantu provenance of the spirit.

It is important to note some differences between these two earlier periods and the present. First, one who observes contemporary Lango possession dances or discusses them with adepts is not likely to find any signs of the Bantu provenance of spirit possession. The term *Jok Nam* is no longer used, nor is an adept called *abanwa*. Most younger Langi take spirit possession for granted, as something that originated in some very early period in Lango history. Many people over the age of forty state that spirit possession has become more widespread and that they can remember a time when there was very little possession and when there were few dances to cure it. Only one informant, a very old man, suggested that it had been introduced into Lango from a Bantu society, and he did not name Nyoro specifically. It is clear that spirit possession has become fully incorporated into Lango religious beliefs and practice. Possession is now the most im-

2. For descriptions of spirit possession in Nyoro, see Beattie 1961, 1968, 1969, 1971:48–51.

portant activity of the adepts, and it gives rise to the most frequently performed ceremony in Obanya Kura, the possession dance.

The possession complex derives from a set of beliefs in spirits and can be fully understood only in the light of those beliefs. The Lango belief system is rich and complex, and (like religious practices) it has undergone considerable change. Because religious beliefs are not the main subject of this study, we shall discuss only those religious beliefs which pertain to spirit possession.

Like other Nilotic peoples, the Langi have a generalized concept of a spiritual being called Jok (Evans-Pritchard 1956; Lienhardt 1961; Southall 1969). This name refers to a force which permeates the universe, which controls natural phenomena, and which created mankind and consequently controls much of human behavior. In the normal course of events little attention is paid to Jok, for it is an abstraction with which men need not concern themselves. Although Jok is discussed from time to time at a metaphysical level, few people profess to understand its nature, and none of the Langi I spoke with were much given to lengthy discourse on Jok. Those who would discuss Jok at all would make a few brief remarks on the omnipotence of Jok or its ubiquity and then break off with some remark to the effect that "no one can know Jok."

The truth of this remark was borne out during the course of investigation when informants displayed a remarkable lack of consensus in their responses to the question, "What is Jok?" The descriptions offered by various informants fell along a spectrum with a very abstract concept of *Jok* at one end, and a host of specific attributes clustered at the other. In other words, some people saw Jok primarily as an abstract concept, and others saw it as a particular spirit or spirits which can sometimes be perceived sensuously. When pressed, the informants admitted that there were two facets to Jok: (1) it is an abstract conception of the supernatural; and (2) it sometimes manifests itself in particular forms. In other words, Jok is sometimes general, sometimes specific. When a speaker wants to distinguish between these two aspects of Jok, he can do so by speaking of "the Creator Jok" (*Jok a cweyo jo*, "the spirit that created people") in contradistinction to a more concrete form of Jok.

We have said that in the normal course of events people pay little attention to *Jok*. This is true—but the course of events is seldom normal. Misfortunes, illnesses, and injustices alter the course of events, not to mention natural phenomena that oppose the Lango idea of an orderly universe. Such phenomena cry out for explanation, and the explanation can be found through recourse to the concept of Jok. In 1966, when the onset of the rainy season was about two months late, some people explained that Jok was unhappy with the world of men and had delayed the rains. When lightning struck an old woman asleep at night, the event was ascribed to the malicious nature of the shades, which are believed to be manifestations of Jok. When a person suffers from a chronic illness that does not respond to medical treatment at the government clinic or to traditional medicines, the illness may be explained as the result of spirit possession: Jok has chosen to enter the person's body and do him harm.

Geertz calls attention to the efficacy of religion in enabling men to transcend intellectual chaos by providing them with concepts that explain phenomena "which lack not just interpretation but interpretability" (1966:14). He cites Evans-Pritchard's well-known discussion (1937) of how the Azande sought to explain the sudden collapse of a granary. The event was not unusual in itself; what was puzzling was that, in falling, the granary injured a man. Such discussions bring out the pragmatic nature of religion by showing that people often remain unconcerned with the philosophical niceties of their religious belief system and merely *use* it to order whatever phenomena their secular beliefs fail to explain. In Lango, such phenomena are not explained through recourse to the abstract concept of Jok, but are seen as resulting from the activities of spirits, which have concrete attributes and are aspects of Jok. Although Jok itself is formless and cannot be perceived, it is capable of assuming many forms. In these forms, it enters into its relations with men. Jok power can reside in a natural object, such as a tree or an animal. Such an object is visible, and the presence of Jok power within it may be well known to the people of the area, who will take care to avoid the object. Jok power can also reside in a spirit. A spirit is normally invisible to people, and people are normally unaware of its presence. From time to time, the spirit seeks to make its presence known, and it enters the head of its human victim, bringing on spirit possession and causing acute discomfort which can be fully cured only when the spirit is driven out of the head by an adept.

Jok, the universal supernatural force, does not possess people. Only the lesser spirits do. There are two principal types of lesser spirits: the shades (*tipu*) and the winds (*yamo*).

Shades

We have described the aspects of shades that relate to the *etogo*. Each person contains a fragment of the power of Jok, which pervades the universe. This fragment is the shade (*tipu*), which is responsible for the shadow the person casts. The shade comes into being at coition, when a fragment of the mother's shade breaks off and implants itself in the embryo within the womb. The shade grows within the embryo, and continues to grow after the child is born. Shortly after birth, the shade splits into two parts; one part takes up residence in the head, the other in the heart. The role of the shade in the affairs of a living person is unclear, except that the shade represents a life-force, entering the person at birth and leaving him at death. The part of the shade that resides in the head can be observed in an infant as one watches the pulsations at the frontal suture of the cranium. The other part of the shade, that which resides in the heart, can be observed throughout the person's life in the form of the heartbeat.

The concept of the shade is thus significant in a philosophical sense, for it forms an explanation of life itself. The shade does not generally become important in social relations, however, until the person dies. This proposition can be stated in another way: as long as the shade of a living person remains inside his body, it is of little import and people are therefore not concerned with it. There are two situations in which a shade can leave the body of its living owner, and both situations can have serious consequences for the owner as well as for others.

First, there is the phenomenon known in the literature of religious studies as "soul loss." This phenomenon occurs only after someone employs an especially powerful adept to lure the shade out of a victim's head in order to drive the victim mad. One young woman went to an adept in Obanya Kura to be treated for soul loss which had given rise to symptoms of madness, most notably glossolalia. Her former husband was angered because his bridewealth had not been returned to him after his wife had left him for another man. After numerous attempts to regain the bridewealth, he employed an adept, who lured the woman's shade out of her head and sealed it in a rain barrel.

The second situation in which a shade leaves the body of its owner is less drastic than soul loss. This situation is the dream. The Lango explanation of dreaming is that it is caused by the wanderings of the shade when its owner lies down to sleep at night. When a man dreams of another person it is said that his shade in the course of its wanderings has encountered the shade of the other person, for shades are believed to experience loneliness and to seek out one another's company.

Apart from soul loss and dreaming, the shade does not enter into human affairs until its owner has died. In examining the burial ceremony, Standing on the Grave, we discussed what happens to the shade after death. The most noteworthy development is that the shade undergoes a sort of personality growth after the death of its owner; put another way, the attributes of the shade must, for the first time, be taken into account by the owner's kinsmen. The most prominent of these attributes is the tremendous grief that every shade feels at the death of its owner. Consequently, the shade is wont to place great emphasis on the observance of funeral rites to commemorate its owner. In other respects as well the shade serves as the spiritual representative of the deceased kinsman. For example, if there is dissension between the co-wives of a deceased man, the shade of that man experiences anger and bitterness, and may seek to act on the matter by spirit possession. From its vantage point in the bush some 100 yards away from the grave of its owner, the shade is believed to be an astute and highly sensitive observer of human affairs. As it observes the behavior of its kinsmen, it experiences the same emotional responses to particular situations that one would expect of the deceased were he living.

For example, a woman died, leaving her husband and sixteen-year-old son as survivors. Her shade continued to look after the interest of her son in his quest for cattle and money to pay bridewealth. The boy quarreled with his father over the use of the father's cattle, and the shade of the woman was said to have experienced the same sort of emotion as most living women who find themselves in the same circumstances—that is, it sided with the son against the father. More important, as we shall come to see, is that the woman was able to act on the situation more effectively as a shade than if she had still been alive.

Occupying its place in the supernatural world, the shade is the logical extension of the social persona of its owner. It looks after the affairs of the owner when he is no longer able to do so.

Another facet of the relation between the shade and its owner is that the efficacy of a shade in possessing people and affecting social relations is a function of personal attributes of its owner during his lifetime. For example, a man who dies in the prime of life is likely to have a more powerful shade than that of a man who dies at a very old age, when he is weak and senile. If the strength of the shade is determined partly by the personal strength of its former owner, this does not mean that the world of shades is a mirror image of the world of men. The status or social rank of the owner does not determine the power of the shades; what counts is rather a vaguely defined strength of character. By this logic, a person of low social status may turn out to have had a powerful shade if that person possessed a strong character which had somehow gone unrecognized during his lifetime. What is significant about this concept is that it is not just the shades of high-status persons that one must be careful of. There is considerably more equality in the world of shades than in the world of men, for shades are free to act on their emotions, whereas living men are subject to restraints. It is true that shades vary in their ability to act on their impulses, but their power is not determined solely by the social status of their former owners.

The world of shades, then, stands in contradistinction to the world of the living, because the former is a more equitable arrangement, in which power is not determined by sex, age, or genealogical position. Women and children have considerable power as shades, whereas very little formal authority is granted

to them according to Lango norms. The statistics on spirit possession (see Appendix II) show that the shades of women, infants,
and children attack people more often than do the shades of
men.[3] Consequently, it is difficult to determine which shade is
attacking a person; within the universe of the recently deceased
kinsmen of a patient, any one of them is as likely to have brought
on possession as any other. It is true that strength of character
partly determines the effectiveness of the shades, but it is very
difficult to judge the relative strengths of shades, for the attributes of their owners that make shades powerful may have been
unrecognized during the owners' lifetimes.

Winds

The second type of spirit that can cause spirit possession is a
wind (*yamo*). Like the shade, it is a particular manifestation of
Jok. The concept of *yamo*, however, is much less specific than
that of *tipu*, and virtually every adept has her own explanation of
what a *yamo* is and what it does. It is possible to put the varying
views together and make some general statements about *yamo*.

First, *yamo* are sometimes visible. They can take the form of
almost any animate (or imaginary) being. They can exist in the
form of frogs, snakes, living human beings (generally non-Lango),
and elflike creatures of six inches in height. The only limitation
on their form is the imagination of the beholder.

Second, *yamo* live in communities that resemble human communities, and these are most likely to be found near rocks,
springs, and streams and on hilltops. Because of the presence of
yamo, it is considered unsafe to go to such places. People con-
sistently avoid hilltops and rocks because of the dangers therein.
Unfortunately, they must visit springs, boreholes, and streams
to obtain water, and it is at these sites that women have most of
their encounters with *yamo*.

Third, the motives of winds and shades differ. Both shades and
winds have a strong appetite for the things that human beings
enjoy. Shades, being free from the restraints on men, have a
strong desire for food, clothing, and money, and they can sometimes be tricked as a result of their greed. Winds carry this greed

3. In the cases I was able to learn about, 72 percent of the shades were shades
of females.

to an extreme, however; they will go to great lengths to satisfy their wants. Moreover, winds are motivated exclusively by greed, whereas shades are motivated primarily by their interest in human affairs.

Fourth—to continue the comparison—although winds are motivated solely by greed, and although they have no use for men, they are not so dangerous as shades, because they have less power. They are more numerous and less predictable than shades, but in the end they are not capable of inflicting so much suffering on men as the shades are.

Last, when a shade wishes to intervene in the affairs of men, it almost invariably does so by employing one or more winds as agents. The shades have a remarkable ability to observe all that goes on among their living kinsmen. Much of their knowledge is provided by the winds whom they employ as messengers. There is something of a patron-client relation between shades and winds. Shades constantly rely on the services of winds. Each shade assigns a wind to observe the behavior of one or two people and to report regularly on their activities. When a shade desires to possess someone it relies on the winds to carry out the task, assigning one or more of them to enter the person and cause him to fall ill. In one instance, an adept reported that she removed 120 winds from the head of a patient, although this is an exceptionally high number.

Thus, shades and winds are distinct from each other in their forms, social habits, motives, power, and actions. Ultimately, both derive their existence and power from the force of Jok. They are forms or refractions of Jok. For this reason, an adept will often report that a person is possessed by Jok without specifying whether the trouble is caused by a shade or by a wind. Only after careful questioning by the ethnographer will the adept make the distinction. This hesitation to identify the possessing spirit is due not to negligence on the part of the adept but to a feature of Lango beliefs which was mentioned above. The beliefs are not codified, nor are they necessarily articulated into a logical system in the mind of each believer. They are to be employed as explanations for particular events, the most important of which is illness, and it matters little whether the explanation for a particular illness is logically consistent with the explanation devised on another occasion. The set of statements we have offered about Lango beliefs leaves many questions unanswered, but so does the belief system itself. Therein lies much of the appeal of the explanations, for the seeming incoherence of the belief system provides the adept with an opportunity to improvise and embellish a diagnosis for any case. There are limits, of course, to the improvisation, and these will be discussed when we consider the set of steps an adept follows in making a diagnosis.

POSSESSION

It is primarily through spirit possession that shades and winds intercede in human affairs. We have noted that the *etogo* ceremonies are directed toward appeasing the shades and preventing them from harming men by causing illness or drought. Langi believe that the shades, as manifestations of Jok, exert some kind of control over the forces of nature, but that this control is significantly manifested only when a shade enters the head of its human victim (accompanied by a wind) or sends a wind emissary to enter the head and cause illness in the victim, or in a close kinsman of the victim, especially his child.

Both shades and winds are capable of possessing people, but shades do not do so by themselves; they invariably employ winds as agents. The two types of spirits possess people from different motives. A shade possesses someone when it feels that it has been slighted by insufficient funeral offerings or when it sees that there is conflict or dissension in the family of the victim. Langi say that a shade attacks when kinsmen are not "staying well," to end the conflict and restore order among the kinsmen. A wind, however, attacks someone either because it was directed to do so by a shade or because it is greedy. A wind attacks to obtain its favorite food, to find a comfortable dwelling place in the head of the victim, or merely to annoy the victim out of sheer maliciousness. Winds sometimes possess people singly, sometimes they attack in groups, and sometimes a wind accompanies a shade.

Three combinations of spirits are possible in any given case of spirit possession. They are listed below in order of frequency.

Type 1 A wind possesses a patient by itself and operates on its own behalf rather than as the agent of a shade.

Type 2 A shade singles out a victim and assigns one or more winds
to carry out the possession.

Type 3 A shade and a wind possess the victim together; the shade
has authority over the wind.

For most purposes, the second and third combinations can be
considered variants of a single type of possession because each is
due primarily to a shade.

In order to define spirit possession in Lango and to distinguish
the three types of spirit possession, let us consider the logical operations that an adept performs when a patient first consults her.
The adept does not carry out a physical examination of the patient but interviews the patient for about an hour. During the
interview, the adept collects information from three domains
which we shall call circumstantial, sociological, and medical.

First, the adept must determine whether the patient is indeed
the victim of spirit possession or is suffering from some ailment
that can be treated at the government clinic or with Lango medicines. Before the adept can offer a diagnosis of spirit possession
she must collect information about the circumstances in which
the patient first developed or noticed the symptoms. Many victims of spirit possession relate that they began to perceive the
symptoms after experiencing some unusual event. One recurrent
type of event is that in which a woman walks to a well or spring
carrying a water pot on her head. At the well or spring she is
startled and loses her balance, and the water pot falls to the
ground. In another type, a person walking along a road or path
at night is frightened by a voice whose source is not apparent or
by an apparition. Events of both types are interpreted as the actions of winds. If the patient can describe to the adept some recent circumstance that included surprise, fear, mysterious noises,
or voices, or some extraordinary mishap like the falling of a water
vessel, the adept offers a diagnosis of wind possession. The reason
is that winds attack people in a violent, somewhat capricious
manner and are likely to interfere with physical objects. The
diagnosis therefore serves to explain not only the disease, but also
a mishap that is slightly outside the normal range of daily
experiences.

Having concluded that the patient is the object of possession,
the adept must decide whether the primary agent of possession

is a wind (type 1) or a shade (type 2). To this end, she employs information from the sociological and medical domains. In the sociological domain, the adept must evaluate the social background of the patient and the relations among her kinsmen. If the adept is acquainted with the patient, as she typically is, she must try to ascertain whether any members of the patient's family are embroiled in an intrafamilial dispute that would displease a shade and move it to take action against the patient. In offering a diagnosis of shade possession (types 2 and 3), the adept not only is making a medical judgment but is commenting upon relations within the family of the patient. The adept often does this by specifying which deceased kinsman the shade represents and, more importantly, why the shade attacked the patient. If the adept is unfamiliar with the patient she may not be able to discern any conduct among the patient's kinsmen that would provoke an attack by a shade. In such cases, the adept might conclude that the possession was caused by a wind acting on its own behalf. Winds tend to attack randomly when they are not acting as the agents of shades. They are unconcerned with the status and the social situation of their victims; they attack people from their own private motives.

Thus a diagnosis of possession by a wind acting as the primary agent (type 1) is not a statement about the social condition of the patient. It does not imply that relations within the family are harmonious, nor does it imply that there is conflict. A diagnosis of type 1 conveys less information than a diagnosis of type 2 or 3, and after a diagnosis of type 1 is made the adept's attention is focused exclusively on the patient rather than on her domestic situation.

To determine whether a shade or a wind is the primary agent, the adept must also obtain information on the medical symptoms of the patient. Severe, chronic illnesses are more likely to be caused by shades than by winds, because shades are more powerful and tend to be more persistent in possessing a person. Physical conditions that are acute and less serious are more likely to be caused by winds. To give an example, a forty-five-year-old woman had been suffering from malarial attacks for a number of years and was afflicted with a recurrent swelling of one leg. During a particularly severe episode of the swelling, she went to an adept.

Her condition was diagnosed as shade possession. The adept informed her that a condition as serious as hers could only have been caused by a shade, and identified the shade as that of the patient's mother. The shade had become upset over a quarrel among the patient's kinsmen. As another example, a twenty-five-year-old woman had two miscarriages shortly after marriage, and her condition was said to be due to possession by a wind. The physical condition of the second woman was not judged serious enough to have been caused by a shade.

TABLE VI

Diagnostic Criteria Used to Determine Whether the Primary Agent of Possession Is a Shade or a Wind

	Primary agent is shade	*Primary agent is wind*
Sociological criteria	A. Adept is *aware* of a situation in patient's personal life that would provoke a shade to attack.	B. Adept is *unaware* of a situation in patient's personal life that would provoke a shade to attack.
Medical criteria	C. Symptoms are *severe*.	D. Symptoms are *not severe*.
	E. Symptoms are part of a *chronic* ailment.	F. Symptoms are *not* part of a *chronic* ailment.

Table VI summarizes the logical operations performed by the adept in making the diagnosis and lists the medical and sociological conditions she considers. These conditions are not weighted equally, for there is a complicated interplay between them. From the adept's perspective, condition A must be present if she is to diagnose shade possession. Then she is free to diagnose shade possession, and decide arbitrarily that criteria C and E have been met. In other words, severity (C) and chronicity (E) are vague criteria, and once the adept has determined the sociological condition of the patient, she has considerable latitude to interpret the medical facts as she sees fit. If she wishes to call attention to a dispute within the patient's family, she traces the immediate medical symptoms back to some earlier, perhaps unrelated physical ailment, and advises the patient that the condition is severe and chronic and, therefore, has been caused by a shade. In an area where numerous parasitic and infectious diseases are endemic, it is certainly not difficult to compile a complete enough medical history for a patient. The *modus operandi* of the adept, then, is to consider the social situation of the patient and then to interpret the situation with reference to both the sociological and the medical conditions.

If the adept has determined that the primary agent of possession is a shade, she must decide whether the possession is type 2 or type 3. This can be done simply enough on the basis of the patient's account of how many spirits visited her and what they said to her. Again, the adept has considerable latitude in interpreting the details.

The dynamics of spirit possession can best be illustrated by two examples from the field.

Example 1: MERIJOSI

Merijosi had been married for three years without becoming pregnant, and she was having difficulties with her affinal kinsmen. Her husband's mother was constantly accusing her of laziness and hinting that Merijosi was inadequate as a wife and should be divorced. Merijosi eventually became pregnant; in the fourth month of pregnancy she walked three miles to her natal home to visit her parents. She stayed until late at night and returned home in the dark. As she walked along the road, she kept hearing the call of an animal that she could not identify, and she tripped on a stone and fell, spilling some objects that she was carrying on her head.

The next morning she had a high fever and nausea; two days later she had a miscarriage. Her mother-in-law was upset over the incident and took Merijosi to an adept who lived nearby. After listening to Merijosi's account, the adept concluded that a wind had attacked her, and that it had not been sent by a shade. The adept tried to lure the wind out of Merijosi's head by preparing some pleasing food and singing songs to charm the wind, but the adept was not certain whether the operation was successful.

Merijosi eventually became pregnant again and gave birth, but her baby died when it was a few months old. While the baby was dying, Merijosi developed chills, nausea, fever, and other symptoms. She went to a different adept and was told again that a wind had attacked her but that it had come on its own account, and that it was not the same wind which had attacked her the first time. On this occasion a dance was held for her, and she has had no more trouble since.

Example 2: KERODIA

Kerodia, a young widow, became ill with severe gastric pains. After the illness had persisted for some months, an adept diagnosed her condition as shade possession. The shade had not entered her itself, but had sent five winds, which entered her head and brought on the pain. The winds had not explained to her why they were attacking her, but the adept discerned that the shade of Kerodia's deceased father had become upset over a protracted quarrel among his sons.

Kerodia's father was survived by two widows, and the sons of one widow were quarreling with the sons of the other widow over bridewealth. The senior wife, Kerodia's mother, had four daughters, and she had given some of the bridewealth received at the marriages of her daughters to the sons of the junior wife. The participants in this dispute are depicted in Figure 12.

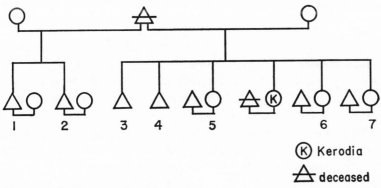

Figure 12: Participants in a Dispute

Participants 1 and 2 were quarreling with 3 and 4 over the bridewealth that the marriages of Kerodia's sisters (5, 6, and 7) had brought into the family established by Kerodia's parents. Normally a man divides his wealth equally among his wives and, most importantly, keeps the wealth of each wife separate. Hence a woman's sons have no right over the cattle held in the name of her co-wife. Each co-wife has full control over the bridewealth received at her daughters' marriages, and the usual practice is for a woman to see that her own sons are given those cattle. Kerodia's mother, however, was generous, and she shared cattle with the sons of her co-wife because they were having difficulty acquiring cattle for their marriages. The conflict arose some years later, when one of Kerodia's brothers needed cattle for his marriage. He approached his half-brothers, but they were unwilling or unable to provide cattle. Their refusal led to hostility between the two sets of brothers. Yet nothing in Lango culture prescribed that the sons of the junior wife return the cattle to their half-brothers. The problem arose because the senior wife did something Lango women normally do not do—that is, she gave cows to the sons of her co-wife.

The adept who treated Kerodia explained which shade was causing the trouble and why it was doing so. The shade had observed the dispute and had become unhappy that there was dissension among its owner's sons. The shade had sent five winds to attack Kerodia. The winds would sometimes talk to her late in the evening and would explain that they intended to kill her, but they did not reveal that they had been sent by a shade. A possession dance was held for Kerodia, and was attended by most of the members of her extended family, including the two sets of brothers engaged in the dispute. Kerodia was cured after the dance, and she reported that the dispute ended shortly thereafter.

Kerodia's case is an example of possession type 2, wherein the actual possession is carried out by a wind, but a shade is the primary agent. Merijosi's case is an example of possession type 1, in which the wind itself is the primary agent. In these cases of possession, as in most, the victims had direct contact only with winds. The winds provide the experiential context of possession: they attack the victim in direct physical encounters and speak to her through some sort of vision. The winds are also immediately responsible for causing the physical symptoms even though a shade may ultimately be responsible. Winds, it will be remembered, have a physical form and can be described in fairly concrete terms, whereas the concept of shades is more abstract.

These examples also tell something of the sociological significance of Lango spirit possession, for in each the diagnosis and treatment reflect the social situation of the patient. In example 1, wherein a wind was the primary agent, the victim was in an unenviable position, as a young wife who had not yet borne children. A woman's marital status is tenuous until she bears children, and the period immediately after marriage is particularly difficult. The problem of adjusting to virilocal residence is a frequent topic of conversation among women, and relations between young wives and their mothers-in-law are invariably strained. Overt hostility is rare, and the young wife is expected to perform her tasks without complaint. As time passes, she comes under greater pressure if she does not bear children; the most frequent cause of divorce is barrenness, for which a man sends his wife back to her natal home and reclaims his bridewealth. In Merijosi, spirit possession was associated with a period of intense personal strain, and the diagnosis provided her and her affines with an explanation of her failure to bear children. Making her the object of attention at curing ceremonies allowed her to save face and to continue in her marriage until she had given birth.

The example of Kerodia is sociologically significant in a different way. A diagnosis of shade possession is a statement about relations among kinsmen: it indicates that conflicts prevail. Aside from offering an explanation and a possible cure for Kerodia's ailment, the diagnosis of shade possession eventually helped resolve the conflict among her kinsmen.

Shade Possession and Intrafamilial Conflict

The logic of shade possession needs clarification, for one might expect that, if a shade observes conflict and wishes to end it, the shade would somehow engage in adjudication and punish wrongdoers. According to Lango beliefs, however, the shade brings pressure to bear on its kinsmen in a roundabout way. First, the shade never possesses individuals who are themselves involved in disputes. The victim is an innocent member of the family. The shade takes pity on this bystander and singles her out for possession.[4]

Informants give two interpretations of what goal the shade has in mind. One interpretation is that the shade merely wishes to call attention to the conflict, to publicize it, and to inform people that it is upset by their behavior. The other interpretation is that the shade is not concerned primarily to end the conflict

4. Strathern has described a very similar attitude toward possession by ancestor spirits among the people of the Mount Hagen sub-district of Australian New Guinea, were ancestors sometimes send sickness "in pity, to draw attention to the wronged person's situation" (1970:573). Also see Strathern (1968:191).

but to alleviate the suffering of the innocent bystander whom it selects. It informs the victim—sometimes by means of a wind, sometimes directly—that it has seen that the victim is living in circumstances marked by conflict and must therefore be very unhappy. The shade states that the only way to alleviate the sorrow of the victim is to end her life. This interpretation is based on the premise that human life is basically unhappy, but that some people are particularly miserable because they belong to families in which kinsmen do not "stay well" together. The only possible solution for these unfortunates is to have their lives ended by some agent such as a shade. The victim then becomes a shade herself and can exercise control over humanity.

Belief in shades and shade possession, then, is a philosophy of suffering, for it recognizes the problem of inequities and injustices among men. Although shades do not necessarily punish evildoers, they intercede in behalf of the innocent. This facet of shade possession often imparts an intensive quality to the possession experience, in that the victim may be told by the possessing spirit what the spirit is going to do, and each successive symptom of illness is perceived as another attempt by the spirit to end the victim's life. For her part, the victim does not accede to the wishes of the spirit. She desperately tries to rid herself of the spirit, recognizing that she must do so if she is to save her life. Although shades are powerful, they cannot kill people immediately, and the victim may find herself in an agonizing struggle with the shade for a long time. As the struggle continues, the shade may kill off the victim's children, particularly infants, for the young are weaker and succumb more readily.

Throughout this discussion, the victims of shade possession have been referred to as females. This does not mean that only women are possessed by spirits; occasionally a man is attacked. The incidence of spirit possession among adult men is extremely low, however; from 1964 through 1966 only one adult man in Obanya Kura was the victim of spirit possession, and he was very old and weak. Other cases of possession among men were reported for earlier years, and all the victims were old. Old men are vulnerable to attacks by spirits, and are so weak that once they are attacked the spirits can cause them great physical harm. Children too are weak, and the deaths of many children, both male and female, are attributed to spirit possession. The spirit usually attacks through the child's mother rather than attacking the child directly.

Shades are aware that women and children are more vulnerable, but shades are said to feel especially sympathetic to women and children, for they are the innocent, unwitting victims of disputes that are waged for the most part by men. If belief in spirit possession is described as a philosophy of suffering, the "suffering" refers to the problems of women, as they are perceived by women in a patrilineal, virilocal society where women hold little formal authority.

Shade possession is not punitive, therefore, but is an attempt to end suffering by freeing innocent bystanders from life. The fact remains, however, that shade possession is associated with intrafamilial disputes and regardless of the interpretation of the shade's motive, the phenomenon of shade possession serves to aid in the resolution of conflict. This is not to say that, whenever a dispute breaks out, an innocent bystander will develop symptoms of spirit possession. Many quarrels can be settled in court, either in the neighborhood court or in the government court. However, not all disputes can be resolved in the courts. Conflicts between members of an extended family, the disputes that serve as the background for shade possession, present two problems. First, a court case between kinsmen of the first degree (brother-brother, father-son, etc.,) is not deemed desirable, for it threatens relations within the family. Second, many disputes between family members do not arise out of particular offenses but are based on vague suspicions, enduring resentment, conflicts of personality, and so forth. Such cases cannot be effectively handled in court, simply because there is no offense that can be charged; or if there once was such an offense, it has long been put aside, even though the bitterness remains.

Kerodia's example shows how an extended family can become so enmeshed in a dispute that it cannot be resolved in court. Kerodia's unmarried brothers envied their married half-brothers for having been able to obtain bridewealth, and relations between co-wives were strained. When the adept made the diagnosis, and placed the blame for Kerodia's symptoms on those who were engaged in the disputes, she made the first public statement of the conflict. All participants in the dispute were asked to attend the dance that was later held for Kerodia. At one point during the dance, the adept again discussed the cause of Kerodia's symptoms, and suggested that the shade would be inclined to leave Kerodia if good will were restored among the kinsmen. In this instance, the dance was not successful in resolving the conflict, but Kerodia and some of her kinsmen reported after it was performed that the members of her family could once again "stay well" with one another, implying that the ceremony, at least while it lasted, had reinforced the sentiment that good will should prevail among kinsmen.

When a shade-possession dance is held and an intrafamilial dispute is discussed, the adept invites only those kinsmen participating in the dispute, and requests that others not attend. In another example, a young married woman was attacked by the shade of her father, which was disturbed over a long-standing dispute between the dead man's widow and his son. The adept held a possession dance for the young woman, but said that the patient's husband and her affinal relatives need not bother to attend. The patient's mother and brother were seated in a prominent position at the dance, and other members of the patient's lineage were invited as well. The adept exhorted the disputants to cease their quarrels so that the shade would no longer trouble the patient.

The adept does not always accuse particular kinsmen. In presenting the diagnosis of shade possession, the adept may not give a specific reason why the shade is attacking the victim. The adept may announce that the shade is unhappy because the kinsmen did not pay the shade sufficient homage through funeral offerings. A shade is said to become annoyed if insufficient beer is served at the funeral ceremonies or if the kinsmen fail to hold a Grave Opening or *Apuny*. Of the fourteen cases of shade possession tabulated in Appendix II, two were attributed to the anger of particular shades over insufficient funeral offerings. But further study of these cases indicates that they were also associated with intrafamilial conflict, even though the adept did not say so when she made the initial diagnosis. In one case, the patient was attacked by the shade of her father's mother, which was said to be upset over the inadequate recognition paid to it at funeral ceremonies. As the patient discussed her case among her neighbors, she became more explicit about the failings of her brothers, and it soon became apparent that the patient was involved in a long series of disagreements with her brothers. The disagreements began at the time of her marriage, when the brothers voiced complaints about the meager size of the bridewealth. On several occasions, the patient had asked her brothers for assistance, but they had never responded generously to her requests. There was no open hostility between the patient and her brothers, but relations were generally strained, and these relations became the focal point of discussion during the patient's illness. It is worth noting that women are expected to abide by the authority of their brothers, and there is virtually no recourse for a woman in those rare instances when a man regularly takes advantage of his sister or refuses to carry out his obligations to her. Like many other cases of shade possession, this one was based on a controversy in which a woman was perceived as an innocent victim and in which the woman herself had no means at her disposal to alleviate the conflict or improve the relations. This situation is the background for many cases of shade possession, even those attributed to insufficient funeral offerings.

THE ACTIVITIES OF THE ADEPT

When a woman develops symptoms of illness she does not immediately go to an adept, but first seeks treatment from other sources. The first choice is usually the government clinic, which is open daily and is within walking distance from Obanya Kura. A woman who has been treated unsuccessfully at the clinic might visit one of the Asian private physicians who practice in Lira, or one of the medical missions operated by the Verona Fathers. These medical missions are situated in Aliwang, which is eleven miles from Obanya Kura, and in Kalongo, which is about sixty miles north. All these alternatives are expensive, however, for there is the cost of transportation in addition to a fee for the medical service.[5] These alternatives are available only to a wage earner or to a person who is able to borrow a sizable sum of money

5. The Asian physicians charge about 20 shillings for an office visit and an injection of penicillin, and the cost of a round-trip bus ticket to Lira is 4 shillings.

in a short time. The patient's choice also depends in part on her symptoms: she may be physically unable to make the journey, or the symptoms may appear so minor that her kinsmen do not regard her condition as serious enough.

If for any of these reasons the woman decides to consult an adept (*imuru*), her first choice will be an adept who lives in her husband's vicinage or in her natal vicinage. The patient will be accompanied by a female kinsman, e.g., mother, mother-in-law, or husband's brother's wife. The patient describes the symptoms to the adept and asks for a diagnosis and for some suggestions how she can be cured.

There is great variation among adepts. Some have achieved exceptionally high status as a result of their diagnostic and curative abilities. At the other end of the scale is the woman who occupies the same status as every other woman in the vicinage except that she has been trained as an adept. The requirements for being an adept are simple. First, a person must have been possessed by a spirit that steadfastly remained with the victim after repeated attempts to eliminate the spirit through dances and other means. Second, the person must then have undergone training by an adept and have been formally initiated at a special possession dance supervised by the trainer. The initiation dance is especially important because during the dance, the spirit possessing the novice transforms itself from a harmful force, which wants to kill its victim, to a beneficial force, which is harnessed to serve the victim and aid her in curing others in her career as an adept. The agonizing struggle between the victim and her spirit ends at the initiation: the victim subjects herself to the spirit, agreeing to obey its commands, builds a special shrine for it, and communicates with it. The spirit, in turn, agrees to advise the victim and help her cure others. The principal barrier to becoming initiated is the capital expense incurred during the training and at the initation. The adept who trains the novice demands a fee of 400 to 1000 shillings, depending on her own reputation, and may charge an additional 500 shillings for the initiation dance. It is not unusual for a novice to begin the training but find herself unable to meet the expenses, while the trainer keeps asking for additional sums and refuses to continue the instruction until they are paid. As might be expected, several women in Obanya Kura had begun the training but could not pay all the expenses, and were therefore never fully initiated as adepts. Such women are in the unfortunate position of being possessed by a spirit that will not leave them, although they are not qualified to serve as adepts. They are prominent figures at possession dances in the vicinage and are often employed to assist the adepts themselves.

Men can become adepts. Although no men in Obanya Kura had been initiated, there were two active male adepts within five miles of Obanya Kura. The most successful adepts, however, were women. They worked full-time as adepts, employing men to grow their food, and maintaining large households which included assistants and novices. Their reputations were such that many of them specialized in particular conditions and commanded very high fees. In contrast, there is the neighborhood adept who is initiated but who has no following to speak of. People say of such an adept that "her spirit is not powerful enough," for Langi believe that the curing power of an adept is determined by the strength of the spirit that possesses her. Between the least successful adept and the most successful lie a wide range, some of whom earn large supplements to their household incomes. The most successful adept in Obanya Kura (see Appendix I) reported that she earned 800 shillings as an adept during 1965 and that she conducted four large dances. Her gross income was 1340 shillings, she said, but she paid large sums to her assistants and to the drummer who worked with her. Of the four adepts in Obanya Kura, she was the only one whose reputation was such that she was asked to treat patients from as far as thirty miles away. She was frequently away from Obanya Kura to consult with patients, to conduct dances, and to visit former patients or with her mentor. She was also the only adept in Obanya Kura who had trained and initiated other adepts; she had trained two women in her vicinage and three from others.

Diagnostic Techniques: Divination

When a woman goes to an adept to learn whether she is possessed by a spirit, the adept employs divination to help in making a diagnosis. There are currently two techniques of divination used in Obanya Kura: reading cowrie shells that have been cast on the ground, and holding a conversation with a spirit. No rules determine which technique is to be used, except that each adept prefers one of the two techniques and uses it more frequently. In offering information to the patient, the adept is expected to reveal events and dispositions of the spirit world; therefore, she must put herself in direct contact with a spirit. The adept receives her powers to diagnose and cure through the tutelary spirit that possesses her, and when she employs divination she is demonstrating to the patient that she maintains an intimate relation with her spirit.

If the adept uses cowrie shells, it is believed, the tutelary spirit determines the pattern that the shells will form on the ground. The adept owns a set of twelve shells, and the shells are held in the right hand and thrown all at once. This is done inside the adept's house, the patient and a few other persons looking on. As the shells fall on the ground, the adept notes three features: whether each shell falls with the orifice facing up (open) or facing down (closed); the distance between shells; and the orientation of each shell relative to the others. The combination of all these features allows the adept to see a miniature sociodrama enacted at each casting of the shells, for each shell is considered to designate one of the patient's kinsmen. The overall pattern of dispersal depicts some significant event in the patient's life. For example, a throw of the shells might show that the patient is about to give birth but that the child will die because of an angry shade in the family. Such sociodramas are created by the intervention of the tutelary spirit, which determines the outcome of each throw of the shells.

In divining with cowrie shells, the adept does not bother to stop and explain each throw to the patient, because only certain throws are relevant to the patient's condition. Therefore, the adept casts the shells, quickly glances at them, sweeps them off the ground, and throws them again. This action is performed swiftly and may be repeated twenty times before the adept feels that the pattern is significant. She will then stop and explain the diagnosis to the patient. The patient and the other onlookers become quite absorbed in this technique of divination; a competent adept can throw the shells with a rhythm and with bodily motions that virtually mesmerize the onlookers.

The second technique of divination is a consultation between the adept and her tutelary spirit. This is accomplished with the adept seated in front of the resting place of her tutelary spirit. When a spirit possesses a person over a long period, it does not always remain in the head of the victim but resides in some spot close by and enters the victim's head only at certain times, causing the victim to go into a trance. The spirit may dwell in a small shrine (*okango*), which the adept builds in her yard from small pieces of wood and grass thatching. Some adepts do not build shrines; the tutelary spirit of such an adept merely resides in a particular spot within a wall of her house.

To communicate with the spirit, the adept places herself near the spirit's resting place and summons the spirit by shaking a gourd rattle in a steady rhythm or by singing some songs that are especially pleasing to her spirit. After the spirit has been summoned, the adept converses with it, asking it questions and responding to its answers. Some adepts merely carry on a one-sided conversation, interrupting from time to time to convey the words of the spirit to those present. Other adepts use ventriloquism to communicate the words of the spirit. The adept asks the question in her customary voice, and the reply is delivered in a very soft falsetto. While the conversation is taking place, the adept continues to shake the rattle, and if she uses ventriloquism the responses can barely be heard.

Curing Techniques

If the adept gives a diagnosis of spirit possession, she is also expected to suggest a cure. The range of possibilities is great, and the adept may suggest a simple procedure that can be performed privately or she may suggest a curing ceremony selected form any of the three ceremonial complexes. If the case is relatively simple, involving only possession by a wind, the adept can suggest a *kwer* ceremony or a Praying for the Sick or a Blessing the Sick from among the *etogo* ceremonies. If the patient has had previous experiences with spirit possession, or if the spirit is a shade, the adept is almost certain to prescribe a possession dance. There is an economic consideration which adepts do not openly discuss but which is undoubtedly crucial in the selection of a curing ceremony. If the adept selects a *kwer* or *etogo* ceremony, she does not stand to gain financially, except in a few instances in which the adept supervises an *etogo* ceremony and is paid a little for her services. The adept receives payment for conducting a possession dance, and it is likely that adepts are therefore predisposed toward prescribing the dances.[6] Of the thirty-one cases of possession tabulated in Appendix II, eleven were treated with possession dances.

Catching the Spirit   If the adept wishes to cure the patient herself but does not prescribe a dance, she can carry out a ritual known as "Catching the Wind" or "Catching the Shade" (*mako yamo, mako tipu*). This ritual is considered effective only in driving away spirits that have not been with the patient long or spirits that are not especially powerful or determined in their actions against the patient. It is doubtful whether a Catching the Spirit of either type can be classified as a ceremony, since it is attended by very few persons. To be effective, it must be performed at the exact site where the patient was attacked by the spirit. The ritual is attended by the patient and a few female kinsmen. I observed three rituals of this type, and no men except me were present at any of them. The purpose of Catching the Spirit is to lure the spirit out of the head of its victim and then enclose it in a pot. Because winds and shades enjoy food and music, Langi believe, they can sometimes be tricked into leaving their victims. A meal is brought to the site and placed before the victim, who seats herself in the center of the circle of women. One of the women beats a drum, while the others shake rattles and sing songs that are believed to please the spirit. The adept brings a food pot with a mouth of about eight inches and prepares some mud, preferably with a high clay content. It is hoped that, at one point during the singing, the spirit will leave the head and go toward the plate containing the food. This moment is signaled by the patient's going into a brief swoon or trance. Her eyes roll upward, the upper part of her body may tremble, and she is likely to fall backward. As soon as this happens, the adept grasps the pot and quickly inverts it over the plate of food. The next step is

6. An adept who is not fully initiated and whose reputation is slight may earn as little as 15 shillings for assisting at a possession dance, but some adepts command fees as high as 300 shillings for especially difficult cases.

to seal the pot with mud, a difficult operation because the spirit has been aroused and can easily escape from the pot. The adept must work quickly. When the pot has been sealed, she carries it out to the bush and leaves it in a hiding place. An adept receives a fee of 20 to 40 shillings to carry out this ritual, but the patient may ask for a refund if the spirit comes back to bother her. In many instances, the spirit manages to escape from the pot after a while and reenter the victim. This event is attributed to the adept's negligence in not having sealed the pot adequately or not having placed it in some spot that would confuse the spirit if it managed to get out of the pot. Catching the Spirit is seldom effective for long, and it is considered a simple and inexpensive expedient to be carried out when the patient cannot obtain enough support from her kinsmen to permit a possession dance.

The Possession Dance   The purpose of the possession dance is the same as that of the ritual just described: to lure the spirit out of the head of its victim and prevent it from returning. In the possession dance, this is accomplished by arousing the spirit through music and dance. The adept must summon her own spirit, which should induce a trance state in her. It is hoped that the patient's spirit will be aroused by the music and dancing and will cause the patient to go into a trance. During the trance, the patient is believed to be engaged in a struggle with her spirit, and the adept frightens the spirit and at the same time encourages the patient in her struggle. There is no certainty that the spirit will be driven away at the dance. The only proof of success is that the patient does not develop any further symptoms of illness for a year or so after the dance. There is one sure indication of an unsuccessful dance, however: that the patient does not go into a possession trance. Absence of a trance is taken as an indication that the spirit was not aroused by the music and dancing and that it will stay with the patient.

A possession dance requires little preparation, for beer drinking is not part of the ceremony, and women do not have to plan to prepare beer well in advance. If the adept and the patient live near each other, the dance is held at the house of the adept. If the patient lives more than a mile from the adept, she may ask the adept to bring her paraphernalia to the patient's house and hold the dance there. The location of the dance is a matter of convenience; it does not affect the success of the dance.

Some adepts build a small structure in the yard of the house where the dance is to be held. This structure is made of saplings bent and lashed together to form a frame, which is covered with grass thatching. The completed structure is about three feet high and six feet long, with an entrance hole at one end and an exit hole at the other. It is just large enough for one person to crawl into and to remain inside in a reclining position. The word for this building is *gony* (*gonyo*: "to separate, to set free"), and the etymology of the word offers a clue to the way the building is used during the possession dance. When the adept or one of her attendants becomes possessed by a spirit and dances excitedly for a long time, she may become exhausted and want to get rid of the spirit in order to return to her normal state. She can then crawl into the *gony*, where the spirit will release itself and set the woman free. The *gony* is used in the same way at the climax of the dance to separate the patient from her spirit once and for all. After the patient has crawled into the *gony*, the adept exhorts the spirit to leave the patient, and the patient quickly crawls out the exit hole while the spirit is resting inside the *gony*. An offering of food may be placed inside the *gony* to distract the spirit, and the two holes may then be blocked off with sticks and mud so that the spirit will not be able to leave. Although the *gony* plays an important role in many possession dances, it is not used in all; its presence depends on the inclination of the adept who is conducting the dance.

The adept must also make arrangements in advance with people who will serve as assistants. Each adept has a coterie of about a half-dozen women in her vicinage, whom she employs to dance, play drums, shake rattles, and sing. The possession dance is, among other things, a dramatic performance, and a successful dance depends largely on an adept's ability to recruit performers.[7] Women who have been possessed by spirits and have never really been cured make good assistants, as do women who have actually been initiated as adepts but have not built up a practice. The

7. The theatrical aspect of spirit possession has been described by Leiris in his study of Ethiopia (1958). This aspect has also been noted by Metraux, who used the term "ritual comedy" in reference to Haitian voodoo rites (1955).

assistants are almost invariably women, although one adept employed her husband from time to time as well as a crippled man who was unable to work in the fields.

The adept, the patient, the assistants, and those kinsmen who have been invited assemble shortly after dark on the designated evening. There is no formal schedule, and activities do not begin until the adept decides to take the initiative. Before the dancing begins, people sit in the yard discussing the case in a casual, conversational manner. The adept should offer an interpretation of the case, repeating the diagnosis, and if the patient is possessed by a shade, the adept should pay particular attention to the shade's reasons for attacking. She does not admonish the patient's kinsmen, but she makes clear that the patient is the defenseless victim of a familial dispute and will not be cured until the dispute ends.

Beer may be served just before the dance, but Lango possession dances do not necessarily entail the consumption of large amounts of beer. At two dances of the seven I attended, the adept and her assistants stopped the proceedings from time to time and drank small portions of distilled millet beer (*waragi*). Never did I observe drunkenness at a possession dance, and, as far as I know, none of the participants took narcotics or stimulants.

After several hours of preliminary discussion, everyone enters the house, and the adept begins to sing songs. The hypnotic effect of the dance is enhanced considerably by the intense crowding within the house. Lango houses are approximately twelve feet in diameter, and about forty-five people may be in attendance, all of them sitting in the house. The adept distributes gourd rattles to people, and there are always two drums. As a result, the music is loud and intense and is characterized by a constant rhythmic beat, which is not utilized to such an extent in other forms of Lango music.[8]

8. My own impression was that the loudness and repetitiveness of the drumbeat and the rattling of the gourds may have helped to precipitate a change in the psychological states of those who were present. Informants sometimes commented that the drumming "bothered" them and hurt their ears, and as an outside observer I found that I could not think clearly after listening to the drum music for an hour or so. The psychologist Andrew Neher attempted to replicate this sort of rhythmic experience in a laboratory, and he observed marked changes in the psychological states of the persons who participated in his experiment (Neher 1963). The ethnographer Beidelman has also made suggestions along these lines

The purpose of the music is to arouse the spirits, and when any woman feels that her spirit "grabs" her, she gets up from her seat and dances. The dancing is improvisational and individualistic. A small area in the center of the floor is cleared for dancing, and only one woman dances at a time. At first, the dancer's style is relatively relaxed and sedate; it becomes less so as the spirit gains more control over her, and finally she begins to go into a trance. The dancer may fall onto the floor or into someone's lap, an indication that she has lost control of herself. One set of movements is much more overtly erotic than anything seen in conventional Lango dancing. The dancer makes lewd gestures or arches her head and shoulders backward while touching her breasts. Another common style of dancing is patterned after military marches. In this form, the dancer stands stiffly upright blowing a police whistle and perhaps carrying a baton, and marches around the room, sometimes adding an about-face or coming to attention.

Whatever the style, it becomes exaggerated as the spirit begins to possess the dancer. After twenty minutes or so the dancer falls on the floor with her face down, and completely loses touch with the rhythm. Spectators gather to help her, for it is clear that at this point the spirit has "grabbed" her. She has a seizure in which she utters several short shrieks, her eyes roll upward, and her body shakes uncontrollably. This state lasts about a minute. When the dancer regains control of her muscles she moves to the side of the room or to the *gony* to rest. The seizure is followed by heavy breathing, profuse sweating, and exclamations of pain and fatigue.

This possession dance is repeated by several women, while the adept sits beside the patient consoling her and singing to summon the spirits. Eventually the adept dances, and her dance differs little from those of the other women, except that a good adept displays virtuosity and creativity. The following is an extract

---

as a result of observing possession dances among the Kaguru of Tanzania. Beidelman writes: "The most commonly possessed persons are women, especially young girls and women approaching menopause. There seems to be much latent sexual frustration associated with such possession. The usual treatment is for the women's relatives to hold a marathon drumming session at which the spirit is danced and drummed out of the woman. Continuous dancing and drumming may well have complex psychophysiological effects upon a disturbed person" (1971:40–41).

from field notes written immediately after observing the dance of an adept.

After the musicians rested, the drumming began again and Elia began to dance, swaying from left to right in a loose-limbed manner. Someone brought out a policeman's cap from a box and placed it on her head. After a moment of music, her step changed. Her body became stiff and upright. Her step changed to the knee-high step reminiscent of a drum majorette. Her eyes became glassy. At no point did she lose control of her muscles, and her dancing remained patterned. Steps varied: a military march backward and forward toward where we were sitting, and her baton carried over her shoulder like a rifle. Could hear hard, short breaths and repeated muttering. About halfway through the tune, she suddenly became possessed by her spirit and fell down again and began to tremble for about 15 seconds. Rose up and indicated to the drummers what sort of rhythm her spirit had requested. The drummers made several attempts to duplicate the beat, but she kept correcting them. After their third attempt, she was satisfied. She danced excitedly and ran out of the house and threw herself on the ground before the entrance to the *gony* and crawled into the *gony* and lay down there, trembling for several minutes and finally relaxing.

Dancing of this sort continues all evening, except for long intervals when no music is played, during such intervals people rest and perhaps food is served. As the evening continues, people become increasingly concerned over the mood of the patient and look for indications that her spirit is about to possess her. The patient is encouraged to dance in the hope that the dancing will activate the spirit, but often the patient remains unaffected and unmoved by the spirit. The dance should continue until the patient goes into a possession trance, and the activities may therefore last for several nights. People rest during the day; those who live nearby return home, and the adept may spend the day talking with the patient and divining with cowrie shells to determine the outcome of the dance.

The culmination of the possession dance occurs when the patient enters a trance. If she does not, after three or four nights of dancing the adept decides that the dance is a failure and should be halted. If the patient does not enter a trance, she is not obliged to pay the adept, and the adept, therefore, cannot pay her assistants and musicians.[9] This rule has some bearing on the economics of spirit possession, since approximately 20 percent of possession dances are unsuccessful.

The dancing and trance of the patient do not differ stylistically from those of the other participants. When the patient finally goes into her trance, the adept may remove her to the *gony*, if one has been constructed, or the adept may simply continue singing and dancing to encourage the patient in her struggle with the spirit. Meanwhile, other women comfort the patient and assist her, bringing her water to drink or removing objects that might injure her as she moves about uncontrollably.

After the patient has entered a trance she is considered to be free of the spirit that has been possessing her, and any further dancing or activity constitutes a sort of epilogue. However, a possession dance never ends at the moment when the patient is freed of her possessing spirit. The dancing may continue for another night or two. There is no fixed duration of a possession dance nor any formal way of determining its conclusion. Like many other features of the possession dance, the time to end is left primarily to the adept. In this regard, the possession dance stands in contrast to the *etogo* and *kwer* ceremonies, each of which has a regular form in which certain ritual acts are performed at certain times and there is a reasonable degree of consensus on when the ceremony should begin and end. In the possession dance, however, there is more room for the adept and even for some of the other participants to improvise the form as the dance progresses. Each adept has her own style of dancing and her own method of conducting the dance, and it is largely her virtuosity in these endeavors that determines her success as an adept.

The same individuality and virtuosity help to make the possession dance more popular than any of the *etogo* or *kwer* ceremonies, which, although rich in symbolic meaning, lack the brilliance and spontaneity of a possession dance. Before going to a possession dance, one is never certain what will take place, and each dancer leaves her personal mark on the performance. Spectators become involved in possession dances in a way that does

9. An assistant or a musician is generally paid 2 shillings per night. If the adept earns an especially large sum for conducting the dance, say, more than 100 shillings, she is likely to pay her assistants and musicians more.

not seem to be possible for the *kwer* and *etogo* ceremonies, which are marked by a seriousness of intent and a temporary feeling of group solidarity facilitated by commensality. At possession dances, spectators sit in rapt fascination as they watch the dancers. Afterward they discuss the high points of the dance and evaluate the intensity of each dancer's possession experience. Little discussion of any similar sort follows a *kwer* or *etogo* ceremony, and it is fair to say that, as a dramatic performance, the possession dance is far more satisfying than any ceremony of the other two types.

Sexual Liminality in the Possession Dance   Lango possession dances follow a general form, which we have outlined although every possession dance differs from every other. The general form includes women's use of gestures, words, and objects that are customarily appropriate only for men. Such behavior suggests a concept of "sexual liminality."

Rituals in which the members of one sex enact behavior appropriate to members of the opposite sex are well known in African ethnographic literature, having been included by Gluckman under the rubric "rituals of rebellion" (1960:133; 1963: 110–136). In Lango spirit-possession dances, the symbolic sex reversal has a different form and meaning than the sex reversal in the ceremonies described by Gluckman. During the dance, the adept uses symbols that are associated with male behavior. Sometimes the symbols are used by the other woman dancers—mostly the assistants, who are often experienced dancers in their own right. Because each dance is largely improvised, not all adepts and dancers use the same symbols, but all adepts use some. I compiled the following list of symbols from observations made at seven spirit-possession dances.

Symbols of Sexual Liminality: handshaking, smoking cigarettes, drinking distilled liquor, wearing men's shoes, carrying a walking stick, listening to a radio, eating chicken or eggs, or announcing that the spirit has requested an offering of chicken or eggs (poultry products are forbidden to women because they are believed to affect a woman's fertility), using words not customarily spoken by women (e.g., *loni*, "this fellow"; *loca*, "that fellow") and using a speech style normally used by men only, blowing a policeman's whistle, wearing a military cap, dancing in a march step.

The last three items are not forms of behavior that men regularly engage in; nonetheless, normally they are masculine activities. The other items are more straightforward, in that under normal circumstances men enact these forms of behavior and women do not. As enacted in the possession dance, all eleven forms of behavior seem to represent a conscious attempt on the part of the adept to alter or invert the normal sex role, although adepts would not make explicit reference to this inversion or to the way they develop it through the manipulation of symbols during their performances.

On the face of it, this manipulation of symbols would appear similar to an actual dramatization of the role of the opposite sex, as discussed by Gluckman (1960:110–116). This is not true in Lango possession dances, however, for in enacting her dancing performance, the adept does not disguise herself as a man, nor does she employ all or nearly all of the symbols she could use if she were consciously trying to imitate men. Instead, the adept utilizes one or a few symbols associated with maleness. She does not make any reference to her own maleness during the dancing; in fact, she does quite the opposite, for, we have seen, lewdness and explicit female sexuality are also part of the possession dance. In other words, behavior exaggerating the femaleness of the dancer is juxtaposed against symbols expressing maleness. For example, in one dance, the adept removed a hat from the head of a male spectator to wear while dancing. She then took some cigarettes from another man (snatching them out of his hands in an unfeminine manner) and began to smoke one. As her dance continued she unfastened the upper part of her clothing to expose her breasts, and she made erotic gestures expressing her own female sexuality.

In a series of essays, Turner (1967, 1969) has discussed the juxtaposition of symbols that denote opposite attributes, e.g., male/female, animal/human. Turner contends that rituals derive much of their impact from this juxtaposition. In the ritual, attributes that in the normal scheme of things are dissimilar or even opposite are brought together in a grotesque distortion of normal categories of thought. Beidelman (1966a) has offered a brilliant analysis of the Swazi *Incwala* ceremony, following a similar line of reasoning. The mixing of symbols denoting oppo-

site attributes has the effect of isolating the central actor in the
ceremony and ritually removing him from the social order. By
using symbols of maleness and femaleness, the adept places herself in a "liminal" state, or a condition that is "betwixt and between," to use Turner's phrases. In this state of sexual liminality
she sets herself apart from others and dramatizes the supernatural
aspect of herself by showing that she is both male and female—
and at the same time neither male nor female.

There is another form of liminality in the possession dance,
for the dance (like the entire spirit-possession complex) juxta-
poses another pair of opposites: men and spirits. The two categories are brought together as spirits possess men and endanger
them with sickness. At the dance, the liminal state is induced
through music and dance, and during her trance the dancer is
caught "betwixt and between" spirits and men as the spectators
watch her struggle to resume her normal (human) state and
eliminate her abnormal (spiritual), illness-bearing state.

How are the two forms of liminality—the male/female liminality and the human/spiritual liminality—related? Turner (1969:
38) has argued that ritual is built up of the "crisscrossing binary
opposition" of several "planes of classification." Let us apply this
mode of analysis to Lango possession dances. The sexual liminality is employed dramatically as one plane of classification which
enhances and calls attention to another, more important plane
of classification, the opposition between men and spirits. Figure
13 diagrams the two planes of classification.

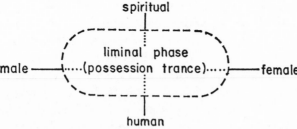

Figure 13: Planes of Classification

But of all the possible planes of classification that might be
dramatized in the possession dance, why is the male/female
opposition dramatized? This theme does not appear in *kwer* or

etogo ceremonies, some of which are concerned with opposition between men and spirits and use symbols that illustrate this opposition. The male/female distinction in the possession dance is certainly related to the most overwhelming feature of the spirit-possession complex—that it is women who become possessed, that women are seen as the innocent victims of intrafamilial disputes, and that women become adepts and conduct the dances.[10]

CONCLUSION

Judging from the ethnographic reports of Driberg (1923) and Hayley (1947), spirit possession is a relatively recent phenomenon in Lango. At present the possession dance is held more frequently than any ceremony of the *kwer* or *etogo* complex. Possession is believed to cause many illnesses and is often invoked as an *ex post facto* explanation when a woman or her child is sick. The possession dance is primarily a curative dance, designed to dispose of the spirit or spirits affecting the victim. Coincidentally, we have seen that some forms of spirit possession—those in which a shade is the primary agent—are associated with intrafamilial dispute in which the patient is seen as an innocent bystander attacked by a well-meaning shade that wishes to remove her from the bitterness of human existence. At the possession dance, the adept and other women become possessed by their spirits through dancing in which symbols of maleness are combined with expressions of female sexuality.

Spirit possession is by no means unique to Lango, and it is not surprising that Lango women have adopted the spirit-possession complex from Nyoro and popularized it during the last fifty years. Lewis (1966:309) has commented on the prominence of women in spirit-possession activities in many societies and has stated that possession activities are especially prevalent in male-dominated societies. Lewis' hypothesis that spirit possession is associated with sexual antagonisms, or the "sex war" (1966:315–316), seems relevant to Lango, where a strong ideology of male superiority is combined with patrilineal descent and virilocal residence.

10. For other examples of East African societies in which women are more active in spirit-possession activities than men, see Harris 1957, Beidelman 1971, and Swantz 1970.

Peter J. Wilson (1967:366) has criticized Lewis' hypothesis "that [spirit possession] may be traced to the innate conflict between men and women in certain types of society where men monopolize the social structure." Wilson argues instead that spirit possession is associated with "conflict, competition, tension, rivalry, or jealousy between members of the same sex rather than between members of opposite sexes" (1967:316). Wilson uses the concept "status ambiguity" to account for spirit possession. He explains status ambiguity as follows.

The women of a community in a society where the rule of postmarital residence is patrilocal, virilocal, or avunculocal will include the following:

1. Those born into the community—sisters, daughters, or generally speaking unmarried females related by birth to resident males and often to each other;
2. Those married into the community. These women are likely to have come from a number of other communities and to be unknown to each other before their arrival as spouses. Exceptions do occur, of course, as when there are preferential marriage arrangements. Women thus married into a community are affinally related to resident males and may or may not be affinally related to each other. Their status, their very social identity is derived from that of their husbands. (1966:373)

Wilson goes on to say that spirit-possession activity is a sort of rite of passage, whereby women attempt to resolve the problem of status ambiguity and define a new identity for themselves (1966:374).

But there is another dimension to status ambiguity, one that Wilson overlooks. According to his definition, a woman's status is ambiguous because of her standing with respect to other women in her husband's community. By Wilson's admission, however, a woman derives her social identity from that of her husband. It is only logical that the husband-wife relationship should be a crucial determinant. The sort of status ambiguity we have seen in Lango is related to the changes in sex roles during the last fifty years. During the period when spirit possession was becoming popular, the status of women became increasingly ambiguous as women made only minimal economic gains while men continued to monopolize jural and political authority. At the same time, women remained peripheral in Lango society because women marry into their husbands' villages, and their rights and duties are largely dependent on the status of their husbands.

My findings in Lango support the arguments of both Lewis and Wilson, and reconcile the positions of these writers. With respect to Lewis' hypothesis, we have seen that Lango spirit possession is related to opposition between the sexes. This opposition is reflected in the jural and political authority of men as well as in the Lango ideal of male superiority, but it does not express itself in overt hostility between the sexes. Sexual opposition in Lango arises out of the combination of patrilineality with virilocality. The model of a unilineal, unilocal society is built on the principle that sexual differences are as logical a means as any for classifying persons and distributing them in space. It is reasonable to expect that a unilineal, unilocal society would express sexual antagonism symbolically, for the issue of sexual antagonism is at the very core of its social life (Murphy 1959).

In support of Wilson's argument, I have shown that the increase in spirit-possession activities is related to the status ambiguity of women, which has intensified during the last fifty years of social change. Lango women, like Lango men, witness the processes of change and develop new wants and expectations; their wants and expectations are not so likely to be satisfied as those of men. Spirit possession is an attempt to solve the problem of women (Ardener 1972), which is derived from the patrilineality and virilocality of Lango society but which has been exacerbated by recent developments.

Two themes recur in Lango spirit possession. The first is the view that wives are the innocent victims of disputes among their kinsmen. The second is the constant concern over a woman's responsibility to bear children for her husband's lineage. These problems are expressed during possession dances by the dramatic opposition of symbols of male atributes to the actuality of female attributes. To some extent, a woman can gain an identity for herself by becoming the vehicle through which a particular spirit carries out its intentions against human beings, and a few women even attain considerable status and earning power as adepts who minister to the needs of their peers.

VI

Conclusion

I have examined the ceremonial activities of a single locale in Lango and have found that some traditional Lango ceremonies are still practiced there and remain meaningful to the people who participate in them. Other ceremonies, particularly those associated with the *etogo* elders, are rarely practiced and are gradually being relegated to the domain of memory culture. Finally, a host of ceremonial activities have been introduced in the last fifty years, and these have been described in Chapter V. In seeking to explain why some elements of Lango ceremonial life have persisted while others have not, I have placed each ceremonial complex in the wider context of Lango social organization, showing how the ceremonies express particular problems and features of Lango society and how ceremonial change is related to the general course of social change in Lango.

This study has not fully described the religious belief system, nor has it mentioned numerous private and semiprivate religious activities that can be called rituals. Its concern has been with religious activities in which groups of about fifteen people or more take part.

I have avoided a discussion of witchcraft and sorcery because they do not figure prominently in contemporary Lango life, and because they have little to do with ceremonies. The practice of sorcery is a private matter and usually occurs during disputes between individuals. One of the parties to the dispute may purchase a magic substance called *lwit*, which is sold both privately and in the marketplace by persons who have specialized knowledge of the various types of *lwit*. The magic substance may be a twig which can be stuck in the ground near a victim's house or in his fields. *Lwit* may also be a root or a powder which can be placed on a victim's chair or in his food. Sorcerers act in other ways; for example, a sorcerer may be able to steal a person's shade, causing the victim to become mad because of soul loss, or he may know of oaths that can cause sickness or destroy the victim's crops. Most sorcerers will perform their services for a fee, but some operate only for personal motives and do not sell their services.

In addition to the practice of sorcery, there is a belief in the existence of depraved persons who work harm against the innocent by using special innate powers. In conventional anthropological usage, this belief falls under the heading of witchcraft. I was frequently told that there were no witches in Obanya Kura, although everyone agreed that there were witches in other locales because peoples in those areas committed incest, and witches are believed to be the offspring of incestuous unions. There are no ceremonies to protect people from witchcraft or sorcery; the only protection for a person who believes sorcery is being used against him is the purchase and use of a countervailing magic substance.

The absence of any discussion of Christianity and missionary activities might be taken as a glaring omission, and a brief explanation is in order. Although Christian missions were established in Lango District as early as 1914, they have had little effect on Lango religion. The degree to which Christianty has influenced people depends primarily on the accessibility of a mission church or school in the particular locality. The people of Obanya Kura can walk to the Protestant (Church of Uganda) mission church at Aloi corner, three miles away, or to the Catholic church five miles away. Both missions offer services every Sunday. The Protestant mission is permanently staffed by two Lango clergymen, whereas the Catholic mission is maintained by a visiting European missonary priest, who opens the church only on Sunday. It is a branch of a larger Catholic mission, which includes a school and a hospital and is located eleven miles from Obanya Kura. None of the residents of Obanya Kura attended Sunday services, although 45 percent of residents over the age of twenty and 60 percent of those between ten and twenty had been baptized and professed to be Christians. Their participaton in Christian activities was confined to undergoing a brief instruction period before they were baptized, usually at about age twelve. In addition, a few people attended church at Christmas or Easter, and almost everyone celebrated these holidays by canceling work for the day and joining in beer drinking and a feast of beef. The most frequently expressed reason for becoming a Christian was that baptism enables a person to append a Christian first name to his Lango name. In short, the effects of Christian missionary activity in Obanya Kura are minimal. There is little awareness of or interest in the principles of Christianity, other than a belief in the existence of a supreme deity which had created people. This diety is alternatively referred to as "the Creator Jok" (*Jok a cweyo jo*) or as *Obanya*, which is a Ganda word evidently introduced by missionaries who had first worked with Banta-speaking peoples in southern Uganda. The concept of a Creator Jok existed in Lango well before the introduction of Christianity, and it appears that the name *Obanya* has merely been applied to a pre-existing Lango religious concept.

Christian missionary activities do not serve to explain the changes that have taken place in the ceremonial life of Obanya Kura. Nor, to my knowledge, have any religious groups or particular persons made an effort to suppress or discourage any of the three ceremonial complexes and promote other religious activities. A Christian separatist movement arose at an early date in Lango, but its influence did not extend to the northern part of Lango District, where Obanya Kura is located (Barrett 1968: 113). The one area of ceremonial change in which diffusion has played a role is the spirit-possession complex; some features of the possession dance are strikingly similar to Nyoro possession activities, and extensive contact between the Lango and Nyoro peoples may account for some of the popularity of this ceremony.[1] Ultimately, however, the explanation for the surge in possession activities and for changes in the other two ceremonial complexes must be sought in changes within Lango itself.

The two most important historical developments in Lango

1. Sudden surges of interest in spirit-possession activities are by no means unusual. For example, Middleton, Southall, and Horton have reported such phenomena among the Lugbara, Alur, and Kalabari respectively (Middleton 1960: 228–264, 1963; Southall 1969:258; Horton 1970).

were the introduction of a cash-crop economy and the establishment of a government. These changes were introduced by the colonial administration in the period after 1914, and many later developments are ramifications of these two far-reaching changes. For example, the tendency to abandon villages and follow a residential pattern based on dispersed households is largely a result of the curtailment of intervillage warfare as government agents began to control intergroup hostility. The introduction of new crops afforded a measure of protection against famine. The introduction of a market system and the use of currency gave more alternatives to the subsistence cultivator: in a year when food crops were bad, the income earned from cotton could be used to purchase foods grown in another locality. The political stability that accompanied the *Pax Britannica* and the greater emphasis placed on agricultural pursuits led to a decrease in internal migration.

These political and economic changes had their effects on the household and on the relation between husband and wife. Cash crops allowed families to earn modest incomes, and there arose the problem of how to distribute such income. The traditional Lango ideal was that the wife should have control over household resources, but this ideal had been formed in a subsistence economy that did not include cash.

The matter became even more complicated when men were able to earn money from time to time working as laborers. At the same time, women were able to supplement their household earnings by selling foodstuffs in the marketplace, by making and selling beer, or by working as adepts. The problem of distributing the earnings from these activities was no more easily solved than the problem of distributing agricultural earnings. More often than not, the ideal that women should control the earnings was overlooked, and the greater portion of the money went to the men, who purchased consumer goods, such as clothing, bicycles, radios, and cigarettes. In this economic system, a woman's best opportunity was to sell beer to groups of men and keep the profits to purchase a few consumer items of her own. Even so, she would still be denied access to many of the amenities of culture change, such as wage labor and high social status.

To generalize, it can be said that, during the period of social change, the roles of men and women were reversed. In the past, Lango men controlled ritual and had less control over household resources than they now have. At present, men have gained more control over household resources, whereas most of the ritual is carried out by women.

Perhaps least affected by the economic and political developments were traditional ideals of patrilineality, virilocality, polygyny, and the subordinate position of women. Bridewealth continues to be the only means by which a birth can be legitimated. Church marriages are unknown in Obanya Kura, and long-term concubinage is condemned. Although polygynous unions are rare because of the difficulty of accumulating bridewealth, most men continue to see polygyny as the ideal form of marriage and strive to achieve this state. Similarly, the pattern of virilocal residence still prevails, men tending to marry women whose natal residences are about six miles from their own.

The preceding facts of change and continuity in Lango, discussed in earlier chapters, are reviewed here in their relation to persistence and change in the three ceremonial complexes. The *etogo* ceremonies have declined; there is little interest in them. Langi say that they do not hold *etogo* ceremonies because the ceremonies are too expensive, yet they spend large sums on possession dances and *kwer* ceremonies. They are reluctant to spend the money because the *etogo* ceremonies deal with existential problems that are not so meaningful today as they were in the precontact period. The primary function of these ceremonies is to inculcate male solidarity at a local level and to maintain good relations among the members of several clans over a fairly large area. Economic changes, together with the tendency toward more permanently settled but isolated homesteads, have made these ideals of male solidarity and interclan relations less important than they once were. Furthermore, a man no longer needs the protection of an *etogo* member when moving to a new locality. Another reason for the lack of interest is that young men are no longer willing to submit to the authority of the *etogo* elders, as they must do during the ceremonies. And the *etogo* curing ceremonies must compete with the government clinic and the adepts; some people believe that *etogo* ceremonies are no longer successful in curing people. The disappearance of *etogo* ceremonies can be safely predicted.

The second ceremonial complex consists of the *kwer* ceremonies, which focus on the problem of maintaining the health of a married woman and her children. These ceremonies persist because they express a problem that still exists: the incorporation of a married woman into her husband's lineage without severing her ties with her natal lineage. In addition, the *kwer* ceremonies are concerned with a woman's ability to bear chldren, which is still the principal determinant of status for a Lango wife.

The last ceremonial complex to be considered was the spirit-possession complex. Spirit possession has become increasingly popular in the last fifty years and is now the most important of the three ceremonial complexes; it is especially popular among women, who serve both as adepts and as patients. In the possession dances, adepts make use of consumer items and forms of behavior that have recently been introduced into Lango—e.g., cigarettes, shoes, and military marches. The ceremonies also contain the reversal of sex roles, women taking on masculine behavior. Participants in possession dances are introducing into Lango religious life an entirely new set of symbols and manipulating these symbols in an effort to address some problems of Lango womanhood. These ceremonies are working toward a resolution of problems traditionally associated with womanhood: adjustment to virilocality, incorporation into the husband's lineage, and the responsibility to bear children. In addition, the possession ceremonies are concerned with that problem of women which is related to social change: differential access to household income, consumer items, and socal status.

Anthropological literature now contains excellent descriptive material on individual African religions as they exist or existed in one or another single period. Furthermore, recent efforts in the analysis of African religious symbols appear to be promising in that they relate religious symbols to social structure (Beidelman 1964, 1966a, 1966b; Douglas 1967; Turner 1967, 1968, 1969). If it is possible to arrive at an understanding of social structure through religious symbols, and vice versa, anthropologists must endeavor to study African symbolic systems as they change through time. Monica Wilson has recently noted that "in spite of piles of mission reports and anthropological books which discuss religion, we have few detailed accounts of how religious beliefs and practices have actually changed in a given community" (1971:4). The symbolism employed in Lango possession dances indicates that people can transform objects recently introduced into their everyday world into meaningful religious symbols. If, as Wilson suggests, the study of ritual is "the key to the understanding of human society" (1954:241), the study of rituals in transition should be a prime consideration of those interested in social change.

Appendix I

The Career of an Adept: Elia Adongo

Elia, the most successful adept in Obanya Kura, is sometimes called on to supervise spirit-possession treatments for people living as far as thirty miles away. In 1966, she earned about 600 shillings from her activities as an adept, but she distributed half of this income among her assistants. They are women who attend all her possession ceremonies and who would themselves qualify as adepts if they could afford the training. There is also a crippled man who regularly plays the drum at her ceremonies and is paid for his services.

When Elia had been married for about six years, her husband, Obua, joined the King's African Rifles. He was gone for two years and returned in 1946. At this time, Elia had three children. One night at the beginning of the rainy season, she brought the children outside with her to collect white ants. After collecting the ants she returned to her house and lay down to sleep beside her husband's father's mother, who was visiting her. Elia's husband was also sleeping in the house. Soon after she lay down, she heard voices coming from the yard behind her house. There seemed to be a group of people in the yard, and the cry of a baby could be heard among the voices. Obua's grandmother was awakened by the noise and began to scold Elia, thinking that Elia had left her baby at the anthill and that the two women were hearing the cries of the baby. Obua then awoke and said that the voices were not those of people but those of spirits.

As they listened more closely, they heard the voices call out the name of Elia's baby several times. Nothing further happened that night, but the next morning Elia's baby became sick, and there was a wound on the chest of Elia's oldest child, a five-year-old boy. His chest had been smashed by the spirits, and two of his ribs had been broken. He became sick but recovered a few weeks later, although he is still bothered by chronic headaches, which began after the first visitation. The baby's condition worsened, however, and she died two days later. The middle child, a four-year-old girl, did not become ill at that time, but five years later she developed leprosy, which was explained as a result of the spirits' first visit. Elia herself felt a swelling in one leg from the thigh to the heel. This swelling began a few minutes after she first heard the voices of the spirits and did not subside for two months.

Just after Elia's leg had returned to normal, the spirits visited her again. This time, one of them entered her house while she was asleep and sat down on the left side of the bed. She awoke in a fright and pushed the spirit off the bed, whereupon he ran out the door. The next morning, she had an intense pain in the left side of her head, but it went away after several hours.

A few days later, four spirits appeared to Elia. This visitation was the first real interaction that Elia had with the spirits. One spirit was a European named Kar Kamili, who spoke only the language of Europeans—i.e., English—and sometimes even forced Elia to speak it. He was the leader of the group and the spirit who was to have the most to do with Elia. He was tall and fat, and an agreeable sort of spirit. When he found that Elia did not understand English, he learned Lango so that he could talk with her. The second spirit, an Acholi named Ocera, served as an interpreter for Elia and the European until Kar Kamili learned Lango. There was also a Lango man who never said anything but served as an assistant to Kar Kamili. The fourth spirit, a leper, sometimes accompanied the others on their visits until he was driven from Elia in a dance. The leper made Elia ill, and she was glad to be rid of him.

On the third visit, these four spirits brought a table, a lamp, a book, and chairs, and told Elia to pray as Europeans pray. She acquiesced and knelt on the floor as they read passages from the book. As she prayed, the leper crawled along the floor of the house making fearful noises.

From that time, the spirits visited her every night, and told her that they were going to stay with her. The visits sometimes ended in fierce arguments, in which Elia would tell the spirits that she wished to have nothing to do with them; they would then beat her into compliance. If she had been especially recalcitrant during one of these sessions she would wake up the next morning with aches, pains, swollen limbs, and a high fever. On several occasions they threatened to kill her, and once she tried to run away from them. She told her husband that she could not stay with him any longer and returned to the home of her parents, thinking the spirits would not follow her there. On the first night of her visit, however, they broke down the door of her parents' house and threatened her again. Realizing that her flight was useless, Elia returned to her husband, and the spirits followed her back.

While these confrontations were taking place, Elia sought help to cure herself of the ailments brought on by the spirits and hoped that the treatments might somehow manage to drive the spirits away. She went to the government clinic about once a week, and although the medical assistants were able to cure many of her ailments, the symptoms recurred and she remained in bad health. She also consulted two old women in Obanya Kura who had some knowledge of medicinal plants. They did not manage to cure her, and the spirits continued to visit her almost nightly.

About two years after Elia had first been visited by the spirits, she consulted her father's sister, who had recently been initiated as an adept. A dance was organized for Elia, and Obua paid 150 shillings and donated a goat and two chickens to Elia's father's sister. The dance was held at the adept's house, and it lasted all night. When it was over, the adept felt that it had been a success and that she had driven away all the spirits. Late in the afternoon of the day following the dance, three of the spirits returned to Elia and told her that they were very angry because the dance had driven away the leprous spirit. They swore to remain with Elia until she died, and they recommended again that she accept her condition peacefully. One of the spirits was so angry that he hit Elia on the leg with a heavy wooden pestle and broke the tibia.

Elia asked the adept who had performed the dance whether she should not give up the attempt to be cured and undergo training to become an adept. The adept told her that she was too young to be trained as an adept (Elia was about thirty), and that she should continue to have dances performed for her in an effort to drive away the spirits.

The spirits, however, were of a different mind. They directed Elia to undergo the training. They advised her to consult Bladina Awuma, a fairly well-known adept who lived fifteen miles from Obanya Kura. Elia asked Bladina to train her as an adept because she was frightened of her spirits and expected them to torture her with more illnesses if she did not become an adept. In talking about this period of her life, Elia emphasizes the suffering and says that her spirits gave her more trouble than spirits have given any other adept she has known. She did not want to become an adept at that time, because she thought she was too young. Consequently, when Bladina held a dance that was to initiate Elia as an adept, Elia, in a frenzied state, drove Bladina away and beat her severely. Once again, the spirits visited Elia and punished her for resisting. The leprous spirit rejoined the other three, and they beat her mercilessly until she consented again. This time she allowed Bladina to take her into the bush at night and learned how to use medicines and how to divine by throwing the cowrie shells. Before the initiation dance was to be held, however, Bladina informed Elia that she would have to pay 400 shillings and a bull. Elia and her husband replied that they were unable to afford this, so the training was dropped, and Elia continued to seek treatment at the government clinic and from local herbalists.

About ten years later, Obua had saved some money, and he sent Elia to another adept for training. This was a man named Yakobino Okello. After she had stayed at Okello's house for two weeks, he had an initiation dance for her which cost her 370 shillings, four goats, and two bulls. Thus Elia was initiated in 1960, fourteen years after she had originally been visited by the spirits.

After she was initiated, the spirits made their peace with her. They visited her regularly but caused her very little illness or pain. Moreover, the principal spirit, Kar Kamili, revealed to Elia why he had originally singled her out. Kar Kamili was the shade of a European whom Elia's husband had killed during his military service in Burma. Kamili said that he had returned to

punish her and her children. He recognized that they were innocent and that it was Obua who had killed him, but, he explained,
that is the way shades operate. He also explained that it had
taken him almost a year to locate Elia. While living in the land
of shades, he had encountered an Acholi who offered to take him
to Lango and search for the family of the man who had killed
him. It was this same Acholi who regularly went with him when
he visited Elia. The other two spirits—the leper and the Lango
assistant—were winds whom Kar Kamili had employed to assist
him. Kar Kamili said that he had taken this action out of anger
and sorrow, for he had been filled with grief by the thought that
there was no one to look after his wife and children, and this
grief had led him to seek revenge.

After Elia's initiation in 1960, Kar Kamili agreed to assist her
in curing other people and in earning money through her activities as an adept.

Appendix II
Thirty-one Cases of Spirit Possession

Case	Victim of attack	Symptoms	Spirit and provenance
1	Boy, age 2	General pain, mother also attacked	Wind sent by shade of mother's father
2	Infant boy	Fever	Wind met on road
3	Children, ages 7 and 3	Fever and headache	Wind met on road
4	Girl, age 12	Headache	Wind sent by shade of father (in form of 120 bir
5	Married woman, age 22, with no children	Barrenness	Wind met at stream
5a	2 years later, had infant	Infant suffered fever	Same wind
5b	2 years later, age 26	Fever	Same wind
6	Adolescent, age 13	Fever	Wind sent by shade of mother's co-wife
7	Adolescent, age 14	Fever	Wind met at stream
8	Married woman, age 25	Sickness	15 winds sent by shade of husband's mother
9	Married woman, age 20, with 3 children	Shivering, headache; 1 child died	Wind met on road
9a	2 years later, 2 children attacked	Blood in children's urine	Wind sent by shade of father's mother
10	Married woman, age 20	2 miscarriages	Wind met on road
11	Young married woman	Pregnancy difficulties	Wind sent by shades of mother and mother's mother
12	Married woman, age 40	General sickness	Wind met at stream, angered because she wen to stream during postpartum bleeding

Treatment	Outcome	Dispute topic	Disputants
inor adept actice	Not cured	None	
ne	Wind went away	None	
ssession dance	Cured	None	
inor adept actice	Cured	Bride wealth	Mother vs. father's son
ssession dance	Cured	None	
ne	Wind went away	None	
ne	Wind went away	None	
ssession dance	Wind driven away; still sick	Half-brother neglected his mother	Mother's co-wife vs. mother's co-wife's son
ogo: Praying r the sick	Cured	None	
ssession dance	12 winds driven away, 3 remained	Neglect	Husband's mother vs. husband and husband's brothers
possession nces	Not cured	Funeral offerings	Father's mother vs. brothers
ssession dance	Cured	Same	Same
ssession dance	Cured	None	
anda adept ve medicine	Cured, later returned to Lango	Living in Buganda, wanted to return to Lango	Ego vs. husband
dept gave edicine	Cured	None	

Case	Victim of attack	Symptoms	Spirit and provenance
13	Married woman, age 25, with 1 child	Barrenness	Wind sent by shade of mother's twin brother
14	Girl, age 12	General sickness, mother also attacked	Wind met on road
15	Married woman, age 32	Vomiting	Wind sent by shade of daughter
16	Man, age 18	Vomiting	Wind sent by shade of sister
17	Married woman, age 28, with several children	Infant had fever	Wind sent by shade of husband's father
18	Married woman, age 40	Stomach trouble	Wind sent by shade of father's brother
19	Married woman, age 30	General sickness	5 winds sent by shade of father
20	Married woman, age 22, with infant	Sickness, infant died	Shade of father
21	Married woman, age 45	General sickness	Wind met on road
22	Married woman, age 23, with no children	Barrenness, 2 miscarriages	Wind met on road
23	Unmarried girl, age 17	Pain in eyes	Wind met on road
24	Married woman, age 22, with infant	Stricken dumb, infant died	Wind attacked at home
25	Married woman, age 25, with infant	Infant attacked	Wind
26	Married woman, age 23, with infant	Sickness, infant and victim's mother also attacked	Wind sent by shade of fath
27	Married woman, age 40	Children sick	Wind met on road
28	Man, age 60	Diarrhea, sick for a long time	Wind met on road

Treatment	Outcome	Dispute topic	Disputants
...nor *kwer*	Cured	Funeral offerings	Mother's brother vs. mother's brother
...*go*: Praying for ... Sick; went to ...vt. clinic	Cured	Domestic quarrels	Ego vs. husband
...*go*: Praying ... the sick	Not cured	Domestic quarrels; later dispute over bridewealth	
...*go*: Praying ... the sick	Not cured	Bridewealth	Father vs. father's half-brother's son
...*go*: Blessing ... sick	Cured	Domestic quarrels	Ego vs. husband
...ent to Arab ...ept in Lira	Cured	Domestic quarrels	Ego vs. husband
...ssession dance	3 winds and shade driven away	Brothers quarreling over cattle	Brothers vs. brothers
...ssession dance	Victim cured	Bride wealth	Sisters vs. father
...ssession dance	Cured	None	
...ne	Wind still with victim	None	
...tching the ...ind	Cured	None	
...ne	Wind went away	None	
...ssession dance; ...tching the ...ind	Dance failed; cured when wind caught	None	
...*ver*; minor ...*go*	Cured	Domestic quarrel at natal home	Mother vs. brother
...*ogo*: Praying ... the sick	Cured	None	
...ne	Died	None	

References

Ardener, Edwin
  1972. Belief and the Problem of Women. *In* Jean S. La Fontaine, ed., The Interpretation of Ritual: Essays in Honour of A. I. Richards. London: Tavistock Publications.

Barrett, David B.
  1968. Schism and Renewal in Africa. London: Oxford University Press.

Beattie, John H. M.
  1956. Ethnographic and Sociological Research in East Africa. Africa 26:265–276.
  1957. Initiation into the Cwezi Spirit Possession Cult in Bunyoro. African Studies 16:150–161.
  1961. Group Aspects of the Nyoro Spirit Mediumship Cult. Rhodes-Livingstone Journal 30:11–38.
  1968. Aspects of Nyoro Symbolism. Africa 38:413–442.
  1969. Spirit Mediumship in Bunyoro. *In* John Beattie and John Middleton, eds., Spirit Mediumship and Society in Africa. London: Routledge and Kegan Paul.
  1971. The Nyoro State. Oxford: Clarendon Press.

Beidelman, T. O.
  1964. Pig (Guluwe): An Essay on Ngulu Sexual Symbolism and Ceremony. Southwestern Journal of Anthropology 20:359–392.
  1966a. Swazi Royal Ritual. Africa 36:373–405.
  1966b. The Ox and Nuer Sacrifice: Some Freudian Hypotheses about Nuer Symbolism. Man (ns) 1:543–467.
  1971. The Kaguru: A Matrilineal People of East Africa. New York: Holt, Rinehart and Winston.

Buchler, Ira, and Henry A. Selby
  1968. Kinship and Social Organization: An Introduction to Theory and Method. New York: Macmillan.

Colson, Elizabeth
  1955. Ancestral Spirits and Social Structure among the Plateau Tonga. International Archives of Ethnography 47:21–68.
  1958. Marriage and the Family among the Plateau Tonga of Northern Rhodesia. Manchester: Manchester University Press.
  1969. Spirit Possession among the Tonga of Zambia. *In* John Beattie and John Middleton, eds., Spirit Mediumship and Society in Africa. London: Routledge and Kegan Paul.
  1971. The Impact of the Colonial Period on the Definition of Land

Rights. *In* Victor Turner, ed., Colonialism in Africa: 1870–1960, Vol. III. Cambridge: Cambridge University Press.

Curley, Alberta
1971.   Social Process: Clanship and Neighborhood in Lango District, Uganda. Unpublished master's thesis. California State University at Sacramento.

Dahlberg, Frances M.
1971.   The Emergence of a Dual Governing Elite in Uganda. Journal of Modern African Studies 9:618–625.

Douglas, Mary T.
1967.   Purity and Danger. New York: Frederick A. Praeger.

Driberg, Jack H.
1923.   The Lango: A Nilotic Tribe of Uganda. London: T. Fisher and Unwin.

Elliot, A. J. A.
1955.   Chinese Spirit-Medium Cults in Singapore. London: Athlone Press.

Evans-Pritchard, E. E.
1937.   Witchcraft, Oracles, and Magic among the Azande. London: Oxford University Press.
1940.   The Nuer. London: Oxford University Press.
1956.   Nuer Religion. Oxford: Clarendon Press.
1960.   The Sudan: An Ethnographic Survey. *In* Stanley Diamond, ed., Culture in History: Essays in Honor of Paul Radin. New York: Columbia University Press.

Field, Margaret J.
1937.   Religion and Medicine of the Ga People. London: Oxford University Press.
1969.   Spirit Possession in Ghana. *In* John Beattie and John Middleton, eds., Spirit Mediumship and Society in Africa. London: Routledge and Kegan Paul.

Fortes, Meyer
1949.   Time and Social Structure: An Ashanti Case Study. *In* Meyer Fortes, ed., Social Structure. London: Oxford University Press.

Fox, Robin
1967.   Kinship and Marriage: An Anthropological Perspective. Baltimore: Penguin Books.

Geertz, Clifford
1966.   Religion as a Cultural System. *In* Michael Banton, ed., Anthropological Approaches to the Study of Religion. A.S.A. Monograph No. 3. London: Tavistock Publications.

Gluckman, Max
1960.   Custom and Conflict in Africa. Oxford: Blackwell.
1963.   Order and Rebellion in Tribal Africa. London: Cohen and West.

Goffman, Erving M.
1959.   The Presentation of Self in Everyday Life. Garden City, N.Y.: Doubleday (Anchor Books).

Goody, Jack
1958.   The Developmental Cycle in Domestic Groups. Cambridge Papers in Social Anthropology No. 1. Cambridge: Cambridge University Press.

1962. Death, Property, and the Ancestors: A Study of the Mortuary Customs of the LoDagaa of West Africa. Stanford: Stanford University Press.

Harris, Grace
1957. Possession "Hysteria" in a Kenya Tribe. American Anthropologist 59:258–272.

Harwood, Alan
1970. Witchcraft, Sorcery, and Social Categories among the Safwa. London: Oxford University Press.

Hayley, T. T. S.
1947. The Anatomy of Lango Religion and Groups. Cambridge: Cambridge University Press.

Horton, Robin
1964. Ritual Man in Africa. Africa 34:85–104.
1970. A Hundred Years of Change in Kalabari Religion. In John Middleton, ed., Black Africa: Its Peoples and Their Cultures Today. New York: Macmillan.

Ingham, Kenneth
1955. British Administration in Lango District, 1907–1935. Uganda Journal 19:156–168.

Jay, Edward
1964. On the Concepts of 'Network' and 'Field.' Man 177:137–139.

Krige, J. D.
1939. The Significance of Cattle Exchange in Lovedu Social Structure. Africa 12:393–424.

Langdale-Brown, I.
1960. The Vegetation of Uganda. In Vegetation. Uganda Department of Agriculture, Research Division, Memoirs, Series 2, No. 6. Entebbe: Government Printer.

Leach, Edmund R.
1961. Rethinking Anthropology. London School of Economics, Monographs on Social Anthropology, No. 22. London: Athlone Press.

Leiris, Michael
1958. La Possession et ses aspects theatraux chez les Ethiopiens de Gondar. Paris: Plon.

LeVine, Robert A.
1966. Sex Roles and Economic Change in Africa. Ethnology 5:186–193.

Lewis, I. M.
1966. Spirit Possession and Deprivation Cults. Man (ns) 1:307–329.
1971. Ecstatic Religion: An Anthropological Study of Spirit Possession and Shamanism. Middlesex: Penguin Books.

Lienhardt, Godfrey
1961. Divinity and Experience: The Religion of the Dinka. London: Oxford University Press.

MacGaffey, Wyatt
1970. Custom and Government in the Lower Congo. Berkeley: University of California Press.

Malinowski, Bronislaw
1925. Magic, Science, and Religion. In James Needham, ed., Science, Religion, and Reality. London: Macmillan.

1927.   Coral Gardens and Their Magic. London: Routledge and Kegan Paul.

Metraux, Alfred
1955.   La Comédie Rituelle dans le possession. Diogene 11:18–36.

Middleton, John
1960.   Lugbara Religion: Ritual and Authority among an East African People. London: Oxford University Press.
1963.   The Yakan or Allah Water Cult among the Lugbara. Journal of the Royal Anthropological Institute 93:80–108.
1971.   Some Effects of Colonial Rule among the Lugbara. *In* Victor Turner, ed., Colonialism in Africa: 1870–1960, Vol. III. Cambridge: Cambridge University Press.

Moore, Omar Khayyam
1957.   Divination—A New Perspective. American Anthropologist 59: 64–74.

Murphy, Robert
1959.   Social Structure and Sex Antagonism. Southwestern Journal of Anthropology 15:89–98.

Nash, Manning
1966.   Primitive and Peasant Economic Systems. San Francisco: Chandler.

Neher, Andrew P.
1962.   A Physiological Explanation of Unusual Behavior in Ceremonies Involving Drums. Human Biology 34:151–160.

Oyler, D. S.
1920.   The Shilluk Peace Ceremony. Sudan Notes and Records, IV, 4.

Parkin, David
1969.   Neighbors and Nationals in an African City Ward. Berkeley: University of California Press.

Radcliffe-Brown, A. R.
1952.   Structure and Function in Primitive Society. Glencoe: Free Press.

Rappaport, Roy
1968.   Pigs for the Ancestors: Ritual in the Ecology of a New Guinea People. New Haven: Yale University Press.

Rouch, Jean
1956.   Migrations au Ghana. Journal de la Société des Africanistes 26.

Smith, Mary
1954.   Baba of Karo. London: Faber and Faber.

Southall, Aidan
1969.   Spirit Possession among the Alur. *In* John Beattie and John Middleton, eds., Spirit Mediumship and Society in Africa. London: Routledge and Kegan Paul.

Strathern, Andrew M.
1968.   Marsupials and Magic: A Study of Spell Symbolism among the Mbowamb. *In* Edmund R. Leach, ed., Dialectic in Practical Religion. Cambridge Papers in Social Anthropology, No. 5. Cambridge: Cambridge University Press.
1970.   The Female and Male Spirit Cults. Man (ns) 5:572–585.

Swantz, Marja-Liisa
1970.   Ritual and Symbol in Transitional Zaramo Society. Studia Missionalia Upsaliensia, XVI. Uppsala: Gleerup.

Tarantino, Rev. Angelo G.
  1949*a*. Lango Clans. Uganda Journal 13:109–111.
  1949*b*. Lango Wars. Uganda Journal 13:230–234.
  1949*c*. Notes on the Lango. Uganda Journal 13:145–153.
Tosh, John
  1971. Precolonial Cooperation and the Decline in Political Scale. Unpublished manuscript.
Turner, Victor W.
  1967. The Forest of Symbols. Ithaca: Cornell University Press.
  1968. The Drums of Affliction: A Study of the Religious Processes of the Ndembu of Zambia. London: Oxford University Press.
  1969. The Ritual Process: Structure and Anti-Structure. Chicago. Aldine.
Van Gennep, Arnold
  1960. The Rites of Passage. London: Routledge and Kegan Paul.
White, C. M. N.
  1961. Elements in Luvale Beliefs and Rituals. Rhodes-Livingstone Institute Papers, No. 32.
Wilson, Monica
  1954. Nyakusa Ritual and Symbolism. American Anthropologist 56:228–241.
  1971. Religion and the Transformation of Society: A Study of Social Change in Africa. Cambridge: Cambridge University Press.
Wilson, Peter J.
  1967. Status Ambiguity and Spirit Possession. Man (ns) 3:366–378.